R - 9/25 ✓

D1551655

HOME RUN

Allied Escape and Evasion in World War II

HOWARD R. SIMKIN

CASEMATE

Philadelphia & Oxford

AN AUSA BOOK
Association of the United States Army
2425 Wilson Boulevard, Arlington, Virginia, 22201, USA

Published in the United States of America and Great Britain in 2022 by
CASEMATE PUBLISHERS
1950 Lawrence Road, Havertown, PA 19083, USA
and
The Old Music Hall, 106–108 Cowley Road, Oxford OX4 1JE, UK

© 2022 Association of the U.S. Army

Copyright 2022 © Howard R. Simkin

Hardcover Edition: ISBN 978-1-63624-195-1
Digital Edition: ISBN 978-1-63624-196-8

A CIP record for this book is available from the British Library

All rights reserved. No part of this book may be reproduced or transmitted in any form or by
any means, electronic or mechanical including photocopying, recording or by any information
storage and retrieval system, without permission from the publisher in writing.

The views expressed in this publication are those of the author and do not necessarily reflect the
official policy or position of the Department of Defense or the U.S. government.

Printed and bound in the United Kingdom by TJ Books

Typeset by DiTech Publishing Services

For a complete list of Casemate titles, please contact:

CASEMATE PUBLISHERS (US)
Telephone (610) 853-9131
Fax (610) 853-9146
Email: casemate@casematepublishers.com
www.casematepublishers.com

CASEMATE PUBLISHERS (UK)
Telephone (01865) 241249
Email: casemate-uk@casematepublishers.co.uk
www.casematepublishers.co.uk

Front cover: Curtis Wright Maps and design by Declan Ingram.

Contents

IRELAND

GREAT
BRITAIN

HOLLAND

Mons

BELGIUM

GERMANY

Colditz Castle

Falmouth

Lille

Amiens

Rouen

Plouha

PARIS

Rheims

Rennes

Orleans

Dijon

SWITZ.

Nevers

OCCUPIED FRANCE

Montlucon

Limoges

Clermont

Lyons
Ferrand

ITALY

Perigueux

VICHY FRANCE

Toulouse

Arles

Avignon

Allied Front Line May 1944

Bilbao

Bayonne

Beziers

Marseilles

San
Sebastian

Perpignan

Rome

Anzio
Beachhead

Barcelona

PORTUGAL

N

MADRID

SPAIN

COMET LINE

SHELBURNE LINE

Gibraltar

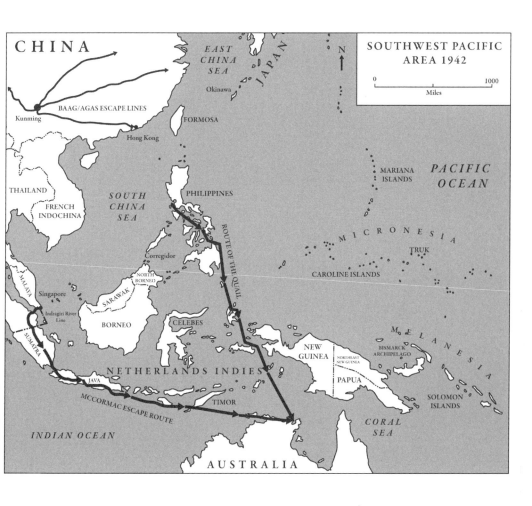

CHINA

EAST
CHINA
SEA

JAPAN

Okinawa

N

SOUTHWEST PACIFIC
AREA 1942

0   1000
Miles

BAAG/AGAS ESCAPE LINES

Kunming

FORMOSA

Hong Kong

PACIFIC
OCEAN

MARIANA
ISLANDS

THAILAND

FRENCH
INDOCHINA

SOUTH
CHINA
SEA

PHILIPPINES

MICRONESIA

TRUK

CAROLINE ISLANDS

Corregidor

MALAYA

Singapore

NORTH
BORNEO

SARAWAK

Indragiri River
Line

BORNEO

CELEBES

ROUTE OF THE QUAIL

MELANESIA

NEW
GUINEA

BISMARCK
ARCHIPELAGO

SUMATRA

NETHERLANDS INDIES

NORTHEAST
NEW GUINEA

PAPUA

SOLOMON
ISLANDS

JAVA

MCCORMAC ESCAPE ROUTE

TIMOR

CORAL
SEA

INDIAN OCEAN

AUSTRALIA

Foreword

This book offers an excellent overview of the heroic escapers and evaders of World War II, their escape kit, and the organizations which aided them. The product of two years of painstaking research, it is written in a highly understandable, almost conversational style. Having known the author for nearly 40 years, I know that he strives above all else to help others understand with his writing, and I believe that *Home Run* does just that. It is a "soup to nuts" book which gives the reader a firm grasp of escape (by someone who was taken prisoner by the enemy and managed to gain their freedom) and evasion (by those who have never been in enemy hands and are seeking to return to friendly control) in World War II. As the world again stares at the possibility of global war, *Home Run* reminds us of an inevitable and dark consequence, while recalling the ingenuity, spirit, and strength of the Allied soldiers and the lengths to which their fellow citizens will go to bring them home.

Home Run introduces us to the British and American Allied escape organizations, MI9 and MIS-X respectively. Both provided evaders and escapers with the necessary training and escape kit to make what was commonly referred to as a "Home Run"—a return from behind enemy lines. MI9 and MIS-X also provided money, agents, and equipment to run escape organizations in occupied areas. These organizations—referred to as lines—provided vital support to evaders and escapers, giving downed Allied aircrew in Occupied Europe—Belgium, France, Holland, and Luxembourg—as much as a 50 percent chance of making a Home Run.

Those servicemen unfortunate enough to be taken prisoner faced a different challenge: escape from a prisoner of war camp. *Home Run* places their trials in context with an examination of camps in the European and

Pacific Theaters. The descriptions of the Berga and Cabanatuan camps are monuments to the barbarity of two totalitarian systems which must never be allowed to happen again.

The author then takes us on a tour of some of the most successful escape lines including the Comet Line—brainchild of a 23-year-old Belgian woman nicknamed Dédée, which rescued over 800 Allied escapers and evaders—and the Indragiri River line, set up by the Special Operations Executive to allow British and Commonwealth troops and civilians to escape the fall of Singapore. In its short life from February 13 to March 17, 1942, it allowed 2,586 military personnel to avoid capture, along with an estimated 4,000–7,000 civilians.

Successful escapes were made by both small and large groups. We follow Airey Neave and Toni Luteyn in their perilous flight from the supposedly escape-proof Colditz Castle in Germany to Switzerland and then across France, Spain and Gibraltar to safety in England. The author then relates how US Army Air Corps Second Lieutenant Edgar Whitcomb, destined to be Indiana's 43rd governor, made his escape and astonishing 11,000-mile Home Run by masquerading as a civilian. Despite being repatriated, he then managed to get back into the Pacific War, ending it at Clark Field on Luzon where he had seen the Japanese attack on December 8, 1941.

Prisoners who escaped en masse faced different challenges. The mass escapes detailed in *Home Run* were from Singapore to Australia and Corregidor to Australia, respectively. The courage and determination of Allied servicemen take center stage in the tale of 18 men in a 36-foot motorboat, led by the intrepid Commander John Morrill, as they made a 31-day, 2,000-mile journey through enemy waters to freedom.

Home Run does not forget those unable to escape: the penultimate chapter covers the liberation experience in the European and Pacific theaters. It focuses on three examples: Colditz Castle (Oflag IV C), Moosburg (Stalag VII A), and Cabanatuan. The liberation of Colditz was unique, as the prisoners had already obtained the surrender of the German force guarding the castle prior to the arrival of any friendly forces. Moosburg was more typical of liberation in Germany, with US tanks and infantry taking control of the camp and freeing the prisoners.

Cabanatuan provides the thrilling story of the rescue of 511 emaciated prisoners by Lieutenant Colonel Henry Mucci and the 6th Ranger Battalion. That daring raid is still studied in military academies today.

The book concludes with a chapter on the aftermath of the war. It provides some closure on the ultimate fate of many of the people—both prisoner and warder—in the book, and also recounts the uneven justice that was meted out by the victors. The POWs returned home to countries many of them hardly recognized, particularly those captured early in the war, where they were subject to varying treatment by governments that had many other priorities at hand.

I would recommend this book to anyone seeking to know about escape and evasion in World War II, whether out of a pure interest in history or to glean lessons and considerations in preparation for our next large-scale conventional conflict. Howard Simkin, a retired green beret and one of unconventional warfare's best thinkers, has done a masterful job. He has woven a brilliant tapestry from fading and disparate threads on an important but understudied topic.

Lieutenant General (Retired) Charles T. Cleveland
US Army

CHAPTER I

Introduction

Imagine that you are deep behind enemy lines during World War II. Your plane was shot down or perhaps you have just escaped from a prisoner of war camp. The enemy is hunting you, seeking to throw you behind barbed wire for the duration of the war. What will you do? Do you have what it takes to make it to friendly territory?

This book tells the story of the brave members of the British Commonwealth and United States Armed Forces during World War II who either evaded capture entirely or were taken prisoner and escaped. During the war, the Germans and Japanese held over 306,000 British Commonwealth and 105,000 US service members as prisoners, but these numbers can only be approximations. The numbers held by the Germans are reasonably solid, as they generally adhered to the reporting requirements of the Geneva Conventions. The Japanese were another matter entirely. Many prisoners of the Japanese were killed before their capture was ever reported, such as those who perished during the Bataan death march.

When deciding which escapes and escape lines to address in detail I had to be selective. What I sought was to bring stories forward that were either unique or neglected. In doing so I passed over the considerable accomplishments of the Pat Line which operated for two years before being penetrated by the Nazis.[1] The remarkable evasion by survivors of the 1st British Airborne Division in the aftermath of *Market Garden* also is omitted. The Dutch Resistance and MI9 managed to mount two operations, *Pegasus I* and *II*, to repatriate evading "Red Devils" from the far side of the Rhine River. The first operation was an unqualified success, with 138 paratroopers crossing the Rhine to freedom. The Germans detected the second, which brought only seven safely home, with the rest of the evaders being killed, captured, or scattered.[2]

This work also does not include the travails of the up to 1.8 million French troops captured by the Germans in 1940. Most were sent to camps in Germany and kept on as forced labor. Starting in 1940, the Germans released a trickle of prisoners—mostly reservists—but retained the bulk of the prisoners until they were liberated by advancing Allied forces.[3] After 1942, they repatriated around 100,000 prisoners based on the *relève* system, where a civilian volunteer took the place of a prisoner.

On the whole, the French attitude toward the returning prisoners was not very positive. As a result, there is not the breadth and depth of literature on the subject that there is for British and American troops. Indeed, there is a lack of hard statistics about all aspects of French escapers and evaders. One estimate puts the number of escaped prisoners at around 70,000.[4] How many of those who escaped later joined the Resistance or the Free French Forces is impossible to say with any accuracy.

The number of successful evaders and escapers, both American and British, exceeded 35,000. This book will relate how they fared in enemy hands or managed to remain free. To avoid confusion over terminology, I will refer to those who never fell into enemy hands as evaders and those who managed to escape from enemy hands and avoid recapture as escapers. This is the same definition used by the Allied escape organizations. The total numbers of escapers and evaders are reflected in the British MI9's end of war report. The table below gives a roll up of those statistics.[5]

Table 1: Total Evaders & Escapers from WO 208/3242, 65

	American	British & Commonwealth	
Western Europe	3,415	3,631	
India and Southeast Asia	39	3,346	
Switzerland	227	4,916	
Mediterranean (West)	3,466	11,910	
Mediterranean (East)	351	4,546	
Total	7,498	28,349	
Grand Total			35,847

Of course, not everyone who surrendered was taken prisoner. In the heat of battle, anyone might be shot out of hand because they would slow down their potential captors or perhaps had fought too well. The German SS were particularly callous in this regard. Allied troops frequently returned the compliment when dealing with SS prisoners. Bomber crews downed over Germany after 1943 or over the home islands of Japan at any time were at peril from enraged civilians. Often their best hope was to fall into the hands of the enemy police or military. Sometimes racial factors came into play, with Black and indigenous troops being treated with particular harshness. This work is about those who either successfully evaded or were taken prisoner and escaped. It will not, therefore, go into detail on these matters.

Simply discussing the lives of the evaders and escapers would leave out a significant part of the story. Both the British and the US built escape organizations to aid evaders and escapers in their return to freedom. The British organization MI9 was formed in August 1939. The American equivalent, MIS-X, began operations in 1942. Together, they developed agent networks as well as ingenious means to smuggle escape aids into POW camps. They are a significant part of the story as well.

No story of evasion and escape would be complete without paying tribute to the brave men and women who ran escape lines in enemy-occupied territory at great peril to their lives. For example, in its over two years of operation, the Comet Line had 156 of its members shot or murdered in Nazi concentration camps. Both the Germans and the Japanese reacted with ferocious cruelty when they discovered escape lines. Imprisonment, torture, and death were certainties for those caught running escape lines or simply aiding evaders. Yet they carried on their work despite the terror. Heroism, betrayal, sacrifice, and cowardice are all elements of this fascinating portion of the rich tapestry of World War II.

This book discusses the essential problems facing Allied evaders and escapers. The most pressing problem was obtaining a few essentials needed by every evader in both theaters of war—food, water, maps, and a compass. In the European Theater, papers and appropriate civilian clothing were an added requirement. The ingenuity displayed by the prisoners in obtaining or manufacturing these essentials is astounding.

Before proceeding further, it is important to understand that evasion and escape have different but related meanings. Evasion consists of the art and science needed to avoid falling into enemy hands and could take place before or as part of an escape after capture. During World War II, downed airmen were the most frequent pre-capture evaders, coming down in occupied or enemy territory and playing a high-stakes game of hide-and-seek with enemy forces. Those evaders who succeeded were almost invariably assisted by a resistance network that provided them with food, shelter, false papers, transportation, and guides.

Escape was a different matter. The escaper was already in the hands of the enemy. The first problem an escaper had to solve was that of breaking free from captivity. The best time to do so was immediately after capture. The troops guarding the prisoner were not trained for the task and friendly forces were often in close proximity. The more difficult alternative was to escape from a POW camp deep in enemy territory staffed by guards who knew their job. Once free, the escaper faced two choices for how to avoid recapture.

First, they could choose to find their way to neutral or friendly territory unassisted. Alternatively, they could link up with a resistance network to make their way to freedom—in POW slang, to "score a Home Run." Most of the early escapers did so on their own, because in many countries the resistance had not coalesced and networks to aid evaders were not yet in place. Later in the war escapers had a better chance of receiving organized assistance. Evading recapture by the enemy took skill, courage, and an element of luck. However, the evader usually had a very narrow window of opportunity to contact a resistance cell for assistance.

Prisoner of war (POW) camps posed their own set of problems for the escaper. As noted above, the POW camp guards were trained for their job. The camps were usually constructed to retain prisoners and cut them off from outside aid. However, through the Allied escape organizations such as the British MI9 and American MIS-X, as well as those POW-run organizations which sprung up in most camps, the POW could receive the essential escape aids of food, money, false papers, maps, a compass, and clothing. They were often assisted by their comrades in other essential aspects of their escape. This could range from diversions staged by other prisoners to distract the guards to participation in an escape through a tunnel.

From whom did evaders and escapers receive their escape aids? Aircrew, who made up most of the evaders, were issued their escape aids prior to each flight. Prisoners often manufactured escape aids such as false papers, clothing, food, wire cutters, and other tools. There were two external sources of such aids. The first were issued by MI9 beginning in 1941,[6] followed by MIS-X in 1942. Much of the story of how they aided prisoners and evaders was left untold for many years due to security concerns. Of particular concern was maintaining the secrecy of the ingenious methods devised to smuggle escape aids into the camps—methods the US and Britain planned to use if the Cold War ever became hot.

This work will bring to life the evaders and prisoners who fell into the hands of the Germans and the Japanese in World War II. Most of them have heard "Taps" or "Last Call" played over their graves, which makes the task of telling their stories tougher. Fortunately, there is a wealth of information with which to work, including letters, debriefings, oral history, and books written by those who evaded and/or escaped.

During World War II, the Japanese and Germans ran hundreds of camps. To make a discussion of camp life comprehensible, I will focus on representative camps in each theater, mentioning other camps as necessary. The camps will include Dulag Luft, Stalag Luft III, and Oflag IVC (Colditz), Stalag IX B (Bad Orb) in Europe and Seoul, Cabanatuan, Omori in Japan, and Changi and the Thai Burma Railway camps in the Asia Pacific. These chapters will include information on how the Germans and Japanese moved prisoners to and from the camps, along with brief descriptions of the "Hell Ships" in the Pacific and the forced marches to avoid the advancing Allied armies in Europe.

To put the treatment of POWs by the Germans and Japanese in perspective, it is important to understand the legal framework provided by the 1907 Hague Convention and the 1929 Geneva Convention. The Hague Convention refers to the *1907 Convention (IV) respecting the Laws and Customs of War on Land* and its annex, *Regulations concerning the Laws and Customs of War on Land*. The Geneva Convention refers to the

1929 Convention relative to the Treatment of Prisoners of War. When World War II began, all the combatants had ratified the Hague Convention, and all but Japan and the Soviet Union had ratified the Geneva Convention. Interestingly, Japan signed but did not ratify the Geneva Convention.

Both conventions expressly forbade the mistreatment of prisoners of war, requiring that they be treated "humanely."[7] The 1929 Geneva Convention was an amplification and clarification of the 1907 Hague Convention. As noted by the International Committee of the Red Cross, "The most important innovations consisted in the prohibition of reprisals and collective penalties, the organization of prisoners' work, the designation, by the prisoners, of representatives and the control exercised by protecting Powers."[8]

All that can be said about their treatment of POWs is that the Germans violated the conventions less blatantly than the Japanese. For example, the conventions required that POWs be fed on the same scale as the capturing power's armed forces in garrison.[9] The Germans violated this standard by providing around 1,500 calories per day when their garrison ration standard was 2,500 calories throughout 1944. In 1945, that standard declined considerably both for the German Armed Forces and for their POWs as well. However, the Germans allowed intact Red Cross food parcels through to the camps on an irregular basis—usually at least once every six weeks. While the average prisoner lost considerable weight, they were able to keep body and soul together until the Third Reich began to crumble under the hammer blows from the Allies in the West and the Soviets in the East.

The Red Cross parcels varied in composition depending on their country of origin. All contained some form of canned meat, crackers, candy, margarine or butter, sugar, powdered or condensed milk, cigarettes, and medicine—quinine or sulfa drugs were the most common.[10] American parcels almost invariably contained Spam and canned powdered milk referred to as Klim. The cans were almost as highly valued as their contents to use as cookware and escape aids. The signature items for British parcels were bully beef and Condendo—a form of condensed milk.[11] A single package could supplement a prisoner's diet for weeks.

Attitudes toward prisoners differed greatly between the Germans and the Japanese in general. This was evidenced by the difference in survival rates, with over 96 percent of Allied prisoners in German hands making it home. Less than 70 percent of those who were prisoners of the Japanese saw their homelands again. Both statistics have their roots in cultural attitudes and concern for their own prisoners in Allied hands. As in any group, there were those who deviated from the official norm by showing kindness to the prisoners in their charge. However, such acts were the exception, not the rule.

Nazi[12] racial theories, together with the rather lame assertion that the Soviet Union had never signed the 1929 Geneva Convention, provided the Germans with their excuse to savagely mistreat Soviet prisoners of war. Of over six million Soviet prisoners taken by the Germans, slightly more than two million survived—a loss rate of two thirds. The German attitude toward other Allied POWs was less brutal. The Germans were also concerned for their troops who fell into Allied hands: after mid-1943, over 100,000 German troops were already in US and British hands. This was certainly a factor which influenced the Germans to largely observe the Geneva Conventions.

Another factor was undoubtedly the good treatment German prisoners of war received in Allied hands. During the war most were shipped to Canada and, after 1942, the United States as well. Because of the distances involved and the lack of an effective German counterpart to MI9 or MIS-X, there was but a single German "Home Run." It was scored by a Luftwaffe fighter pilot, Franz von Werra, in January 1941. He leapt from a moving train as it neared the US–Canadian border. He managed to cross 30 miles of snowy terrain before crossing the St. Lawrence River near Ogdensburg, New York. Since America was neutral at the time, he was handed over to the German Consul in New York City. When it appeared that he might be returned to Canada, Werra fled to Mexico. From there he made his way home to Germany.[13]

German culture had a strong bias toward upholding treaties, particularly if Germany benefited from them. As signatories to both the Hague and the Geneva Conventions the Germans felt a need to observe at least the form of correct behavior, particularly as the Americans and British began to capture more and more German prisoners. The possibility of Allied retaliation against German POWs in the case of mistreatment of Allied POWs acted as a reality check for an increasingly desperate Nazi regime which contemplated harsh measures against Allied POWs.[14]

For that reason, Field Marshal Herman Goering, who had a genuine concern for captured Luftwaffe personnel, was often a voice for "correct" treatment of Allied POWs. As Hitler's deputy his opinion carried considerable weight, although it gradually eroded as the Allied bombing campaign against Germany became increasingly effective beginning in 1943. This attitude of correct treatment was reflected in the camps holding Allied airmen run by the Luftwaffe. That changed in the wake of the "Great Escape" from Stalag Luft III. This allowed Reichsführer-SS[15] Heinrich Himmler to assume overall control of all POW camps, although the guards and administrative staff were still provided by either the Luftwaffe or the Wehrmacht.

After that, escaped prisoners were often, but not always, sent to concentration camps such as Sachsenhausen. Generally, Wehrmacht camps were more strictly administered than those of the Luftwaffe, but brutal treatment of American and British Commonwealth prisoners was the exception, not the rule, in most camps. The glaring exception was Berga, more properly known as Arbeitsdienstlager[16] 650.

Collocated with the Berga Concentration Camp, it was under the control of SS Obersturmbannführer[17] (SS Lieutenant Colonel) Willi Hack. For the sake of appearances, Berga was guarded by Wehrmacht troops, but it was under the iron control of the SS. Over 20 percent of the 350 American POWs who arrived at Berga from Stalag IX B near Bad Orb ultimately perished.

They were all supposed to be Jewish, but no more than 80 out of 350 were, according to Hans Kasten, a German-American soldier captured during the Battle of the Bulge. Kasten had been the Man of Confidence, an elected position where a senior enlisted man spoke for the other prisoners. At least 70 prisoners died during their two months in the hands of the SS from starvation, overwork, and brutal treatment.

In the matter of disciplining prisoners, the Germans generally adhered to the 1929 Geneva Convention, which required that prisoners be treated humanely and set definite limits on punishments. Prisoners were subject to being sent to solitary confinement, which they called "the cooler", for a variety of offenses for a maximum of 30 days.[18] These offenses included insubordination and escape attempts. The Conventions prohibited mass retaliation or execution for escape attempts.

In the case of Germany, the odious, pseudoscientific claptrap of Nazi racial theory was a minor factor in the treatment of the majority of US and British Commonwealth prisoners of war. In Nazi eyes, they were not subhuman (*Untermensch*) despite being decidedly inferior to Germans. Although the Germans sought the *lebensraum* (living space) detailed in the turgid pages of Hitler's *Mein Kampf*, they envisioned obtaining it through conquests and exterminations of *Untermenschen* such as Jews and Slavs. *Mein Kampf* translates to "My Struggle" and was written by Hitler in Landsberg Prison in 1922–1924 when he was serving a prison sentence for attempting to overthrow the Bavarian government.

The book was published in two volumes, one in 1925 and the other in 1927. Taken together, they laid out exactly what Hitler thought and what he intended to accomplish. Hitler's blueprint for conquest did not envision the destruction of the British Empire, which he viewed as a stabilizing influence in the world. Nonetheless, *Mein Kampf*'s cold-blooded mandates led inexorably to the death of millions to achieve its ends. Even by the standards of the mid-20th century, when many believed in inferior and superior races, *Mein Kampf* stood out for its radical aims and views.

Nazi racial theory was not conjured out of thin air. It was largely based on Houston Stewart Chamberlain's book, *The Foundations of the Nineteenth Century*. Born in England, Chamberlain wrote *Foundations* to purportedly tell the racial history of humanity up to the 19th century. It posited the existence of an "Aryan" race that was superior to all others. This race originally included Germans, Celts, Slavs, Greeks, Latins and—surprisingly—the Berbers.

At the top of the heap were the Germans, who had best preserved the purity of their bloodline. At the bottom were the Slavs, who had so diluted their bloodlines as to no longer be true Aryans. How Chamberlain managed to make the case for German "purity of blood" in the light of the centuries of savage rapine and plunder undergone by the German heartland at the hands of all their neighbors is anyone's guess. *Foundations* also blamed everything bad in history on the Jewish people, repositioning Judaism from being a culture and a religion to a race.[19]

Foundations incorporated elements of the Teutonic myths of Richard Wagner and the racist drivel of Arthur de Gobineau. Everything good, beautiful, and heroic was Aryan. All that was evil, ugly, and cowardly was Jewish. Hitler embraced Chamberlain's views enthusiastically. In 1923 Chamberlain endorsed Hitler and his party for their stated views about racial purity. This toxic tree of knowledge bore bitter fruit in the savage destruction it inspired Hitler and his henchmen to visit upon the world—from the murder of millions of Slavic people to the "Final Solution to the Jewish Question."

The Japanese were a different matter entirely. Their culture had undergone a rapid transformation from medieval to modern in the space of less than a century. During that time, they had not had time to lose their firmly held belief that to be Japanese was to be superior to all other human beings. The doctrine of *Hakkō ichiu,* which translates roughly to "eight corners, one roof" was an expression of this feeling. It was attributed to the first Japanese Emperor Jimmu, although it appears it was a Meiji Restoration theme. The doctrine spoke directly to the emperor's duty to unite the entire world under his rule. It was Manifest Destiny on steroids.

The Japanese military viewed itself as the instrument by which *Hakkō ichiu* would become reality. The noted historian Richard Frank observed when writing about the Rape of Nanking:

> Yet another important contributor to this tragedy and many others to come was the Imperial Army's socialization of officers and men through physical violence. Not only did noncommissioned officers beat common soldiers, but so did officers strike junior officers and enlisted men. Not surprisingly, this instilled in enlisted men the outlook that they were in turn entitled to physically abuse those with still lower status, like civilians and prisoners. Further, by the 1930s the Japanese armed forces inculcated the belief that there was unbearable shame in surrender. Anyone who would offer to surrender was contemptible. Finally, physical violence against women was rampant in Japanese society.[20]

As a result, the Japanese violated the Hague and Geneva Convention standards more blatantly than the Nazis by providing each prisoner with an average of less than 1,000 calories per day even when food was plentiful, and the Japanese ration standard was around 2,500 calories a day. They also rarely issued intact Red Cross parcels to the prisoners. Often all that was left in the looted parcels was cheese or milk-based products. Most prisoners saw one such parcel a year, if that.

The Japanese, who considered themselves as only bound by the 1907 Hague Convention, were still required to treat their prisoners humanely.[21] However, they chose to interpret Chapter II, Article 8 of the Convention which stated that "Prisoners of war shall be subject to the laws, regulations, and orders in force in the army of the State in whose power they are. Any act of insubordination justifies the adoption towards them of such measures of severity as may be considered necessary"[22] as affording them the latitude to beat and even execute prisoners for any infraction of the rules, however minor. Given that beatings at the hands of superiors were a daily fact of life in the Imperial Japanese Armed Forces, this is not entirely surprising.[23] However, as the International Military Tribunal for the Far East (IMTFE) found, the Hague Convention did not excuse their behavior as it went well beyond that of normal Japanese discipline in severity.

Japan had its own cultural baggage which made the brutal mistreatment of prisoners far more likely. The first element was the already-mentioned conviction of racial superiority that was engrained from childhood.[24] The second was the attitude imparted by the *Imperial Rescript to Soldiers and Sailors* of 1882 and the *Senjikun Military Code* of 1941. Both documents emphasized both loyalty to the emperor and the shame of becoming a prisoner. The *Senjikun Military Code* went even further, prohibiting surrender under any circumstances and mandating an honorable death. Thousands of Japanese committed suicide rather than be taken prisoner.

Many Japanese who were taken prisoner were firmly convinced they would be outcasts when they returned home. This belief is reflected in the single Japanese breakout from a POW camp near Cowra, Australia. The camp initially held both Italian and Japanese prisoners, with the Italians being repatriated in late 1943. In the early morning hours of August 4, 1944, almost 900 prisoners attempted to escape with 378 breaching the wire. Over 500 were driven back by machine gun and rifle fire before they could escape. They had agreed before escaping that they would not harm civilians but would cause as much damage to military targets as possible before being killed. They knew that the Infantry Training Centre was nearby and hoped to obtain weapons and ammunition there. However, the Australians were not completely surprised and managed to recapture all but 27 of the prisoners who had committed suicide. In the end, five Australians died, along with 231 Japanese (including the suicides) and 108 Japanese were wounded.[25]

As a result, there were marked differences between being taken prisoner by the Germans in the European Theater and the Japanese in the Asian Pacific Theater. The starkest contrast is the difference in survival rates once in a prisoner of war camp. British Commonwealth and US prisoners suffered a four percent mortality rate in German hands. In the hands of the Japanese, their aggregate mortality figure was 27 percent. When broken out by nationality the mortality figures are: Americans 34 percent, Australians 33 percent, British 32 percent and Dutch 20 percent.[26]

The Germans had no compunction in shooting a prisoner caught breaching the wire. However, with the exception of the cold-blooded execution of 50 Allied prisoners recaptured after their escape from Stalag Luft III, chronicled in Paul Brickhill's *The Great Escape*, the Berga Incident, and the Malmedy Massacre, the Germans did not indulge in wholesale massacre of Western Allied prisoners of war as a matter of policy.[27] Their treatment of Soviet and Eastern European prisoners was unspeakable as it was driven by the twisted Nazi ideology.[28]

This stands in stark contrast to the long tally of Allied prisoners of war intentionally murdered by Imperial Japanese Forces—a list that almost defies description. What is particularly shocking to the Western mind is the number of prisoners murdered *after* the Japanese capitulated.[29] Allied airmen were singled out for especially harsh treatment. The Japanese passed a law in the immediate aftermath of the Doolittle Raid in 1942 classifying all airmen as war criminals. Very few airmen who bombed the home islands after the Doolittle Raid survived capture by the Japanese.

Another contrast between the European and Pacific theaters was the difference in the availability of resistance networks to aid evaders or escapers. In Europe there were several escape lines which sprang up shortly after the fall of France. One example is the outstanding accomplishments of the Comet Line, which carried over 800 Allied evaders—mostly airmen—from Belgium to Spain during the course of the war. The peoples of Nazi-occupied Europe were more likely than not to help or shelter an escaped prisoner or downed airman. Therefore, an assisted escape was far more likely.

Not so in the Pacific. Americans in the Philippines could count on some support from local guerilla organizations or from most Filipinos after the fall of Bataan and Corregidor in 1942. British Commonwealth and American troops in what are now Indonesia, Malaysia, and Burma faced hostile populations for the most part—although there were numerous exceptions as the populace began to get the measure of their Japanese overlords. There were some notable escapes, but except for the lines set up by the Special Operations Executive (SOE) as Singapore fell in 1942, by the British Army Aid Group (BAAG) in Hong Kong and China, and by the American Air Ground Aid Service (AGAS) in China in 1943–45, much of the Pacific Theater did not favor evasion or escape because of the sheer distances involved. In General Douglas MacArthur's domain, the Southwest Pacific Area, MI9 and MIS-X were not allowed to operate independently as in all other areas. MacArthur insisted that, as intelligence entities, they come under his control.

However, Home Runs did occur in both theaters. The most difficult were those which were unassisted by a resistance network. As a percentage, these were few in the European Theater. The population and resource controls of Nazi-occupied territories were stringent. Movement without guides was chancy at best. In the Pacific Theater, a rather larger percentage of overall escapes were unassisted by a formal escape organization. Except in China, where downed airmen could find refuge among a sympathetic population, Pacific escapes usually took the form of striking out for friendly territory in a boat.

For those unable to escape, liberation came in several forms. The Germans repatriated a tiny fraction of prisoners due to their no longer being fit for military service. The Japanese did not repatriate prisoners at any time, preferring to dispose of them through overwork, starvation, or outright execution. The advance of victorious Allied Forces liberated the vast majority of prisoners, either in their camps or as they were on the march. Regardless of the circumstances, liberation was sometimes fraught with peril and always a period of extreme tension. Prisoners in Europe feared that Nazi die-hards would execute them to prevent their liberation, a fear that was not entirely groundless. The Japanese military, on the other hand, had definite plans to murder all the POWs in their hands if the Allies invaded the home islands.[30] Only the shock effect of two atomic bombs that forced their surrender prevented those plans from being carried out.

Once freed from captivity, the former prisoners went home to a reception that did not feature ticker-tape parades. Society little understood the searing psychological trauma they had undergone. In all too many cases officialdom simply ignored their problems. What is so inspiring is how most POWs went on to rebuild their lives in spite of all of their trauma and suffering. They became productive citizens, despite it all. It is to those brave survivors and the honored dead that I dedicate this book.

CHAPTER 2

Allied Escape Organizations

Britain and the United States each had their own organization whose mission was to help evaders and escapers worldwide. The British had MI9, and the US had MIS-X. Both were military intelligence organizations that observed tight security. Since the US entered the war later than Britain, MIS-X owed much but not all its tradecraft and ideas for escape gadgetry to MI9. This chapter traces the history of both organizations from their formative days to their winding-up operations at the end of the war, beginning with MI9.

World War I had taught the British a great deal about evasion and escape. In 1917, they created MI 1a to support escapers from the hands of the Central Powers. Their operations included employing coded letters to maintain two-way communications with officers' camps, but not with other ranks. Shortly after the end of the "War to End All Wars," the British deactivated MI 1a as part of their overall post-war retrenchment. Faced by another large-scale war, the British reactivated MI 1a in August 1939. It became MI9 on December 23, 1939.

According to its original commanding officer, Major (later Brigadier) Norman Crockatt, MI9 had the following objectives:

(a) To facilitate the escapes of British prisoners of war, thereby getting back service personnel and containing additional enemy manpower on guard duties.
(b) To facilitate the return to the United Kingdom of those who succeeded in evading capture in enemy occupied territory.
(c) To collect and distribute information.
(d) To assist in the denial of information to the enemy.
(e) To maintain morale of British prisoners of war in enemy prison camps.[1]

MI9 had a shoestring beginning, consisting only of eight members in early 1940. However, they were all forceful characters who left their mark on MI9 as it grew. None of the founders had more effect than their commander throughout the war, Norman Crockatt. When he took command of MI9, he was a 45-year-old Royal Scots Major. An infantry officer who served with distinction during World War I, he had earned a Distinguished Service Order (DSO) for bravery under fire. Twice wounded, he retired from active service in 1927. When war threatened, he left his lucrative position as a stockbroker to assume command of MI9. Described as "clear-headed, quick witted, a good organizer, a good judge of men, and no respecter of red tape," he was the perfect man for the job.[2]

The other original members of the team included the chief of staff Captain V. R. Isham of the Suffolk Regiment, the executive officer Captain Cecil M. Rait of the Artist's Rifles (a British Regiment that was originally composed of artists), three intelligence officers, Lieutenants H. B. A. De Bruyne, Leslie Winterbottom, and Clayton Hutton, and two liaison officers, Commander Phillip Wood Rhodes, Royal Navy (RN) and Pilot Officer A. J. "Johnny" Evans, Royal Air Force (RAF).

Captain Isham was nicknamed "Tiger." He was by all accounts the consummate chief of staff. His nuanced understanding of the byzantine workings of military bureaucracy helped MI9's requirements work their way through the system with a minimum of delay. Captain Rait was quick thinking, bold but not rash, meticulous, and entirely indifferent to self-promotion. He had served with distinction in World War I, leaving service as a major. He accepted a post under Captain Isham—to whom he was senior—without complaint. He finished the war as MI9's chief of staff in the rank of lieutenant colonel.

Lieutenant H. B. A. De Bruyne, Royal Horse Artillery was an exceptionally talented debriefer of evaders and escapers. As MI9 grew, his techniques and procedures became the framework for British and, later, American evader and escaper debriefings. He preferred the nickname of Bruno, but much to his chagrin he was often called "Bo Peep" because his family had owned a sheep farm in southern Chile before the war. He ended the war as a lieutenant colonel in the Royal Horse Artillery.

Before the war, Lieutenant Leslie Winterbottom had been the personal assistant to an Oxford retail tycoon. The interpersonal skills he learned in that job transferred to his duties as the liaison with British prisoners' families. He oversaw the entire process of sending and receiving coded messages to prisoners of war. Part of this process involved securing the cooperation of family, wives, and sweethearts to write the necessary letters in their own hand. The Axis never discovered—although they suspected—that some sort of coded messages were passing daily through the mail. His tireless efforts allowed MI9 to send and receive messages to the prisoners advising them of clandestine supply shipments and receiving intelligence from them in return. Winterbottom ended the war as a lieutenant colonel in the Intelligence Corps.

From Lieutenant Christopher "Clutty" Clayton Hutton's fertile imagination sprang most of the escape devices used by the Allies during World War II. These ranged from compasses hidden in uniform buttons and hacksaws concealed in boot laces, to a complete evasion kit in an easy-to-carry pouch. Having been a flier in World War I, he was determined to serve his country when war broke out. He dispatched telegrams to dozens of agencies offering his services. This led to an interview with an officer looking to put "square pegs into square holes."[3]

What clinched his entry to MI9 was his interest in "escapology." As a young man, he had issued a £100 challenge to the great Harry Houdini—a challenge which he lost. Clutty had challenged Houdini to escape from a box of Clutty's own design, put together by workmen of Clutty's choosing. It seemed like a sure thing, but Houdini managed to escape anyway. It was only years later that Clutty found out the secret. Houdini had bribed the workmen to nail the box up in such a manner that he could escape! As Clutty observed, it taught him a great deal about the art of escape.

He was perennially at loggerheads with either a civil or military bureaucrat which bothered him not one iota. Recognizing Clutty's value to MI9, Norman Crockatt refused to allow the bureaucrats to hem him in. In a letter to a provost marshal in response to one of Clutty's innumerable scrapes with authority Crockatt wrote, "This officer is eccentric. He cannot be expected to comply with ordinary service discipline, but he is far too valuable for his services to be lost to this department."[4] In spite of all his head butting with authority, Clutty finished the war as a major on the General List.

The liaison officer from the senior service, Commander P. W. Rhodes, was affectionately nicknamed "The Admiral." He had spent over two years as a prisoner of war following the battle of Jutland. Although he had not escaped successfully from captivity during World War I, it was not for want of trying. He remained a steadying influence on the senior leadership of MI9 throughout the war.

A. J. "Johnny" Evans was a famous escaper of World War I and author of *The Escaping Club*. His practical knowledge garnered from two successful escapes—first from the Germans and later from the Turks—would help to direct the evolution of the highly successful escape kits and devices Clutty developed. More than once, he would examine a piece of escape kit and observe quietly, "This won't do Clutty." His comments on the Mark IV escape kit were particularly useful. He also had a formative influence on the briefings MI9 developed to give to aircrew, commandos, paratroops, and others going in harm's way with a high risk of capture.

After the fall of France in May 1940, MI9 expanded rapidly. By December 1941, the organization had five sub-sections that were continually augmented as the war went on. In 1942, MI9 added a subsection (P15) to recruit, train, and employ agents for the purpose of building escape organizations in enemy-occupied territory. One of their most successful operations would be the Shelburne Line. MI6, which was the organization with overall responsibility for British intelligence collection efforts in occupied Europe, always maintained close visibility of all of P15's operations. Indeed, the formidable head of MI6, Sir Claude Dansey, kept a personal eye on the training and employment of MI9 agents in the field. MI9 added an awards bureau in 1944 to recognize those who had helped Allied escapers and evaders. The awards bureau continued its work well into 1946. The table below depicts MI9's designation, functions, and peak manning.

Table 2: MI9 sub-sections and their functions as of December 1941[5,6]

Designation	Functions	Peak manning
B	External liaison; interrogation of returned evaders and escapers (function later transferred to MI9[W])	Section redesignated AB in 1944
D	Training which primarily involved training aircrew, commandos, and paratroops in the art of evasion	15
W	Interrogation of returned evaders and escapers	14
X	Planning and organization of escapes; this included sustaining resistance networks and dispatching agents	7
Y	Codes, to include developing the codes, training selected personnel in their use, dispatching coded letters to prisoners of war, and decoding letters from prisoners	24
Z	Escape aids, to include kits and devices	17
D-P(15)	Employment and training (under auspices of SIS) of agents sent to enemy occupied countries of Western Europe to assist escapers and evaders to return to U.K.; preparation of plans for evacuation of escapers and evaders from France, Belgium and Holland; communication with IS9 (the field arm of MI9) agents in these countries.	5
AB	Validating and rewarding those who helped Allied evaders and escapers; external liaison	90

The Metropole Hotel in London, not far from the War Office, was MI9's original home. In September of 1940, the hotel was slightly damaged during a German air raid. This led to Crockatt shifting the headquarters to the Wilton Park estate in Beaconsfield, a town in the South Bucks district of Buckinghamshire, England, 23 miles west–north–west of central London.[7]

As noted earlier, MI9 wound up the war ensuring that those who aided Allied evaders and escapers received proper recognition. This could range from the award of a decoration to compensation for financial losses. At the end of the war, MI9 filed a detailed end-of-war report with the War Office (WO 208/3242) that was declassified in 2010. Even before the declassification, a number of excellent books were written about MI9 by those who had participated in its operations, including *MI9 Escape and Evasion 1939–1945* by M. R. D. Foot and J. M. Langley as well as *Saturday at MI9* by Airey Neave.

This contrasts rather starkly with how the US's escape and evasion organization, MIS-X, wound up its operations. In August of 1945, the US assistant chief of staff G2, Major General George V. Strong, ordered the destruction of all documents and artifacts relating to MIS-X. He also ordered the destruction of all MIS-X facilities. By the end of the summer, it was done. Except for a few files overlooked in the National Archives and the memories of the MIS-X personnel, the organization went into the memory hole. Unlike MI9, only one authoritative book—*The Escape Factory* by Lloyd Shoemaker—has been written about MIS-X.

MIS-X came into existence in early 1942 in the aftermath of Major General Carl "Tooey" Spaatz's visit to England in February of that year. He was charged with establishing the US Army Air Corps presence in England, a presence that would grow into the "Mighty Eighth" Air Force. Spaatz quickly realized that he would need an organization much like MI9 to support American evaders and escapers. After a month of briefings from the RAF, Major General Spaatz returned to Washington, DC, to—among other things—get the ball rolling on a US evasion and escape organization.

Accompanied by RAF Air Vice-Marshal Charles Mendhurst, Spaatz briefed both Chief of Staff General George C. Marshall and Secretary of War Henry L. Stimson on MI9. They won Marshall over immediately. However, Stimson was initially skeptical of the idea. The arguments made by General Marshall and Major General George V. Strong of Army Intelligence finally won him over. However, it was not until seven months later, in October of 1942, that the War Department ordered the commander of the Prisoner of War Branch, Colonel Catesby ap Jones, to form MIS-X.[8]

Colonel Jones realized he would need liaison at the Pentagon and in England as well as a commander for MIS-X. Colonel J. Edward Johnson, a canny former business executive, ably filled the post at the Pentagon. Johnson was the head of an organization designated PW/X which worked exclusively in the European Theater of Operations (ETO) as a liaison element. However, MIS-X did most of the heavy lifting. Therefore, I will use MIS-X to cover all US evasion and escape efforts, particularly in the ETO. Spaatz had already appointed Lieutenant Colonel W. Stull Holt as liaison with MI9. Although not under Jones' command, Holt met the needs for liaison with MI9. As commander of MIS-X Jones picked Captain Robley Winfrey, who proved himself an ideal commander. Levelheaded, discreet, and a strong leader, Winfrey would end the war as a lieutenant colonel.

The location for MIS-X was never in doubt, at least in Colonel Jones' mind. He picked Fort Hunt, Virginia, a former part of the Civil War defenses of Washington, D.C. His main reason for selecting Fort Hunt was that MIS-Y, the section of Army Military Intelligence which interrogated select German prisoners of war, had been there since early 1942. Tight security was already in place, including military police checkpoints, fences, and patrols. Integrating a few additional personnel into the daily rhythm of Fort Hunt activities would hardly raise anyone's interest. By November of 1942, MIS-X occupied their initial building, nicknamed "the Creamery," as well as several renovated World War I officers' quarters. As the war progressed, so did the building program. A no-frills warehouse was erected near the Creamery, which included space for Winfrey, storage space, as well as an area called "the Shop" where specialists turned out US escape aids and German documentation required by evaders and escapers alike. Later in the war, the technicians in "the Shop" ran off large batches of counterfeit Reichsmarks.

Using the MI9 structure as a template, MIS-X organized into five subsections: interrogation, correspondence, POW locations, training and briefing, and technical. MIS-X had many of the same tasks as MI9, as detailed in a War Department memo entitled "Establishment of a Unit to Deal with Prisoner of War Escape Methods."[9] These included:

- Indoctrinating Air Force and ground force instructors in evasion and escape methods.
- Providing instruction on evasion and escape to air and ground force personnel.
- Providing instruction in proper conduct in the event of capture.
- Debriefing returning evaders or escapers for information with intelligence value.
- Obtaining information from prisoners via coded letters on the condition of their imprisonment, escape opportunities, escape equipment requirements, and other intelligence.
- Preparing and distributing escape kits and emergency kits for personnel with a high risk of capture.
- Planning, developing, and carrying out code correspondence with selected prisoners.
- Maintaining close liaison with MI9.[10]

MIS-X faced several obstacles in becoming operational. The first was funds. Unlike MI9, they had no regular appropriation because Major General Strong had forbidden it on grounds of security. However, while MIS-X was occasionally close to being bankrupt, Winfrey always managed to find enough money to keep the lights on somewhere. The right sort of technical personnel were difficult to find, but the Army personnel system eventually managed to locate volunteers with the right skill sets. In December of 1942, the first five code officers arrived, followed by three additional officers and eight technicians in February of 1943. With their arrival, MIS-X could begin operations.

Much of MIS-X's technical work on escape aids depended on the voluntary cooperation of industry. The British had the 1940 Defence of the Realm and the long-standing Official Secrets Acts to compel any business or individual to cooperate in the war effort and keep quiet about it. MIS-X initially only had the tools of persuasion to get US individuals and businesses to cooperate. It took the passage of the Second War

Powers Act of 1942 to put MIS-X in a position to use coercive power on industry. Much to industry's credit there was little need for coercion, no matter how mystifying the request. This cooperation ensured that "Uncle Sam's General Merc,"[11] the insider nickname for MIS-X, always had the raw materials and finished products to work their magic.

Vital to the functioning of both MI9 and MIS-X in the European Theater were the code users (CU), whose coded letters allowed information to pass back and forth between the prisoner of war camps in Europe and the headquarters at Beaconsfield and Fort Hunt. This system succeeded in Europe because the Germans allowed the prisoners mail on a fairly regular schedule. It had scant success in the Pacific because the Japanese generally denied prisoners any mail. Still, the use of what was known as letter codes allowed prisoners to pass intelligence, and request and confirm the arrival of escape aids. Both the British and the Americans maintained tight security of their respective CU systems. The first sample of a British letter code appeared in 1979 while the first sample of a letter code employed by US POWs surfaced in 1990, 34 and 45 years respectively after the war ended.

In China, MI9 worked through a staff element GS 1(e), later referred to as "E Group," and the British Army Aid Group (BAAG). MIS-X operations were conducted primarily by AGAS. The BAAG, set up by the initiative of Lieutenant Colonel (Sir) Lindsay Ride, provided aid to prisoners in camps in China. Ride was highly motivated to help prisoners, having been captured when Hong Kong fell on Christmas Day of 1941. He escaped to the mainland on January 8, 1942, where he began to develop an organization that clandestinely provided news, food, and medicine to the prisoners being held in the Hong Kong camps. The BAAG assisted evading airmen, even rescuing some who parachuted in sight of the Japanese garrison in Hong Kong. The key factor in their success was the cooperation of the Chinese people, who were thoroughly anti–Japanese after having suffered unspeakable atrocities at the hands of the Imperial Japanese Army. However, this doesn't mean that BAAG operations were without their peculiar challenges. Due to almost a century of intermittent conflict between Britain and China,

Ride had to prove his trustworthiness to the Chinese—particularly the forces of Chiang Kai-shek—daily.

Initially established at New Delhi by Lieutenant Colonel Robin Ridgeway in May 1942, E Group eventually spread its operations across China and Southeast Asia. Besides gathering intelligence on the location and condition of POWs, they ran two highly successful jungle training schools for aircrew and commandos, one in Ceylon[12] and the other northeast of Calcutta. E Group provided BAAG with links to the larger Allied intelligence apparatus as well as providing escape kits, blood chits, and silk maps to aircrew and other troops likely to become isolated. They also funneled £3,000 per quarter (roughly worth £150,000 or $190,000 today) to BAAG to defray operating expenses. E Group worked hand-in-hand with BAAG, AGAS and on occasion the Office of Strategic Services (OSS) throughout the war, continually improving their complementary evasion networks across Asia.

The AGAS came into being when MIS-X dispatched First Lieutenant Barclay P. Schoyer to China in early 1943. A fluent Mandarin speaker, Schoyer went straight to Lt. Col. Ride to see how things were being done. He quickly copied many of BAAG's methods. However, because the US had no significant history of warfare with China, the Chinese trusted Americans to operate radios without supervision. This allowed Schoyer to dispatch teams to widely dispersed and remote areas of China. These teams contacted local Communist guerillas or Kuomintang forces to ensure that any downed airmen would be funneled to the team. The evaders would then be placed into a network of friendly Chinese who would spirit them to safety. At times, AGAS would employ networks set up by BAAG and vice versa. By the end of the war, their combined efforts had rescued at least 898 downed airmen.[13]

MI9 did not operate in General Douglas MacArthur's domain, the Southwest Pacific Area. For that matter, neither did MIS-X, other than providing briefings and escape supplies. General MacArthur refused to have any intelligence organization not under his direct control operate in his domain. Besides, there was precious little MIS-X could do, given that the Japanese largely denied delivery of Red Cross parcels to prisoners and that mail was so infrequent as to be nonexistent.

Throughout the war in both theaters, the cooperation between MI9 and MIS-X was exemplary. Much of this was due to their commanding officers, men of strong character with abundant common sense. They maintained a single-minded—but not blinkered—focus on their mission to aid Allied evaders, prisoners of war, and escapers. They can take a large portion of the credit for the 35,000 British Commonwealth and US military personnel who made successful Home Runs during World War II.[14]

CHAPTER 3

Essentials and Escape Devices

The challenges facing evaders and escapers were many. Some challenges were common to both theaters, others were not. The essentials also varied between the European and Pacific theaters. For simplicity's sake, we will first address the problems common to evaders and escapers in both theaters. Food, water, maps, and a compass were the bare essentials required by all. Evaders were sometimes issued these essentials, but not always. Escapers had to make their own or rely on items smuggled into the camps or manufactured by the prisoners.

So how were these devices and other essentials produced? As mentioned earlier, MI9's Clayton "Clutty" Hutton was the driving force behind the development of most Allied escape aids. Initially working from a cramped office in the Hotel Metropole, he moved to Beaconsfield with the rest of MI9 after the hotel was damaged in a bombing raid. Given a large office and workspace in a Georgian mansion, he nevertheless sought a more private, isolated spot in which to experiment. He built one in a local cemetery, making his workshop look like a tomb! The move succeeded. Except for a curious American co-worker, no one discovered Clutty's secret lair during the course of the war.

The Americans produced their own versions of British escape devices at Fort Hunt, plus a few of their own invention. These included a miniature radio, broken into four pieces and packaged in softballs shipped to the prisoners. Like the British, the US relied heavily on manufacturers to produce items such as game boards and sports equipment loaded with hidden escape aids for insertion in POW packages, which they referred to as "specials" or "dynamite" packages. Since British and American manufacturing methods and material differed, MIS-X was often forced to develop entirely new methods of loading escape devices into innocuous items such as game boards, records, and shaving brushes.

Both MI9 and MIS-X had an iron-clad rule of never using Red Cross parcels to ship contraband of any type. They feared, rightly as post-war interrogations and documents showed, that the Germans would stop all deliveries of these lifesaving parcels if they discovered contraband. Rather, they created front organizations to manage the flow of contraband. MI9 had a total of 36 organizations shipping contraband as a tiny fraction of their overall shipments. Of these, only three had their cover blown during the war.[1] MIS-X had only two such organizations—the War Prisoner's Benefit Foundation and the Servicemen's Relief. Both shipped articles throughout the war without being compromised.[2] In addition to their established organizations, MI9 dispatched packages from a host of fictitious friends and family to the prisoners, of which a percentage would contain loaded items. The letters which often accompanied the "specials" were written by men and women who volunteered to add a missive which boosted the credibility of the package.

The quantity of escape devices shipped by MI9 and MIS-X to the prison camps was based on a combination of experience and special requests. Ultimately, the effectiveness of the system depended on having a CU in the target camp. The capture of bomber crews and ground personnel ensured that CUs eventually found their way into every camp. They were the link that allowed MI9 and MIS-X to alert the POWs that a special package was inbound as well as provide directions on how to access the contents. CUs could also advise Beaconsfield or Fort Hunt of specific needs. This could be the essentials but could include complex items such as radio parts and, in a few rare instances, weapons. The CUs could also signal when they had run out of room to hide escape devices, which happened with increasing frequency during the autumn of 1944. Indeed, by the winter of 1945, almost all shipments of special packages had ceased.

Napoleon said that "an army travels on its stomach." So did evaders and escapers. When hungry, they would often make serious mistakes leading to their capture. Food used by evaders and escapers had to be nutritious, in concentrated form for ease of carry, and resistant to spoilage. Depending on the version of escape kit, the food issued to aircrew, paratroops, and commandos was sufficient for up to 10 days if the evader exercised discipline. The British Mark IV Escape Kit, by far the most common issued in World War II, contained 24 malted milk balls, a bar of chocolate, and a peanut butter bar. It also contained a tube full of pure dairy cream.[3] There were American versions of the Mark IV as well as unique kits designed for pilots which contained several fortified chocolate bars.

In the European Theater, prisoners made their own escape foods from the contents of their Red Cross parcels, from bartered items, or through black market trading. To enable "The Great Escape," the prisoners cooked a large batch of what they nicknamed "fudge." It was made from oatmeal, sugar, chocolate (when available) and condensed milk. Cooked in sheets and cut into squares, it was undoubtedly nutritious and resistant to spoilage. However, it was not a delight to the palate.[4]

In the Pacific Theater, prisoners had little to augment their normally meager supply of food. However, some prisoners did have the discipline to save food for their escape attempts. The most usual method for accumulating food supplies was to trade for it, with cigarettes being the most widely accepted currency. Rice was the staple food, both in camp and during escapes. The prisoners had a saying, "Rice is the greatest food there is—anything you add to it improves it."[5]

While an individual can go without food for up to three weeks, the limit for going without water is three to four days.[6] An escaper in both theaters could normally find water without much difficulty. However, the water sources in the Pacific Theater were more likely to cause illness. Another hazard of the Pacific arose when evading or escaping by boat. Apart from rainwater or water sources found during landfall, the vast expanse of the Pacific afforded no other source of drinkable water.

Evaders in both theaters were issued water purification tablets, which addressed the potability issue, but not that of portability. One obvious requirement for a water carrier was that it fit into an escape kit case. At first, MI9 and MIS-X tried placing rubber bags (which looked a lot like condoms) in the kit, but they tended to burst easily. Besides, the troops didn't care to drink from a canteen which looked like a condom. The next attempt at solving the portability problem was a rubber or plastic water bottle. Unfortunately, they tended to crack when stored for any length of time and therefore to leak. The solution developed by Clayton Hutton was elegant—redesign the escape kit case as a very serviceable canteen. While it would leak if handled too roughly, most evaders rated it highly. Escapers often created makeshift canteens or fabricated drinking cups from Red Cross parcel cans or bits of metal available in their POW camps. Those transiting Germany and the Nazi-occupied territories often relied on water from public sources, particularly if carrying a canteen or drinking cup did not fit their escape persona.

Compasses were a vital part of the evader's escape kit. The fly button of many evaders included a tiny but durable compass. Originally, to extract the compass, one merely had to twist the button counterclockwise. However, a German soldier unknown to posterity discovered the secret during a search of a downed airman. Thereafter every captured airman or paratrooper had their fly buttons tested with a quick counterclockwise twist. On learning this, Clayton Hutton developed and issued a fly button compass which only came apart with a clockwise twist. Hutton was gratified to learn at the end of the war that the Germans never caught on to the change.

MI9 and MIS-X issued at least 1,700,241 compasses in Europe, Africa, and the Middle East.[7] This does not include the miniature compasses smuggled to POW camps for which there are no definitive figures. MI9 and MIS-X showed great ingenuity in smuggling these compasses to prisoners. MI9 and MIS-X hid them in buttons, collar studs, rings, pencils and shaving brushes, to name just a few concealment methods.

However, to offer users as many options as possible, MI9 persuaded Gillette and other safety razor manufacturers to magnetize their blades made in Britain for the duration of the war. MIS-X later got US safety razor manufacturers to follow suit for razors manufactured for issue to the Armed Forces. To use a magnetized razor blade, the evader or escaper suspended it by a thread. It would wobble a bit before steadying up. North was indicated by the first letter in the manufacturer's logo. Another variation of the string-suspended compass was a bar of magnetized metal with two luminous dots on one end to indicate north and a single dot at the other end to indicate south.[8] While not as simple to use on the move as a miniature compass, they were both serviceable navigation aids in a pinch.

Prisoners showed extreme ingenuity in manufacturing compasses. Examples varied in sophistication. The simplest were made by laboriously magnetizing a bit of metal to create a string suspension model. At the extreme were miniature compasses complete with luminous dots and glass covers. Because of the lack of any outside supplies reaching prisoners in Japanese hands, string suspension models were the most common type used by escapers in the Pacific.

Maps provided to evaders in both theaters were normally printed on silk and of high quality. Airey Neave, in *Saturday at MI9*, records that MI9 issued such maps in Europe, Africa, and the Middle East.[9] Prisoners in the European Theater had three other sources of maps—handmade, stolen, and smuggled. Handmade sketch maps were common throughout the war. These sketch maps provided enough information for basic navigation. Stolen maps were filched from visitors or their vehicles by light-fingered prisoners. Since maps were a controlled item in the Third Reich, their loss was often not reported for fear of the consequences such as a transfer to the Russian Front. When not used by an escaper, smuggled or stolen maps often provided the basis for high-quality sketch maps produced in the camps.

Equipped with food, water, a compass and map, the evader or escaper was almost ready to depart. In both theaters, they required suitable clothing. Once in the hands of an escape line or resistance group, evaders and prisoners in both theaters almost invariably received suitable civilian clothing. This is remarkable as clothing in Nazi-occupied Europe was rationed and very hard to get. In Europe, civilian clothing was necessary to blend with the population. Such clothing was either produced in the camps or obtained from guards using bribes of cigarettes or chocolate from Red Cross parcels.

Prisoners and Allied escape organizations employed many ingenious means to ensure that escapers were properly clothed. Prisoners could barter for or steal items of civilian clothing. One enterprising sergeant got himself detailed to a work party handling civilian clothes and managed to steal a full set to aid in his successful escape.[10] Another escaper, Lieutenant D. P. James, RN, actually travelled in the full-dress uniform of the Royal Navy, reasoning that the Germans would not be familiar with it. It almost worked. Using a forged identity card bearing the prosaic name of "I. Bagerov," Lieutenant James made it from Marlag-Milag Nord to the gates of the Lübeck dockyard before being recaptured. Undismayed by his failure, Lieutenant James subsequently escaped disguised as a Swedish sailor and made a Home Run.[11]

Prisoners in Europe would use blankets, mattress covers, and their own altered uniforms to produce a wardrobe suitable for their escape persona. They used items as simple as bleach or boot polish to change the color of the cloth. To aid the prisoner's ingenuity, MI9 and MIS-X provided dyes and easily alterable replacement uniforms. In this form of aid, MI9 really stood out. Clutty Hutton invented a working pen which had a dye capsule in the ink well. Once removed, it was sufficient to dye a single uniform.

Taking advantage of the Geneva Convention requirement that prisoners be allowed to receive replacement uniforms, MI9 invented two new but very adaptable replacements intended for use by prisoners. The first was a mess dress uniform that was almost identical in cut to its Luftwaffe counterpart. It even included metallic thread piping which could be fashioned into German decorations! The other example was a reversible fatigue uniform that could be quickly converted with minimal effort into civilian work clothes. To ensure that the Germans didn't become suspicious, the RAF and the British Army published official announcements of the two uniforms' debut. These made their way into neutral country magazines and from there to the Germans.

In the Pacific, there was no chance of an evader or escaper of European descent blending with the population, but clothing still performed its basic function of protecting the body. Prisoners of the Japanese were frequently dressed in not much more than loincloths. They frequently lacked any form of foot protection, whether sandals, shoes, or boots. However, once escapers encountered Filipino or Chinese guerillas, they usually received some form of clothing which, even if ill-fitting, was far better than what they had arrived wearing.

A good example is that of the 11 survivors of the December 1944 Palawan Massacre who were all provided with footwear and clothing by the Filipino guerillas who eventually took them under their wing.[12] For both the evader and the escaper, clothing offered no chance to blend with the populace except when viewed from a distance. Concealment from enemy sight was the best option in the Pacific.

Carrying or losing an escape kit was often a problem for aircrew. The RAF designed the Beadon suit to solve that problem in China and Southeast Asia. When worn, it prevented RAF aircrew from leaving their escape devices behind or losing them during bailout. A lightweight overgarment, it kept all of the devices and rations in buttoned pockets. It included maps, a hacksaw, a machete, a compass, anti-malarial pills and a Mark IV escape kit. The US forces initially met the problem with an E-kit that attached to the parachute harness. It contained all of the equipment of a Beadon suit, plus a mess kit, frying pan and smokeless cooker. Due to reports of the E-kit tangling with suspension lines during a bailout, the E-kit evolved into a pocketed mesh garment, the "E-vest."[13]

Papers were an absolute requirement for both evaders and escapers in occupied Europe where the Germans had imposed a police state requiring multiple documents for simple existence, much less travel. There were several ways to obtain the required documentation. Forgery was the primary means. Therefore, forgers were a vital part of the escape organizations in the POW camps in Europe. The adept band of forgers in Stalag Luft III mass produced the documents for 220 escapers who were to have taken part in "The Great Escape."[14] These documents included such details as overstrikes and corrections—all done by hand. Because of the forgers' painstaking attention to detail, the Germans never detected that these fakes were handwritten!

MI9 and MIS-X both produced large quantities of blank documentation such as work permits, identity cards, and travel permits for use by POWs.[15] They included them in packages sent from the bogus prisoner aid societies, along with money, both genuine and counterfeit. The prisoners then simply had to fill them out. Resistance escape lines either forged entire documents or stole authentic blanks to fill out. Mr. Fernand de Greef of the Comet Line worked as a translator for the Germans at the *Kommandantur*[16] in Anglet, France. He purloined blank forms as well as official stamps to provide at least 337 evaders and escapers with very genuine-looking documents between June of 1941 and August of 1944.[17]

In the Pacific, papers were of no real use because the evaders or escapers lacked genetic camouflage and linguistic ability. The exception was the "blood chit," a document written on silk cloth which promised to pay a certain sum to the holder for returning an evader safely to Allied hands. It was written in several local languages and was mostly employed in China and Southeast Asia by MI9, BAAG, and AGAS. It was remarkably successful and certainly contributed to bringing hundreds of downed fliers to safety.

Escape-minded prisoners manufactured many items that were either too bulky or too specialized to be shipped in packages. These included items as diverse as wire cutters, digging tools, ventilation pipes, air pumps, rails, and trolleys. In Stalag Luft III, the prisoners used soft metal strips which they hardened in fire, using sugar as the source of carbon, to produce wire cutters. Digging tools were made in a similar manner, using pilfered metal. At times, the prisoners were able to steal such tools or barter them from "tame" guards. Ventilation pipes for tunnels were made from empty Red Cross food cans. Bellows-style air pumps pushed air down tunnels through makeshift ventilation pipes. They were made in various configurations from scrounged lumber, cloth, and (at times) leather.

While not one of the essentials for escape, radios allowed the prisoners to have a link with the outside world. Surprisingly, even Japanese POW camps had radios. Some were smuggled in, others were built from scratch from scrounged or stolen parts, or from parts sent in via special parcels. Most camps had at least one radio, which boosted morale immensely as the Allies began to pile up victories.

POWs produced a wide range of other items to aid in their escapes. These were mainly props needed to flesh out their escape personas, but they were often ingenious. Briefcases for businessmen, as well as dummy binoculars, rifles, and pistols for Luftwaffe or Wehrmacht officers and soldiers, all served to help camouflage an escaper in plain sight. Airey Neave, who escaped from Colditz in 1941, wore a locally manufactured Wehrmacht uniform, complete down to a dummy side arm and decorations.

Throughout the war, Beaconsfield and Fort Hunt continued to dispatch every aid possible to prisoners and to equip evaders with the best gear possible. Prisoners continued to match wits with their Germans and Japanese captors, usually coming out on top. Equipped with the essentials, evaders and escapers had a much better chance of eventually coming under the wing of an escape line which would assist them in their escape to friendly hands—a Home Run.

Escape lines in both theaters concentrated on recovering aircrew for a number of reasons. One was that it took up to a year to train certain aircrew members. Making extraordinary efforts to recover such highly trained personnel made the hardest sort of sense. Another reason was maintaining morale, particularly among bomber crews with their high attrition rates.[18] The sudden reappearance in their midst of aircrew who had been given up as lost was a real shot in the arm for unit morale. Finally, prisoners of war were in guarded camps. The differences between the theaters required that they be treated separately.

Once an evader hit the ground or a prisoner escaped, Nazi-occupied Europe had escape lines directed and staffed primarily or totally by local resistance members. Three outstanding but very different examples were the Comet, Rome, and Shelburne lines. Their efficiency in locating and helping downed Allied aircrew was a large part of the reason that by mid-1942, an Allied airman shot down over Holland, Belgium, Luxembourg, or France had a 50 percent chance of eventually making it home safely. The time in transit could vary from a week to several months, depending on the circumstances. In Germany, prisoners of war seeking to escape were detained in a police state where escape lines had little or no chance of operating. Once across the German border, the evader had a much better chance of linking up with an escape line and making a Home Run. The trick was getting out of Germany.

In the Pacific, escape lines were differently organized and led. One major escape line only operated for a short while, that of Singapore, set up by the Special Operations Executive (SOE) in 1942. Some might argue that it was really an evacuation line, but it helped thousands evade capture. BAAG and the American organization AGAS worked throughout the war, assisting evaders and escapers. It is their story which we will explore in some of the following chapters. In Southeast Asia, the Office of Strategic Services (OSS) also dabbled in escape lines.

Japanese camps were either in Japan or in terrain which did not favor the escaper, particularly when weakened by systematic starvation and maltreatment. Some camps were located where escapes were possible, but the Japanese policy of executing a number of prisoners (usually at a 10-to-one ratio) in retaliation for an escape put a damper on escape fervor. So did their almost invariable habit of executing recaptured prisoners in a very public and brutal manner. Once the Japanese had occupied an area for about six months, locals were willing to provide aid, but it was not generally as part of an organized escape line. The usual process would involve linking the evaders or escapers with a guerilla unit who would then handle their return to friendly hands.

CHAPTER 4

POW Camp Organization

Prisoner of war camp organization varied depending on whether the camp was located in Europe, Asia, or the Pacific. From 1940 to 1943, both the Nazis and the Italian Fascists had POW camps located throughout their respective countries. After the Italian surrender in September 1943, all permanent POW camps for Allied personnel were in Germany. Whether in Italian or German hands, the prisoners quickly established highly efficient internal organizations. This was only possible because in the main the Germans adhered to the Geneva Conventions. In Asia and the Pacific, it was rather more hit or miss because the Japanese rarely observed even the forms of the Geneva or Hague Conventions. Permanent camps such as those in Hong Kong normally had some form of organization, as did some camps in Korea, Manchuria, and the Philippines.

But the conditions in many of the work camps where the Japanese employed soldier slaves, such as the Bangkok to Rangoon railway and almost all the camps in Japan, prevented any but the most rudimentary organization. Regardless of the camp's location, the Japanese practice of executing recaptured prisoners or killing 10 prisoners for every escapee put a damper on most escape attempts.[1] For that reason, this chapter covers the internal POW camp organizations most often found in the European Theater.

Camps in Germany normally held either officers or enlisted men, regardless of whether they were administered by the Wehrmacht, Luftwaffe, or the Kriegsmarine. There was an overt POW chain of command in each camp. The head of each officer's camp was the Senior

Allied Officer (SAO), who was senior in grade as the name implies. Depending on the camp, the senior officer might be referred to as the Senior British Officer (SBO) or, to confuse things further as in the North Camp of Stalag Luft III, the Senior American Officer (SAO). To simplify matters, this work will use Senior Allied Officer (SAO). In enlisted camps, the spokesman for the prisoners was known as the Man of Confidence—an elected post. Each block (or barracks) had their senior person in charge. They all looked fine on parade, performed the overt administration within the camps, and acted as official liaison with the enemy camp administration. However, with respect to camp organization they were usually the tip of the iceberg.

Buried beneath the surface was a shadow organization dedicated to supporting escapes. The two key figures were the Big X, in overall charge of the escape organization, and the Big S, in charge of security. Both were vital to a successful escape organization. There were other sub-organizations which dealt with supplies and intelligence, all of them important to getting as many POWs beyond the wire as possible. Those running the escape organizations and most of the escapers understood that they would probably be caught short of a Home Run. However, escaping was not just about Home Runs.

The idea behind escaping was to tie up as many enemy resources as possible in keeping the POWs in place or hunting them down when escapes occurred. As Paul Brickhill recorded of the aftermath of the "Great Escape" by 76 POWs from Stalag Luft III in March 1944, "There was only one bright point in the whole affair. Bit by bit we pieced together information brought in by the tame guards and eventually established the fact that the rather staggering figure of 5,000,000 Germans had spent some of their time looking for the prisoners, and many thousands of them were on the job full time for weeks."[2] This is remarkable considering that only three out of 76 prisoners made a Home Run.

Regrettably, the mass escape did have two unintended consequences. First, on Hitler's orders the Nazis executed 50 of the recaptured POWs. Second, Hitler placed the head of the SS and Gestapo, Reichsführer Heinrich Himmler, in overall charge of all POW camps. The various armed services still manned and administered the camps, but under

Himmler's control. It also meant that troublesome prisoners could find themselves sent to a concentration camp. Several of the escapers from Stalag Luft III were confined in Sachsenhausen concentration camp until the end of the war. Word of these actions had a chilling effect on further mass escape attempts but did not stop them all.

Almost every camp in Germany had a "Big X." Normally selected by the SAO, the Big X was rarely part of the visible camp administration. The Big X headed up the escape committee, which listened to prisoners' escape plans, made helpful suggestions, provided needed logistical support, and ultimately approved the escape attempt. While there were occasional spur-of-the-moment escapes such as hiding in a garbage bin being hauled from camp, they were usually unsuccessful. The Big X was assisted in his labors by the Block Xs, who extended his reach into every block, barracks, or hut in camp. The Block Xs kept a close eye on their domains to ensure that no worthwhile escape idea went unnoticed. They also did their best to scotch some of the more harebrained ideas.

The "Big S" normally sat on the escape committee as well, as he arranged the security necessary to cover escape activities. The Big S was also in charge of the organization that kept tabs on the camp guards—known universally to the prisoners as goons—as well as developing a detailed understanding of all enemy security measures. Like the Big X, he had subordinates in every barracks, block, and hut.

Because security was personnel intensive, the Big S might have a quarter of the camp personnel under his control. For example, in Colditz beginning in January 1941 the prisoners kept a 24-hour watch on everything so that "every sentry's beat, every arc light's timetable, the entire routine of the garrison were studied as intensely as any young lover ever watched his beloved: the enemy's methods received such painstaking attention that no chink in his restraining armour could go unspotted."[3] This system, known as the duty pilot system in RAF camps or stooging in US Army Air Corps-dominated camps, maintained an actual log of how many Germans were in the compound at any given time, including their entry and exit times.

At Stalag Luft III, the German camp sergeant major knew about the log. He would often say when passing the duty officer (or stooge),

"Mark me in." One afternoon, he asked to see the log out of curiosity. He was surprised to see that two of his men had made a quick visit to the compound and departed. Visibly angry, he said as he left, "Mark me out." The prisoners later learned that the two guards were caught getting ready for an unauthorized trip into town. The sergeant major punished them both.[4]

In addition to the duty watch, there was security throughout the compound safeguarding escape activity such as tunneling, manufacturing, tailoring, or forgery; keeping track of the movement of the guards; and maintaining a close watch on a special breed of guard known to the prisoners as a ferret. The ferrets were specially trained, and they prowled throughout the camp, sniffing out evidence of illicit activity. They were normally unsuccessful, but they did inevitably score some successes like discovering spoil from a tunnel or finding various sorts of contraband during searches of the barracks. At Stalag Luft III and at Colditz, they confiscated enough evidence to start museums stocked with displays of escape equipment. New guards and ferrets went through the museum on a regular basis to impress on them the ingenuity of their guests.[5]

Beside goon-watching, key parts of camp security were the arts of goon-taming and goon-baiting, practiced with varying degrees of success in all camps. Goon-taming began with sharing hard-to-get items such as cigarettes, coffee, or chocolate from Red Cross or personal parcels with a guard. Since the guards were strictly prohibited from taking anything from the prisoners, as soon as they took something, they became vulnerable to blackmail. Even if the guard could not be persuaded into providing bits of uniform or documents, at the very least they could be induced to look the other way and keep their mouths shut.[6]

Goon-baiting was a rather more hazardous activity. Prisoners would engage a guard in conversation designed to provoke anger but stop short of a physical response. It distracted the guards while lowering their morale. However, practitioners had to be careful not to overstep the mark, provoking a lethal response.[7] Sometimes, goon-baiting could be humorous, while still achieving its aim. At Colditz in May of 1941 the Germans were holding what the prisoners regarded as an inordinate number of surprise barracks rollcalls. Prisoners were expected to stand at the foot of their bunks to be counted by the guards. The process often took 30 minutes of precious sack time away from the prisoners. Fed up, the response by 25 French POWs to the next rollcall was to turn out stark naked. The unexpected nature of their action brought the rollcall to a halt.[8] There were no further surprise rollcalls for several weeks.

Every escape organization had an intelligence section which handled counterintelligence and radio use, maintained coded letter communications, and provided forged documents, maps, and escape intelligence. It was normally the largest section of the camp escape organization aside from security. Counterintelligence was vital to maintaining security. Occasionally, the Germans would attempt to insert an English-speaking German soldier into the camps.

Such infiltrators rarely lasted more than a few days under the relentless scrutiny of the prisoners. Purported Americans would be asked questions about baseball and those posing as British would be asked about cricket. Combined with these details were a series of questions relating to their military jobs and the daily routine of service life. The difficulty for someone who was not genuine in providing answers to these questions meant that the outsider had little chance of passing muster.

There was the occasional turncoat who had offered to inform on his fellow prisoners, but even they were almost invariably exposed. At Colditz there was one who managed to do significant damage, even though he was there but a short time during March 1944. Sub Lieutenant E. W. Purdy was a naval officer who had been broadcasting propaganda for the Nazis. After a disagreement with his superiors in Berlin, Purdy was packed off to Colditz. He promptly offered his services to the Camp Security Officer, Reinhold Eggers. With his help, Eggers discovered a tunnel and a cache of escape aids. Fortunately, Purdy did not compromise the camp radios before he was identified as a traitor.[9]

No escape plan had much chance of success unless it was supported by up-to-date intelligence on the local area. This included information every escaper would need such as railway timetables, what trains to take and which to avoid, and what areas were heavily patrolled. Many escaped prisoners were recaptured because they didn't know which foods or drinks could be bought without a ration coupon, or that civilians could only travel in specific cars on certain trains, or that everyone had to head for an air raid shelter when the alarm sounded. When these recaptured prisoners returned to the fold, the intelligence section debriefed them and spread their knowledge to aid future escapers. Newly arrived prisoners provided useful information, as did tame goons.

Nearly every camp in both theaters had a radio, which some camps referred to as a canary.[10] The radios were small—for the time—the smallest of which was the size of a cigarette pack if it could draw power from the camp electrical system; mobile versions requiring batteries were the equivalent of two cigarette cartons in size.[11] They were carefully guarded for several reasons. First and foremost, they provided a valuable source of intelligence about life outside the camp. Second, as the war went on, the news of Allied advances they provided boosted morale tremendously. Lastly, while in Europe possession of a radio led to a trip to solitary confinement in what was known as "the cooler," in the Pacific it meant a painful death. The usual protocol for radio use involved at least two men taking down verbatim transcripts of BBC or American broadcasts while heavy concentric rings of security encompassed the room in which they worked.

As soon as the radio operators transcribed the broadcast, they would tear down the radio and secrete it. While the radio operators were hiding the radio, others would take the transcripts to the Intelligence section. After a quick review, the Intelligence section would brief a number of men with good memories to carry the news of the day throughout the camp.[12] News which could affect the prospects for successful escapes went straight to the Big X. Late in the war, several camps had radios which could both receive and transmit smuggled in via clandestine packages.

The Intelligence section had another means of two-way communication with the outside world at their disposal. By 1942 every camp in the European Theater had at least one CU. This practice never took hold in the Pacific because the Japanese generally refused to allow the POWs to receive mail. MI9 developed the first letter code for use by POWs in 1940.[13] It was simple to learn, and it was meant to be used in correspondence between prisoners and fictitious addressees. MIS-X developed its own code system in 1942 and by the end of the war had trained 7,724 CUs in its use.[14] CUs were normally officers or non-commissioned officers, selected by their commanders for intelligence and security-mindedness. They were expected to train others, should they become prisoners. Each CU was assigned a code name and an address to send their coded letters. Captured CUs were instructed to report to the SAO on their arrival in the camp and inform him that they had the means to communicate with the War Office (British) or War Department (American).

As their letters came in, postal officials flagged them and routed them to the appropriate department.[15] This allowed MI9 and MIS-X to communicate information to the camps about upcoming clandestine shipments of special goods, provide information, or request intelligence. The prisoners used their coded letters to MI9 or MIS-X to request supplies or provide intelligence. The system worked well and was never breached by the Germans—although they suspected something was going on.

The camp forgers were inventive in preparing documents to support an escapee in a Home Run attempt. In Colditz the prisoners built a type-writer from scratch to type out identity papers and other documentation.[16] In many camps the prisoners used materials as varied as linoleum tiles and rubber shoe heels to manufacture the stamps needed to impart the final official seal of approval on their documents. At times, the prisoners received special clandestine packages courtesy of MI9 or MIS-X which contained ink, pens, paper, stamps, and even blank documents.[17]

One way or another, the forgers took great pains to produce remarkable quantities of authentic-looking documentation. As they worked, concentric rings of security surrounded them to give them the few seconds' warning they needed to conceal their handiwork. One popular quick concealment method for documents was to shovel them into cut-out books. When the guards arrived in the room, the forgers would be busily drawing pictures of birds, or taking notes on a lecture, without an incriminating document in sight.

The Intelligence section also provided maps, either brought in from the outside, stolen from the enemy, or produced in the camp by the ever-busy forgers.[18] The reproduction of maps was probably the greatest source of escape maps, particularly to support large attempts.

Escape intelligence was a high priority for the Intelligence section. Without a detailed knowledge of what lay beyond the wire, no escapee could expect to get far. This sort of information came from tame guards or from escapees who had been captured and returned to camp.

As in all militaries, logistics came under the purview of a supply section charged with obtaining, storing, and issuing escape kit. This included maps, compasses, rations, and clothing to name the most essential items. Obtaining escape kit called for a combination of skill at stealing from the Germans, converting materials at hand, bribing the guards or bypassing searches of packages containing contraband.

The production of clothing appropriate for escapers in Nazi Germany is an illustration of the ingenuity of MI9, MIS-X, and the prisoners themselves. MI9's Clayton Hutton was the author of a particularly ingenious way to get clothing into the camps, right under the noses of the Germans. Hutton reasoned that since officers and enlisted men were entitled to receive uniforms under the Geneva Convention, he might be able to send some trick clothing in regular parcels.

To prepare the way, Hutton had several articles published in official pamphlets certain to come to German attention that the RAF was issuing new mess and walking-out uniforms, complete with illustrations of the uniforms. Once he learned from intelligence sources that the Germans had swallowed the bait, he dispatched the uniforms. The mess dress MI9 dispatched could be converted with minimal effort into a convincing Luftwaffe uniform, while the walking-out uniform was reversible and could become working man's clothing. The mess dress uniform was particularly ingenious in design. It had wire facings which could be used to manufacture Iron Crosses. Additionally, "we thought it would help if we sent them packets of handkerchiefs tied up with strips of black and white material, from which the right ribbons could be made. Our agents across the Channel managed to smuggle out rolls of German leather, which served admirably for the manufacture of Luftwaffe boots."[19]

Most camps had a few professional or self-taught tailors who were able to convert blankets into clothing. Since by mid-war the German populace was increasingly poorly dressed, the use of blanket material for clothing did not attract undue attention. Articles of escape clothing also came from parcels from home, although they were normally limited to scarves, socks, and gloves. Another source of clothing, although a minor one, was clothing left unsecured by German workmen in the camp. Most of the time, the escaping prisoners were adequately dressed and equipped to attempt their Home Run.

Once equipped for the journey, there were three basic types of escape plan: walk out, tunnel, and wire. The first could be as simple as absconding from a work detail or as complex as attempting to leave camp disguised as a workman or even a German officer. Airey Neave's escape, described later in this book, was of the walk-out variety. Tunnel plans could involve most of the camp, as did the "Great Escape" from Stalag Luft III in March 1944 where 76 prisoners managed to break free—with three making a Home Run.

Tunnel plans could also be on a much smaller scale, such as the three British officers whose escape is detailed in *The Wooden Horse* by Eric Williams. Williams and two fellow POWs built a wooden vaulting horse, upon which they exercised for several hours every day. Unbeknownst to the Germans, when the wooden vaulting horse was carried out each day, it had a man concealed inside. When the horse was in place, he would tunnel through the sandy soil with the ultimate goal of getting clear of the wire. The spoil from the digging would be placed in bags which were hung inside the wooden horse. When they left at the end of the day, they concealed the entrance to the hole with a wooden hatch and spread dirt over it. By dint of hard labor, they eventually succeeded in getting beyond the wire. The three who used the tunnel all made a Home Run.[20]

Wire schemes could involve going over or through the wire fences around the camp. They could also involve cutting the wire in a location not likely to be noticed, as done by Sergeant Hans Kasten in his escape from Berga concentration camp. Marked for death by the camp commandant, Kasten and two other soldiers found a spot out of sight of the guard towers and snipped through the wire to escape. Although recaptured after several days, they were spared execution by the timely arrival of Allied ground forces.[21]

CHAPTER 5

German POW Camps

This chapter covers five representative camps administered by the Germans. Stalag Luft III, Colditz, Stalag IX (Bad Orb) and Berga—all in Germany—are presented a logical best to worst progression. One unique German camp, Dulag Luft, also deserves mention as it was the camp through which all Allied aircrew were routed for interrogation.

Of all the World War II POW camps, Stalag Luft III is probably the most famous. It features prominently in a number of books as well as in the movie *The Great Escape*. Located in a densely wooded area near Sagan (now Zagan in Poland), a small town halfway between Berlin and Breslau, it began in March 1942 with a single compound for captured Allied aircrew.

By late 1944 it had grown into a sprawling complex of five compounds rather unimaginatively named North, South, East, West, and Center. At their peak the compounds held around 15,000 Allied aircrew. Each was bordered by two 12-foot barbed-wire fences built six feet apart with concertina wire filling in the gap between. Inside the compound and 25 feet away from the inner fence was the warning wire, a single strand of wire on stakes 30 inches off the ground. Any prisoner crossing that wire could be shot by one of the guards in the many towers (nicknamed goon boxes by the prisoners) surrounding the compound.[1] Warning shots were not required.

Inside each compound were rows of barracks, a cook house, a theater, and a sports field. The German administrative buildings and guard billets separated Center and East camps from the other three camps.

The infamous "cooler" along with a camp hospital was in a separate wired enclosure just outside North camp. Like most POW camps, Stalag Luft III bore the impression of its commander's character. In this case, for two years that was Oberstleutnant (Lieutenant Colonel) Friedrich Wilhelm von Lindeiner-Wildau, a loyal German but decidedly anti-Nazi. He had fought in the trenches during World War I with distinction, being wounded, promoted, and decorated several times. As World War II approached, he sought a position where he could serve Germany but not the Nazi party. He found it by joining the Luftwaffe in 1937—at Herman Goering's invitation—and taking command of Stalag Luft III in March of 1942. He held command until relieved in the aftermath of the "Great Escape" in March 1944. Although threatened with court-martial, he ended the war in a military hospital after being wounded in February 1945 leading an infantry unit against the advancing Soviet Army.

He was a humane man who kept a tight rein on his guard force. He also insisted on delivery of Red Cross parcels without delay—although he was no fool. The security measures he imposed uncovered a number of escape attempts as well discovering some of the means used by MIS-X and MI9 to smuggle contraband into the camps. Even after Von Lindeiner's relief, the new *Kommandant* (the former second in command), Major Gustav Simoleit, continued his generally humane policies until the camp was abandoned in January of 1945 and the prisoners marched westward to avoid the advancing Soviet Army. Although by no means a luxury resort, Stalag Luft III was humanely administered, and the prisoners were cared for to the best of the camp administration's ability.

Running a close second to Stalag Luft III in notoriety is Oflag[2] IVC, otherwise known as Colditz. The Germans referred to it as a *Sonderlager*, a "special camp" for those who were considered particularly anti-German or given to escaping. In World War I it had been heralded as an "escape proof" camp.[3] Perhaps that is why the Germans decided to put so many of their most determined escapers within its walls.

In World War II, despite formidable security measures, a number of POWs made Home Runs from Colditz. Among these was Airey Neave, whose successful escape is described in Chapter 12. Reinhold Eggers was a German officer stationed at Colditz from November 1940 until the

Allies liberated it in April 1945, most of the time as the camp security officer. He wrote a memoir called *Colditz, The German Viewpoint* in which he observed, "You might think at first sight that the place was impregnable. It probably was, but apart from putting bars on the windows it had never really been built for the purpose of keeping people in. As time went on I realized that while Colditz, like so many other castles, might be impregnable from without, it certainly was not 'impregnable' from within. Breaking out was shown to be much easier than breaking in!"[4] Eggers was an efficient, formidable adversary. He foiled many escape attempts, located hidden caches of escape gear, found the prisoners' "Treasury," and established a camp museum of escape artifacts he used to train his guard force. Yet, because of his unfailing "correctness" he was still regarded with respect by the prisoners. Following his release from Soviet imprisonment in 1956 a former POW, Wing Commander Douglas Bader, flew him to England and became his champion.[5]

Oflag IVC was centered on a Renaissance castle built by Augustus, the Elector of Saxony in the late 1500s. The castle was built atop a rocky outcrop and had two courtyards. Located halfway between Leipzig and Dresden, the castle housed POWs from all Allied nations from its opening in November of 1939 until May of 1943, when the Germans decided that Colditz would hold only British and American prisoners. It also held a number of prominent individuals such as a nephew each of King George V and of Winston Churchill. The so called *prominente* were kept there as potential bargaining chips. Regardless of their status, all the prisoners were kept in the older inner courtyard, while the German administration and guard force occupied the newer outer courtyard. The upper courtyard included solitary confinement cells, a guard house, a theater, a kitchen, guard force barracks, and a canteen.

Colditz's only serious shortcoming was that there was insufficient room for exercise. The Germans established a fenced-in exercise area nearby, but security considerations really did not allow the prisoners as much access as they, or for that matter the Germans, would have liked. Naturally, the prisoners—all die-hard escapers—channeled their energies into building tunnels, planning escapes, and even building a two-man glider in the attic of the castle. They also established two radio rooms, one of which was never found by the Germans.

The camp went through a series of commanders, the first of which was Oberstleutnant[6] Schmidt, an elderly World War I veteran who favored correct treatment of the prisoners, rarely entered the upper courtyard, and ruled with a loose hand.[7] He retired in July 1942 on reaching the age of 70, to be succeeded by the self-important Oberst (Colonel) Edgar Glaesche. While still observing the Geneva Conventions, Glaesche insisted on being saluted by the prisoners and imposed a few petty regulations.[8] In February 1943 he left to take command of prison camps in Ukraine and was replaced by Oberst Prawitt—a martinet of the Prussian school who commanded the castle until its liberation. Prawitt interpreted the tolerance shown by Eggers and others as slackness and moved to stop it. Although not a brutal man, his methods almost caused an open revolt which Eggers managed to defuse. Overall, the Germans treated the prisoners at Colditz according to the Geneva Conventions, but Prawitt had been prone to imposing collective punishments expressly forbidden by the Convention. Still, most prisoners did not feel they had been treated harshly while at Colditz.

Last from the bottom of the list of German POW camps is Stalag IX B, located at Bad Orb, about 30 miles north-northwest of Frankfurt-am-Main. The *Kommandant* of Stalag IX B was Oberst Karl Sieber, and his second-in-command was Oberstleutnant Albert Wodarg. They were both old-school soldiers who believed in ruling with a rod of iron. At times, their behavior crossed the line of the Geneva Conventions, such as turning a blind eye to violence against the prisoners. Once, a German guard was assaulted by two prisoners who had broken into the mess hall in search of food. Sieber threatened to withhold food, coffee, and firewood until the culprits were found and handed over.[9]

Fortunately, the rigid attitude of Oberst Sieber did not infect the majority of the guard force, who were men from Landesschützen Battalion 633.[10] Like others of their type, the men were classified as not fit for front-line service. Bad Orb had been the site of a concentration camp and a camp for Soviet POWs prior to being used as a POW camp for US soldiers captured during the Battle of the Bulge. In peacetime, it had been the site of a spa and a children's summer camp. The onset of war brought Bad Orb under Wehrmacht control, then that of the SS, and back to Wehrmacht control again. Its layout and security measures were not that different from those of other *Stalags*. What was exceptional was the overcrowding, the starvation rations, denial of mail, scant medical supplies, and random beatings by the some of the guards, many of whom were used to maltreating Soviet POWs.

The *Stalag* had 16 barracks which each housed between 290 and 500 men. Of the 13,000 prisoners at Bad Orb, 1,500 slept on concrete floors in unheated buildings.[11] Their daily fare was soup made from grass and turnip greens along with a few slices of black bread made partially of sawdust. To be fair, the German civil population had been eating the same bread since 1941. Called *Schwartzbrod* (black bread) it was "50% bruised rye grain, 20% sliced sugar beets, 20% tree flour (sawdust), and 10% minced leaves and straw."[12] It barely provided 1,000 calories per day, whereas the average prisoner needed 1,700 calories just to ward off starvation. The arrival of 2,300 Red Cross packages in early March 1945 probably saved quite a number of lives. Whitlock says, "The standard Red Cross package contained a can each of corned beef, pork luncheon meat, powdered milk, margarine, salmon, orange concentrate, coffee, and liver paste, a package of cheese, two chocolate bars, a box of sugar cubes, a box of raisins, a package of biscuits, several bars of soap, and four packs of cigarettes."[13] This went a long way toward filling the nutritional needs of the semi-starved prisoners in Bad Orb.

During their entire time at Bad Orb, the POWs were only allowed to send one postcard. Although there was a nearby military hospital where the prisoners could receive treatment, the camp medical staff had hardly any medicines. There were also scant facilities for the prisoners to wash themselves or their clothes. On average, 160 men shared one cold water tap with very low water pressure. This, combined with the lice left behind by the concentration camp inmates, made the prisoners' lives even more unbearable.

One other aspect of Stalag IX B deserves mention: the segregation of Jewish prisoners from those of other religions. This was done in a number of other camps, but nowhere else did the *Kommandant* become so personally involved. When the prisoners had arrived at Bad Orb, they were asked to state their religion. Several prisoners declined to state their religion (even though it was on their dog tags). As a reward, they were beaten with rifle butts and made to stand for hours in the snow.[14] Thereafter, almost all inprocessing prisoners gave their religion as Protestant.

Being aware of American demographics, the Germans did not believe that 13,000 prisoners did not include any Jews. So, they issued orders that all Jewish prisoners would be segregated, using as an excuse the example of how Black soldiers were segregated in the US Armed Forces. Some prisoners bought off on this logic, but most did not. The Germans threatened to start shooting prisoners if Jewish POWs did not identify themselves. Seventy-eight prisoners, whatever their reasons, decided to identify themselves. Given the reputation the Nazis had gained for brutality, many Jewish prisoners prudently decided to hide their religious affiliation. As one Jewish soldier put it, "I didn't think the Germans had the Jews identify themselves because they were doing a term paper or some sociological study on the prisoners in Stalag IX B."[15] As events would show, they certainly were not.

This brings us to the worst of the camps, Berga. More properly known as Arbeitsdienstlager 650, it was collocated with the Berga concentration camp, a sub-camp of Buchenwald. It was under the control of SS Obersturmbannführer Willi Hack whose consuming purpose was Project Swallow, building a synthetic oil plant in tunnels carved by slave labor in the mountain near the camp. Germany had no natural petroleum resources and the fields in Romania and Poland on which they relied to run their war machine had first been damaged by Allied bombers before falling to the advancing Red Army, so the need to develop synthetic fuels was a top priority. Hack was behind schedule, and he needed relatively healthy laborers. The emaciated European Jewish prisoners from Berga were dying without getting much done. Hack made a deal with the *Kommandant* of Stalag IX B, Oberst Karl Sieber, to take his troublemakers off his hands, along with any Jewish prisoners. For the sake of appearances, Berga was guarded by Wehrmacht troops commanded by Hauptmann (Captain) Ludwig Merz and Sergeant Erwin Metz, but it was under the iron control of the SS.

Hauptmann Merz had been a member of the Nazi Party since May 1, 1933, so he was a logical choice as Kommandant from the SS point of view. The guard force was drawn from Landesschützen Battalion 621 headquartered near Leipzig.[16] It was a typical POW compound, with barracks, a double barbed-wire fence, guard towers, searchlights, and a warning wire. What was atypical was its location within a concentration camp.

In mid-February of 1945, 350 enlisted American POWs arrived at Berga from Stalag IX B near Bad Orb.[17] During the trip they had been crammed into rail cars with no food, water, or sanitary facilities. Although nominally under Wehrmacht control, the prisoners were starved, beaten, and brutalized by the SS. They were treated no differently than the Jewish inmates of Berga concentration camp. Prisoners worked in 12-hour shifts, 24 hours a day, seven days a week. They inhaled massive amounts of rock dust generated by the explosives used to blast the tunnels because they were driven in to work before the dust had even settled. Their rations were so meager that many recalled the rations from Bad Orb fondly.

Two weeks after their arrival Hans Kasten and a barracks full of prisoners refused to report for work. Hack brought in heavily armed SS troops with Alsatian dogs to enforce compliance. He got what he wanted. As the Man of Confidence for Berga, Kasten had tried to better the conditions of his fellow prisoners but merely earned the enmity of Obersturmbannführer Hack. In the aftermath of the attempted work stoppage, Hack beat Kasten nearly to death. After the beating, Kasten resolved to escape. Along with two other prisoners and aided by the camp escape organization, Kasten made his bid for freedom on March 3, 1945. The trio headed west cross country seeking the advancing American lines. Although recaptured by the Germans two days later in the small town of Göschwitz, they were liberated by advancing US forces before they could be returned to the hell of Berga. Once liberated, Kasten went hunting for Hack amid the ruins of a defeated Germany. Much to his regret, he never found him.[18]

Of the 350 Americans imprisoned at Berga, at least 70 died as the result of maltreatment. That represents 20 percent of the prisoners at Berga and an astonishing six percent of the total deaths of all American

POWs in German hands during World War II. On April 3, the Germans forced the prisoners onto the road, marching them south, away from the approaching US forces. Hauptmann Merz deserted his charges somewhere along their route of march, fearing retribution. The story of the final liberation of the Berga POWs is reserved for the end of this chapter.

This brings us to this chapter's final camp, Durchgangslager der Luftwaffe (transit camp of the air force) or, more simply, Dulag Luft.[19] Located near the town of Oberursel, northwest of Frankfurt-am-Main, it grew into a sprawling complex that at the peak of its operations in 1944 processed an average of 2,000 downed Allied airmen a month.[20] Its sole job was to interrogate prisoners for whatever information the highly skilled Luftwaffe interrogators could extract. No other branch of the German Armed Forces had such a camp; nor did the Japanese. Originally, the term Dulag Luft only applied to the interrogation center proper and the original transit camp nearby. However, as the Germans added a hospital and additional transit camps, Dulag Luft took on a more expansive meaning. One of the final transit camps was built in Wetzlar, 37 miles north of Oberursel.

The camp had two sets of interrogators. One specialized in bomber crews, while the other focused on fighter pilots. Each had their own distinct approach to extracting information, as discussed below. A formidable intelligence organization supported the interrogators in building a picture of the Allied Air Forces arrayed against them. The Documents section was the most productive, producing an estimated 80 percent of the intelligence Dulag Luft, obtained mostly from the pockets of the downed airmen, recovered from aircraft downed over German territory, or gleaned from newspapers.

The Yellow File section (so called because the file folders they used were yellow) built biographies of Allied personnel gotten from what would today be called Open Source Intelligence (OSINT). The Squadron History section built detailed pictures of the location, activity, and organization of every Allied squadron. The Attack section ran two situation rooms which tracked all activity in the past 24 hours, which the interrogators could visit prior to coming on shift.[21]

Fighter pilots were better treated than bomber crews, partially because of the difference in psychological approach to quickly extract tactically valuable information. With fighter pilots, the interrogators normally used a comradely approach which might include having a brandy in an almost social setting. Probably the best fighter pilot interrogator was Hans Joachim Scharff. The Allied pilots he interrogated almost universally acclaimed him as the most humane, yet skilled of all the Dulag Luft interrogators.

One of his favorite approaches was to gather fighter pilots from the same wing in his interrogation room, set out some schnapps, and sit back and listen to the conversation (which was also recorded by hidden microphones). Regardless of the situation, he never raised his voice or threatened. Perhaps the best summary of Scharff's skills came from Colonel Hubert Zemke, a top US fighter ace with 19.5 kills whom Scharff interrogated.[22] Zemke noted, "I had the impression that it might even be dangerous just to talk about the weather with him as he'd probably gain some important or confidential information from it."[23]

The Germans might use similar interrogation tactics on bomber crews. If they were resistant, they were much more likely to receive rougher treatment. This could include being placed in detention cells with the heat turned up to an almost unbearable level, denied the ability to wash, and fed very meager rations. Escaped prisoners brought back word on the various German interrogation tactics. As Keith W. Simmons, a B-24 bombardier who went through Dulag Luft, noted in his book *Kriegie, Prisoner of War*, "My four crew members and I had received the full training course on Dulag Luft, and we entered its grounds with determination to survive the ordeal before us."[24]

The Germans used every trick to get them to part with more information than their name, rank, and serial number. They gave them bogus Red Cross forms to fill out, which contained many personal questions and led into detailed questions about military matters. The prisoners were told that if they did not answer questions, they might be handed over to the Gestapo as spies. Simmons spent 17 days confined in a solitary cell. On the morning of the last day, he was close to "calling the guard and telling the captain everything." Much to his relief, he was released from the cell and shipped along with a group of 168 American and British aircrew to Stalag Luft III.[25] Dulag Luft continued to function until it was overrun by the US 7th Armored Division on March 29, 1945.

As the war drew to a close, the Germans attempted to keep prisoners of war from being liberated by advancing Allied forces. Evacuation would usually begin by road marching the prisoners deeper into the steadily shrinking Third Reich. Depending on the situation, the prisoners might be moved in cramped rail cars to their final destinations. This chapter will touch on two of these evacuations, the first from Stalag Luft III and the second from Berga. Both were arduous, but for entirely different reasons.

The prisoners in Stalag Luft III knew that the Soviet Army was coming ever closer to the camp because of their clandestine radios. The Germans lent this idea further credence when they made an unprecedented announcement on January 17, 1945, of Soviet advances toward the camp. This was enough to get the camp organization preparing for a move. The SAO put everyone on full rations to prepare for the journey ahead. The organization made sure everyone packed a bedroll, set aside some food, and redistributed clothing formerly hoarded for escape purposes. The Germans noticed the preparations, of course, and even made moves to confiscate the bedrolls. When the prisoners signed paroles that they would not try to escape, the Germans relented. The leadership of the various compounds organized each marching group to ensure that it included leaders, engineers, and medics. They also made contingency plans in case the German guards deserted them or tried to massacre them.

Allied Command knew that the Germans planned to move the prisoners, and had the BBC broadcast an order for the prisoners to stay together if evacuated and not to attempt to escape.[26] After all, the Third Reich was collapsing like a punctured balloon and escapers would most likely be safer in a guarded group rather than unarmed and on their own. On January 25, the Soviet Army was less than 50 miles from the camp. The 26th passed with no orders to move. Finally, on January 27, 1945, the evacuation order came. The first group of prisoners from South Compound hit the road at 11 p.m. in the bitter cold and falling snow. Within 24 hours around 14,000 prisoners were marching westward.

There were still 500 prisoners that were too sick to move. They followed in trucks and by rail on February 9.

The first leg of the march was from Sagan to Bad Muskau, a distance of around 40 miles. According to Article 7 of the Geneva Convention, prisoners could not be marched more than 20 kilometers (12.5 miles) per day. The men of South Compound moved over 34 miles in the first 27 hours. After a short four-hour rest, they resumed the march and arrived in Bad Muskau where they were quartered briefly in a brick factory and a heating plant which had running water—a blessing! From there they headed for Spremberg, a railway center a little over 15 miles distant. There they were crammed into boxcars and sent to various destinations. The other march groups followed the same route as the men of South Compound. They had all entrained by February 3.

It was obvious to everyone who marched from Sagan to Spremberg that the Germans had made little preparation to care for the prisoners during the move. There were no rations available, although most prisoners had brought food along. Water was a different matter; the prisoners had to get it wherever they could find it. This included melting snow to slake their thirst. The weather was a factor, with the wind chill hitting minus 20 degrees Fahrenheit. Many of the prisoners became so frozen that they could not move without assistance. Still, there was little overt brutality and nearly all the prisoners made it safely to their destinations. While difficult, the evacuation of Stalag Luft III paled by comparison with the movement of the emaciated prisoners from Berga.

In late March 1945, the Allied armies approaching from the west had breached the Rhine River defensive line. The Soviet Army was closing in on Berlin from the east, hammering the now desperate German defenders. On April 2, 1945, the US Army liberated the prisoners in Stalag IX B after a brief fight in Bad Orb.[27] With American forces approaching Berga from the north and west, on April 3 the Germans forced 280 of the original 350 of Berga's prisoners of war onto the road south toward Bavaria. Twenty-five of the original number were already dead, having died of mistreatment or been shot, often on the whim of a guard. Around 20 had escaped and the remainder had been sent to hospitals as too sick to move. With the callous Hauptmann Merz and

Sergeant Metz in charge, the column moved slowly south in the early spring weather. The weak, emaciated prisoners straggled along for several days through Greiz, then Plauen, until they reached the city of Hof, near the Czech border, on April 9. By then an additional 10 prisoners had died. Although only 30 miles from Berga, around 50 of the sickest and weakest prisoners could march no further. They were taken care of by the local populace who fed them bread and soup until soldiers from the 90th Infantry Division liberated them.

The prisoners rested at Hof until April 13, when they took to the roads again. With the sick and weak disposed of, Hauptmann Merz forced the pace to keep the prisoners out of friendly hands. The prisoners staggered on though the towns of Rehau, Schönwald and uphill to the plateau near Thierstein. Eight more prisoners died by the time the column reached Rehau. At Thierstein four more were buried. Covering 9 to 18 miles a day, the prisoners remained just ahead of the advancing American Third Army. At Fuchsmühl, Merz allowed more of the sickest prisoners to be left in the town's hospital, where they were freed by troops of the 90th Infantry Division's 357th Regiment. On April 20, a different set of guards replaced Merz and his men.

The new guards brought an immediate improvement in treatment as well as better rations. Still, the prisoners were at the end of their tether. On April 22, the 160 remaining prisoners reached the town of Rötz. They had covered 186 miles and could go no further. As a body, they decided that if the Germans tried to get them to move, they would refuse. Fortunately, in the morning hours of April 23 troops of the 11th Armored Division came to the rescue. The Berga death march was finally over.[28]

CHAPTER 6

Japanese POW Camps

This chapter follows the best-to-worst pattern of the German camps. It covers the Seoul, Changi, Thai–Burma Railway, Omori, and Cabanatuan camps. Seoul and Changi were among the best administered, while Cabanatuan was typical of most Japanese camps in the Philippines. The Bangkok to Rangoon Railway and the Omori camps deserve coverage as camps unique in their callous and sometimes studied brutality.

By the opening of the war in the Pacific, the Japanese had occupied Korea for 31 years. During that time, they did their level best to eradicate Korean culture. The Japanese occupiers banned Korean language, literature, and history from public life. In an attempt to erase documentary evidence of Korea's illustrious history, the occupiers burned over 200,000 irreplaceable manuscripts and scrolls. Korean religion was replaced with Shinto—the Japanese "Way of the Gods." Japanese law coerced Koreans into adopting Japanese surnames by refusing official recognition to anyone who did not do so. Close to a million Korean men were forced to work in Japan's war industries. Hundreds of thousands of Korean women were forced into sexual slavery as "comfort women" for the officers and men of the Imperial Japanese Army. The occupiers even renamed major cities such as Seoul (Keijo), Pusan (Fusan), and Inchon (Jinsen).[1] Their systematic attempt to eradicate Korean culture ultimately failed, but it left deep feelings of resentment of which vestiges persist to this day.

The Seoul War Prisoners Camp was located among the many Japanese barracks in the southern part of the city. It consisted of a stockaded enclosure, guard towers, a parade ground, and a four-story brick cotton storage warehouse into which the Japanese crammed 550 British and Commonwealth officers captured in Singapore, most of whom were from the 2nd Loyal Regiment (North Lancashire), also known as the 2nd Loyals. The warehouse was dusty, with small windows—not good for ventilation but a mercy when the winter winds howled down from Siberia. Each floor was subdivided into four bays designed to hold 30 men each. The SAO, Lieutenant Colonel Elrington,[2] decided not to use the bottom story as living space because of the dirt floor, so all 550 men shoehorned into the top three floors.

The camp commandant was Colonel Noguchi, who gave a long speech in "tortured English" to the arriving prisoners, a speech of which they each received a copy. He warned that they "must be cautious, not spoiling yourselves by punishments." This the prisoners took to mean they should observe camp discipline to avoid punishment. Noguchi catalogued the record of Japanese victory, which he ascribed to "Special Providential Aid." Afterwards the British chaplain remarked wryly that it sounded like "an insurance company."[3]

Unlike in most other camps, Red Cross parcels as well as private parcels arrived and were distributed to the prisoners intact with nothing more inconvenient than an inspection by a Japanese officer for contraband. Some prisoners even received mail, although it was often a year out of date. Surprisingly, several hundred books came to the camp by the good offices of the International YMCA. As winter approached, the Japanese even provided the prisoners with British winter battledress from stocks captured in Hong Kong. For greatcoats, the camp administration issued Japanese Army coats from the Russo-Japanese War of 1904. They were tight fits for many of the prisoners, but they were better than nothing.

Prisoners grew cabbage to supplement their diet, which they wouldn't grow fat on, but which was adequate for survival. Medicine was in short supply, but the Red Cross parcels helped as they often contained sulfa drugs. Still, 16 men died, primarily from amoebic dysentery and diphtheria. Things could have been worse, but the camp had several skilled doctors who managed to contain the outbreaks. In a unique coda to the loss of 16 prisoners, Colonel Noguchi had their remains cremated and buried with full military honors. He also tried each Christmas to provide extra food and a day of rest for the prisoners in his charge. Although the prisoners were sent on work details, there was no brutal mistreatment. Not that there was no corporal punishment, but it did not exceed the limits of normal Imperial Japanese Army discipline.

While on work detail some of the prisoners engaged in small acts of sabotage, such as switching labels on crates in the Seoul Railway station to misroute freight. However, the manual labor most prisoners performed generally ruled out such mischief. Taken all in all, life in the Seoul War Prisoners Camp was a tough but not brutal experience. As Tom Wade, one of the captured British officers, assessed it: "The truth was, Colonel Noguchi was an honourable man, not inclined to cruelty or harsh punishments, and Lieutenant Colonel Elrington, DSO, MC, was equally honourable, presenting our case to the Japanese in a calm, quiet voice, which Colonel Noguchi respected. Thanks to the character of these two men, life in the camp was bearable, correct and decent; there were no abuses and a satisfactory discipline."[4]

The Changi prisoner of war camp was "arguably one of the best places in the Greater Asian Co-Prosperity Sphere to be a prisoner of Nippon."[5] Changi was on a peninsula which juts out into the Johore Strait at the eastern end of Singapore Island. Established when Singapore fell, it had been the main British Army base on the island. Initially, Colonel Sugita commanded the camp; his second in command was Lieutenant Okazaki who handled the day-to-day administration. In August 1942, Major General Shimpei Fukuye who was in command of all the Malayan POW camps took direct control of Changi. He left Lieutenant Okazaki in place as the administrator. Fukuye was an enigma to many of the prisoners. On one hand, he made an honest effort to feed the prisoners and did not condone violence against them. However, he did compel all of the prisoners to sign a promise not to escape, which led to what became known as the Selarang Barracks Incident.

The trigger for the incident was when eight prisoners attempted to escape. In response, Fukuye demanded that all prisoners sign a pledge not to escape. When met with a flat refusal, on August 30, 1942, Fukuye ordered that all 14,000 prisoners be collected into an area of little more than eight acres, be placed on one-third rations, and be given very little water. On September 2 Fukuye ordered the prisoners who had attempted to escape executed by firing squad. On September 5, with men beginning to die from lack of food and water, the British and Australian commanders ordered their men to sign, saying that such a pledge was invalid since it was obtained under duress.[6] For his part in the incident, Fukuye was tried by the International Military Tribunal for the Far East, sentenced to death, and executed by firing squad on April 27, 1946.[7]

The camp encompassed about 9.5 square miles. Into that space, the Japanese initially herded over 68,000 prisoners. By mid-March 1942, that number shrank to around 14,000 due to drafts of prisoners to work on various projects around Singapore. March 1943 found the average camp population at around 2,000 due to work drafts for the infamous Thai–Burma railway. The Japanese ran a barbed-wire fence across the top of the peninsula to cover the landward side. Otherwise, there were no towers and no searchlights, just random perimeter patrols by a tiny force of Japanese guards.

The Japanese gave the prisoners in Changi a surprising amount of autonomy. Indeed, other than the Selarang Barracks Incident, Major General Fukuye provided a ration scale only exceeded by the camps in Korea and Manchuria, even handing out intact Red Cross parcels as they became available. The Japanese rarely patrolled inside the camp, leaving that to the prisoners. Lieutenant General Percival, who had been in command when Singapore fell, had his four senior subordinate commanders to help him run the camp. He divided the camp into five areas for ease of administration.[8] The former Singapore Fortress troops were clustered in the north at the tip of the peninsula in what was called the Southern Troops Area. Troops from the British 18th Division occupied the Kitchener Barracks to the West and the Indian Corps troops were in barracks to the east. The Australians were given Selarang Barracks near the southern border of the camp. In the middle of it all was the Roberts Barracks, which was used as the camp hospital.

In the immediate aftermath of the British surrender, morale was low. Part of the reason was that many of the prisoners believed that they could have put up a better fight if their senior leadership had been up to the mark. They also realized that escape was nearly impossible. In addition, the officers in the camp did not encourage escape-mindedness. Fortunately, when the first troops arrived, they brought in large amounts of food, medicine and, surprisingly, money. Nearly all the cash available for pay and supply purchases for the Army found its way into the compound where it was hoarded for future use. It later made the difference between life and death for some of those sent to work on the Thai–Burma Railway. The Japanese had made it clear that the camp would have to be self-sufficient for everything but rice by April 1942.

The prisoners achieved this by developing a thriving black market, primarily conducted with and through Singapore's decidedly pro-Allied Chinese population. Every night and sometimes during the day, prisoners would regularly go "under the wire" to buy food, tobacco, and medicine. Some were doing so to help others while some were only looking out for themselves. The activities described in James Clavell's novel *King Rat* were based on his experience as a prisoner in Changi. Regardless of their motivation, aided by a sympathetic Chinese population in Singapore, the wire crossers kept the camp better supplied than almost any Japanese POW camp.

One curious episode deserves mention. In June 1942, the Japanese garrison of Singapore was replaced. However, due to some shoddy staff work, the incoming troops did not arrive until five days after the original garrison departed. This gap resulted in hundreds of prisoners being able to simply walk into Singapore town, visiting restaurants, shops, and the red-light district. Tom Wade noted, "Few people on earth have ever been kinder or more generous than the Chinese citizens of Singapore to a few thousand British and Australian prisoners during that unexpected freedom in 1942."[9] When the new garrison arrived, they quickly put the prisoners back in their compounds. Oddly, there were no lasting repercussions.

Eight hundred American prisoners passed through Changi, arriving in September 1942. They were survivors of the heavy cruiser USS *Houston* and the 131st Field Artillery (FA) Battalion, also known among themselves as the "Lost Battalion." The *Houston* survivors had been fished out of the sea in the aftermath of the disastrous battle of the Java Sea. The soldiers of the 131st FA Battalion had surrendered when the Japanese took the island of Java in present-day Indonesia. The Americans in Changi had a uniformly low opinion of the senior British officers administering the camp, which they shared with many of the Australians captured in Java who also passed through the camp. By January 1943, the Japanese shipped all but 69 of the Americans out to work on the Thai–Burma railway.[10]

For the rest of the war, Changi continued to be one of the better Japanese POW camps. When the Japanese surrendered, the prisoners found they were at liberty to trade openly with the Chinese and that the Japanese guard force had ceased to care about their comings and goings. Today, most of the camp is beneath the ultra-modern Changi Airport, but a chapel and museum have been erected on a portion of the camp. They are a fitting memorial to the prisoners who endured captivity there.

The Thai–Burma Railway Camps existed to allow the Imperial Japanese Army to construct a supply line from Bangkok, Thailand to Moulmein, Burma. Stretching approximately 178 miles from Nong Pladuk[11] in Thailand to Thanbyuzayat in Burma, it traversed incredibly tough terrain, mostly mountains and jungles. The construction required the removal of 105 million cubic feet of soil and rock as well as building 141 million cubic feet of embankments—almost all by hand. It also saw the construction of more than 600 bridges totaling over 8 miles.[12]

Supervised by the Imperial Japanese Army's 5th Railway Regiment from Thanbyuzayat in Burma and the 9th Railway Regiment from Nong Pladuk in Thailand, all the manual labor was done by the prisoners of war who were later augmented by civilian workers called *romusha* by the Japanese. The plight of the *romusha* deserves a mention here, even though they were not prisoners of war. Enticed with false promises of regular pay and good working conditions by the Japanese, well over 270,000 Thai and Burmese toiled on the railway. Unfortunately, they lacked medical support, internal organization, and more than a rudimentary sense of field sanitation. A recent estimate for their death rate is a staggering 200,000 or 72 per cent.[13]

The line was originally conceived in the planning for the invasion of Malaya and Burma in October of 1941. However, in the flush of unexpectedly easy victories the plan sat on the shelf. As the Japanese faced stiffening British opposition in Burma and increasingly aggressive and successful US submarine attacks on their shipping in the South China Sea, they dusted off the plans. POWs began to work on the line in March 1942 and continued to toil through October 1943.[14] The Japanese organized the POWs into brigade- and battalion-sized units to perform the work and to have a parallel chain of command to ease the flow of orders.

The prisoners worked in a series of over 40 camps strung out along the railway route. Each camp was much like every other, with thatched huts for everything. There would be sleeping quarters, latrines, and a kitchen. The Japanese engineers and guard force would be housed separately. There was no barbed wire—none was needed. The jungle was an effective boundary and barrier to escape. Most of the camps were constructed by British soldiers. They were neat and orderly. Some were built by unskilled, sick, and starving *romusha* labor. Unsurprisingly, these camps were built to a much lower standard.

Depending on the Japanese administration in a camp, the Allied officers might have a good deal of latitude or none when dealing with the day-to-day running of the camp. Diseases, malnutrition, and overwork combined to kill one third of the POWs overall before the line was completed. As a POW, chances of survival on the railway depended largely on three factors: unit officers, mates (friends in American English), and unit medical officers.

One example of a brigade-sized unit working from the Burma terminus was "A Force." Originally formed in Singapore during May of 1942 from Australian troops, the 3,000-man unit eventually included British, Dutch, and Americans in its ever-shrinking ranks. In command was Australian Brigadier General Arthur Leslie Varley, the commander of 22 Australian Brigade at the end of the Singapore Campaign. A brave man, Varley won the Military Cross twice in the fighting in France during World War I. He was a successful businessman with a wife and three children when he was recalled to the colors as a battalion commander the start of World War II.[15] His leadership of A Force was exemplary. Varley kept a diary which recorded his constant efforts to better the lot of those under his command.[16] Forced to innovate, he ordered that the possessions of the deceased be sold to pay for food and medicine for the living.

His tactful but relentless pressure on the Japanese was instrumental in A Force having the lowest death rate (19 percent) of any railway workforce, despite severe supply difficulties not faced by workforces which arrived later or that worked from the Thailand end of the railway.[17] Varley did not survive the war. "On 6 September 1944 approximately 2300 men under the command of Varley were loaded onto transport 'Rokyo Maru' in very cramped conditions. On 12 September the convoy was attacked by United States submarines and the transport with the prisoners were torpedoed. However, the 'Rokyo Maru' remained afloat for 12 hours which allowed time for the men to escape. The Japanese crew were rescued soon after but the Allied prisoners were left littered in the ocean on bits of the ships debris and some life-rafts. The men in the rafts split into 2 groups and one headed west and the other, with Varley, headed east. The western group was rescued by a Japanese destroyer about 2 days later but Varley and the group that headed to the east did not survive."[18] One of his battalion commanders, Lieutenant Colonel George Ramsay, did. He kept a record throughout his captivity which attested to Varley's leadership style.[19]

Two hundred Americans were attached to A Force, survivors from the heavy cruiser USS *Houston* and the 131st Field Artillery (FA) Battalion. They arrived in Moulmein in January 1943 and were shipped off to Camps Kilo 26 and Kilo 40, so called because they were 26 and 40 kilometers east of Thanbyuzayat respectively. Before A Force left, they listened to a rambling speech from the commander of the 5th Railway Regiment, Colonel Yoshitada Nagatomo. The basic point was clear, though. Escape was impossible. Either the jungle would get you or the Japanese Army would. The result would be the same—death. For his part in executing escaped prisoners, Colonel Nagatomo was executed after the war.[20]

When the Americans departed for Camp Kilo 40, they included in their ranks a Dutch physician. Dr. Henri Hekking had years of experience in the practical aspects of tropical medicine. He had also studied tropical herbs and plants for their medicinal value. His knowledge and abilities would spell the difference between death and life for many from the endemic scourges of dysentery, malaria, beriberi, and jungle ulcers. It took some persistence, but Hekking persuaded the camp commander,

Major Yamada, to allow him to go into the jungle to gather plants such as the *cephaelis ipecacuanha* to treat dysentery.[21] The first patient he treated with *cephaelis* was Jim Gee, from the Marine Detachment of the *Houston*. Gee's recovery was so rapid that Major Yamada let Hekking go harvesting in the jungle for medicinal plants on a regular basis. After all, healthier prisoners could work harder.

Hekking was helped in his efforts by "Packrat" McCone, a veritable genius in taking discarded items and turning them into something useful. A Marine gunnery sergeant from *Houston*, McCone took an instant liking to Hekking, and made it his mission to help him. Tin cans were used as water cups, packing thread for sutures, and spoons as surgical instruments.[22] The Japanese were leery of him, as they thought he was crazy. McCone did nothing to dispel that image, rather he amplified it by the way he walked and constantly talked to himself as he searched for useful items. He organized a group which earned the name "The Forty Thieves" who stole anything from the Japanese that wasn't nailed down. This even extended to stripping a parked truck of everything that could be of use to the prisoners. After they were done, they rolled the chassis into a ravine, camouflaged it, and erased any tracks they (and the truck) had made. They watched with barely suppressed glee as the dumbfounded driver received a succession of beatings from his corporal, sergeant, lieutenant, and finally Major Yamada. In spite of all the corporal punishment, the Japanese never did figure out what happened. McCone's inventiveness and generosity saved the lives of many of his fellow prisoners.[23]

The prisoners at Camp Kilo 40 were fortunate they had a courageous officer to stand up for them. Lieutenant James P. Lattimore of the 131st Field Artillery was a Texas National Guardsman called to active duty. Described as "short and thin with light blue eyes and sandy hair" he was captured with the rest of his battalion when Java fell.[24] He was a tower of strength for the men in his charge. He endured many a beating at the hands of Major Yamada or the guards for insisting on better treatment for the prisoners. This included a particularly savage episode after he organized a work slowdown in a bid for improved rations. Still, he survived the war and many of his fellow prisoners credit their survival to his fearless championship of their wellbeing.

The arrival of Korean guards heightened the misery at Camp Kilo 40—as it did anywhere. At the time, Koreans were at the absolute bottom of the Imperial Japanese Army. Any Japanese private—no matter his station—could look down on his Korean counterpart, who was identified by a "shooting star" patch sewn on the left side of the jacket and shirt.[25] Consequently, Koreans endured constant physical and mental abuse at the hands of their chain of command. Once they became guards, the Koreans had someone to abuse. As the British poet Rudyard Kipling noted, "Single men in barracks don't grow into plaster saints." While deplorable, their behavior is understandable.

After the Americans completed the work at Camp Kilo 40, they moved on to the nearly identical Camp Kilo 75 in May of 1943. This was the beginning of the "Speedo" period, where the completion date for the railway was advanced by four months from December to August 1943. This was in response to the steady American advances in the Pacific and US submarine warfare making the sea lanes increasingly unsafe for Japanese ships. In any event, the line was not completed until October 1943, at the cost of untold misery for the military and *romusha* slave laborers who built it.

Omori—also known as Tokyo Headquarters Camp or Tokyo Main Camp—was located on an artificial island near Yokohama. Prisoners of war had constructed it, primarily as a holding place for "special prisoners," who included among their numbers Lieutenant Louis Zamperini, a former Olympic athlete, and the skippers of the submarines USS *Grenadier* and USS *Tang*.[26] They were brought to Omori for their potential propaganda value. Omori was surrounded by a solid wooden wall instead of barbed wire. Otherwise, it had the features common to most camps. Guard towers dotted the perimeter. Barracks, latrines, a cookhouse, and the buildings for the guard force and administration filled the interior.[27]

Enlisted prisoners at Omori were forced to work every day while officers were not—practically the only part of the Geneva Conventions to which the administration at Omori adhered. However, there was a twist. Because they did not work, officers received half the rations of enlisted personnel. The food in either case was barely sufficient to sustain life. The enlisted prisoners were farmed out by the camp administration to perform hard physical labor, routinely moving 20 to 30 tons of material by hand each day.[28] A few handfuls of rice per day and a few ounces of meat per week, supplemented by a few vegetables, was all the prisoners received on a day-to-day basis. What kept the men alive was the contraband food smuggled into the camp by those on work parties. As Tom Wade noted, "If you watched the men undressing after returning from the jobs, you would see Japanese-issue socks filled with sugar or grain, the ends tied off, come slipping out of sleeves, inside legs, flat against the belly, the small of back, even under the caps of some crafty POWs."[29] The Japanese severely beat anyone caught stealing, but they did not put a dent in the thieving and smuggling.

Omori stood out from other camps during the period of August 1943 to February 1945 because of the presence of one man, Corporal—later Sergeant—Mutsuhiro Watanabe. From a wealthy family, he was well educated, having studied French literature at Waseda University in Tokyo. Shortly after he graduated in 1942, he joined the Imperial Army on a wave of patriotism. He initially had high hopes for his military career, applying to become an officer. His application rejected, Watanabe was given the rank of corporal and assigned to the elite Imperial Guards. Then the blow struck. In late 1943, his superiors assigned him to a POW camp—a dead-end assignment for any Japanese soldier. Humiliated, he descended on Omori and its hapless prisoners like a demon from Japanese folklore.[30]

At first, he seemed rational and intelligent. He spoke with the prisoners in a non-threatening way, often expressing his desire to visit the United States and Europe after the war. Then it all changed. As he was entering a barracks, Clark, the barracks commander, shouted "Gangway." Watanabe misinterpreted it as a warning to cease illicit activities and beat Clark nearly senseless. The fearful reaction of the other prisoners was like blood in the water to a shark. From then on, Watanabe became increasingly erratic and violent. Perhaps because his application for officer training had been rejected, he concentrated his fury on the officers in the camp. Louis Zamperini was one of his favorite targets. As noted author and historian Laura Hillenbrand observed, "From the moment that Watanabe locked eyes with Louie Zamperini, an officer, a famous Olympian, and a man for whom defiance was second nature, no man obsessed him more."[31] Among the tortures Watanabe inflicted on Zamperini was forcing him to "pick up a beam of wood, six feet long by four inches square and hold it at arms length above his head."[32] Incredibly, Zamperini held it up for 37 minutes.

Watanabe had a nickname—The Bird—a name picked because it was innocuous. He was so feared that the prisoners tracked him in the compound to warn of his approach. Their fear was not unreasonable, because Watanabe could not let a day pass without beating at least one prisoner. He did it to maintain fear, but he also did it because he got sexual enjoyment out of it. Prior to his arrival, prisoners had been allowed to send mail and receive the occasional letter from home. He put a stop to it, sometimes bringing prisoners in and burning their unopened letter from home before their eyes. He blocked their receipt of Red Cross parcels as well. He would sometimes apologize to the prisoners after beating them but within a few hours he was back to his old tricks. None of his supervisors made any attempt to restrain him, either.

Still, the prisoners were not entirely cowed by Watanabe. While they were at work, they engaged in a relentless sabotage campaign. This went from simply switching mailing labels on crates to derailing a train. They urinated on any rice they shipped, stole anything small and portable, pilfered anything alcoholic and destroyed items meant for the Nazi ambassador. They even sank two barges—in succession—and were not caught.[33] Sidney Stewart, an American captured in the Philippines and later held in camps in Manchuria and North Korea, had a theory as to why such actions were rarely detected. He felt that the Japanese simply couldn't envision anyone doing work badly![34] Regardless of the cause, the spirit of the men in Omori remained unbroken right up through their liberation.

The Cabanatuan prisoner of war camp was typical of the camps holding Americans and Filipinos captured when the islands fell to the Japanese onslaught from January to May 1942. Located on Luzon north of Manila near the barrio of Plateros, it stood in a rural, agricultural area. The prisoners were survivors of Camp O'Donnell transferred when Cabanatuan opened in late May 1942. Over 30,000 prisoners had already perished at O'Donnell before the transfer, due to Japanese neglect and outright maltreatment. At its peak, the camp held 12,000 prisoners although the number fluctuated considerably as the prisoners were shipped off in the "Hell Ships" to Formosa (present-day Taiwan), Manchuria, and Japan as slave labor. In the end, Cabanatuan held 511 prisoners who were too sick to move.

No discussion of Japanese treatment of prisoners of would be complete without a brief mention of what became known as the Hell Ships. The advances of Allied forces in the Pacific and Southeast Asia combined with the labor shortage in Japan led to the shipment of POWs in merchant ships from the far corners of Japanese-held territory to their home islands. The prisoners at Cabanatuan were no exception, with the final draft of 1,300 prisoners being shipped off to Japan in January 1945. According to the Geneva Conventions, such ships should have been clearly marked. As such, they would have been immune from air or submarine attack. There is not a single recorded instance of the Japanese doing so. This failure alone led to the needless deaths of thousands of POWs.

Reading the various accounts of the Hell Ships, one is struck by their similarity. Crammed below decks with barely room to lie down, the prisoners had very little food and practically no water. In winter they froze and in summer they boiled. Sanitary arrangements were a bucket—if the prisoners were lucky. As prisoners died, they were tossed overboard like so much refuse. If the ships were damaged or sunk by aircraft or submarines, the prisoners were often locked below decks until the ship was nearly under water. In some cases, an orderly evacuation was possible but not in many. Some prisoners had the terrible experience of being sunk, rescued, and put onto another ship. In retrospect, the 511 sick who were left at Cabanatuan were the fortunate ones.

In late May and throughout June 1942 the prisoners trekked from Old Bilibid Prison to Cabanatuan, if they had been taken on Corregidor, or from Camp O'Donnell if they were survivors of the Bataan death march. They would have noted the eight-foot-high barbed-wire fence and the evenly spaced guard towers surrounding the camp. They would also have seen the four guards in each tower armed with at least one Nambu machine gun. It is doubtful they would have known that the camp had originally been a US Department of Agriculture station. Some were sure to have known that it had been a training center for Filipino draftees just before the war. Regardless of what they knew, on arrival they were greeted by Lieutenant Colonel Shigeji Mori,[35] the camp commander. The IMTFE sentenced Mori to life imprisonment for his mistreatment of prisoners. His sentence was commuted in 1951 and he was released.

Had he not held the power of life and death over them, the prisoners would have mocked him openly. Short, squat, sporting a pencil-thin moustache, and with his samurai sword trailing in the dust as he waddled across the compound, he was given the nickname "Charlie Chaplain." But although his appearance was comic, he was deadly serious. One of his first acts was to assign the prisoners to groups of 10. He made it clear that anyone attempting to escape would bring about the deaths of the other nine people in their group.[36] While absolutely against the Geneva Conventions, such action made sense to the Japanese who, at the time, were brought up in a culture of collective responsibility.

The prisoners at Cabanatuan would have had to endure even greater suffering if not for the "Miss U Underground." Named after its guiding spirit, Margaret Utinsky, the organization surreptitiously funneled food and desperately needed medicines into the camp. Born Margaret Doolin in St. Louis, Missouri, Utinsky was a widow when she went to the Philippines in 1934 with her young son.[37] There she met and married Jack Utinsky, an American civil engineer working on Corregidor. When the war began, Jack assumed his rank of captain when called to duty with the US forces fighting on Bataan. Margaret hid in her apartment, aided by Filipino friends, until she heard that Bataan had fallen. She was determined to find her husband and help him if she could. With the help of a forged pass, Margaret transformed herself into Rosena Utinsky (code name Miss U), a Lithuanian born in Kovno. She purposely chose to be a Lithuanian because they were neutrals and had no diplomatic representatives in the Philippines. She volunteered as a nurse with the Philippine Red Cross and as a neutral was allowed to travel relatively freely. When she learned of Jack's death by starvation, she embarked on a crusade to aid the prisoners in Cabanatuan.[38]

In this she was aided by an Irish priest, Father John Lalor (code name Morning Glory), a Filipina beauty shop operator named Naomi Flores (code name Looter), a group of Maryknoll nuns (code name Angels) and a nightclub owner named Clara Phillips who went by Carla Fuentes (code name High Pockets). She recruited two Manila pharmacists as well as a wide variety of helpers of neutral nationalities including Spaniards, Swiss, Italians, and Russians. They established ways to move supplies right under the noses of the dreaded Kempei Tai. Later, members of the Miss U Underground would aid in the liberation of Cabanatuan.

Using an unused garage at a convent in Manila as a staging point, they moved quinine, sulfa drugs, clothing, shoes, and food through trusted couriers to the owner of several market stalls in Cabanatuan City. The prisoners were allowed to make weekly runs under guard into the city to make purchases with the few pesos a month they were given by the Japanese. With the guards distracted by attractive young Filipinas who were there for that purpose, the prisoners would load the contraband goods into the carts. The prisoners nicknamed the process the "Carabao Clipper."

The Miss U Underground even funneled transcripts of short-wave broadcasts with news of Allied victories to the prisoners on a weekly basis. The organization also furnished radio parts which were soon turned into working receivers. Of special value to the network was Elizabeth Kummer. Although she was American born, her husband was German (although anti-Nazi). Kummer was on good terms with a few Japanese officers. As a result, she was able to pass warnings when the network was in danger.[39] Father Lalor also maintained contacts in the Japanese headquarters. It was he who warned Miss U of her impending arrest. She fled Manila just ahead of the Kempei Tai and joined a guerilla unit.

The death rate at Cabanatuan was very high in the first few months. Between June and August over 2,000 prisoners died, mostly survivors of the Bataan death march. At the peak, 60 men died in a single day. By December, the death rate had bottomed out to a few deaths per week. Subsisting on two handfuls of rice per day, supplemented by an occasional bit of carabao meat or some vegetables, the survivors clung to life. But they did more than cling to life. Starving and sick, they still organized plays and vaudeville shows. The chaplains organized church services, which were well attended. There were black marketeers in the ranks, but there were everyday acts of kindness as well.[40] The combined selfless efforts of the prisoners and the courage of the Miss U Underground helped many to survive Cabanatuan who otherwise would not have lived to see the day of liberation.

CHAPTER 7

The Comet Line

The most unique escape line in Europe was founded in August 1941 by Andrée De Jongh, a 24-year-old Belgian nurse known to her Resistance co-workers as Dédée or to her immediate family as the Little Cyclone. Called the *Réseau Comète* (the Comet Line), it received significant support from MI9 but was entirely controlled and run by Belgians throughout the war. As a young girl, Dédée had been awed by stories of the English nurse Edith Cavell, executed by the Germans in World War I for helping prisoners to escape.

In May 1940, she volunteered as a nurse to care for Allied soldiers in hiding. Determined to do all she could to redeem Belgian honor, in August 1941 she helped her first evaders—a young Scottish soldier, Private Colin Cromar of the 1st Gordons, and two Belgians who wanted to fight for the Allies—to reach Spain. It took a week, including a crossing of the Pyrenees on foot, for Dédée and her charges to enter Spain. At first, the British Consul in Bilbao didn't know what to make of her. Was she a German plant? He decided to take a chance and sent her back to Belgium with a purse full of money and a mission to bring back three more evaders. Thus, the Comet Line was born.[1]

Dédée's father Frédéric De Jongh (who used the alias Paul) along with Fernand (l'Oncle) and Elvire De Greef (Tante Go), Peggy van Lier, the Belgian guides Yvonne and Robert Lapeyre and the Basque guide Florentino, Nadine Dumont (Michou), Henriette Hanotte (Monique), Jean-François Nothomb (Franco), Baron Jean Greindl (Nemo), Count Antoine d'Ursel (Jacques Cartier), and Baronne Jean Greindl (Bernadette), were typical of those who formed the line. Their efforts were so successful that the line passed over 800 evaders along to freedom from August 1941 until the liberation of France and Belgium in September 1944. This places the Comet Line in a class of its own as a purely local escape line.

The Germans attacked the line with ferocious determination throughout its operation, but never succeeded in putting it completely out of operation. By war's end, 156 members of the Comet Line had been murdered by the Nazis. Twenty-three were shot outright and 133 died in prison or in concentration camps.[2] But despite all of these threats, there was always someone to step up and assume leadership, act as guides, or keep safe houses.

The northern terminus of the line was in Brussels, the Belgian capital. Members of the Comet Line like Charles Morelle sought out evaders from across Holland and Belgium and funneled them to Brussels. During the early days of the line, he along with his sister Elvire Morelle were the principal guides from Brussels to the border. They worked tirelessly to aid Allied evaders without regard to the risks they ran. Both were eventually betrayed and wound up in concentration camps. Elvire survived, emerging gaunt and emaciated from Ravensbruck concentration camp. Sadly, although American troops liberated Charlie from Dachau concentration camp, he died shortly afterwards from the effects of his maltreatment.[3]

For a time, the husband-and-wife team of Yvonne and Robert Lapeyre would become fixtures of the Paris to Bayonne portion of the line, also working tirelessly to bring evaders, who they called *enfants* (children) to safety. They were finally forced to flee to England via Spain in March 1943, one step ahead of the Gestapo. But others continued to step up and continue the line's work.

Once in the line, the Comet Line's guides would conduct the *enfants* as a party southwest by rail. As a general rule, the line used local trains to travel because the security controls on them were less strict than on express trains. Crossing the border between Belgium and France at Quiévrain was often a heart-pounding moment for both guide and evader alike, yet the Nazis caught surprisingly few evaders. There were several reasons for this. To begin with, the guides brought their charges across during rush hours when inspections were normally cursory. It helped that the *enfants* were in appropriate attire and their papers were in good order. The guides further took care to blend their *enfants* in with the largest group of workmen they could find. In a tough spot, it helped that most of the French and Belgian customs inspectors, referred to as *douaniers*, were sympathetic to the Allied cause.

An example of this was shown during one crossing where Elvire De Greef (Tante Go) was the guide. She loathed the Germans. She had already suffered through an occupation of her native Belgium in World War I. She was cool under pressure and possessed of an ability to think on her feet. These characteristics would stand her in good stead in the situation to come. Unknown to her, the two *enfants* in her care had ignored her directions to ensure their pockets contained no incriminating material. One had unwisely crammed his pockets full of cigarettes—something sure to raise suspicion in a country where cigarettes were strictly rationed.

Unfortunately for the party, a German *Feldgendarme*[4] happened to be on duty at the station, so the French *douaniers* were more thorough than usual. They found the cigarettes. As a result, the *douaniers* bustled both evaders off to an adjacent office, searched them thoroughly, and told them to wait. Much to their surprise, the door to the outside was left open and unguarded. After a short wait, the two evaders simply seized what looked like an opportunity and left. In their haste to be gone, they left most of the cigarettes behind. As they hurried away from the station, they heard a shout from behind. It was one of the *douaniers*, bicycling madly toward them. After he pulled to a stop and dismounted, he returned the rest of their cigarettes with a broad smile on his face! As he did so, he offered some advice to Tante Go: "When you take birds like this about, don't wait for the Customs to empty their pockets. Do it beforehand. Good luck."[5]

Once across the Franco-Belgian border, most parties of evaders would normally take local trains to the busy rail hub at Lille and then change trains to arrive at Corbie, a sleepy town along the river Somme. Security controls to cross the Somme were so strict that the party would detrain and cross by night in a skiff, positioned there by two men who knew the surrounding marshland well. Having crossed the Somme, the party would usually head by train for Paris,[6] where members of the line would temporarily house them before dispatching them with new papers, appropriate clothing, and a different guide.

The party would then head south-southwest toward the Franco–Spanish border near Bayonne. Many parties passed through the town of Anglet, headquarters of the redoubtable Tante Go and L'Oncle. Once convinced of their identity, Tante Go would take them under her wing prior to dispatching them by foot across the Pyrenees in the capable hands of Florentino Goicoechea, a Basque smuggler turned Resistance member. Once across the border, the British Consul would have a car waiting in San Sebastian to conduct the evaders to Bilbao and thence to Gibraltar and England. The guides would return to begin their task anew.

From August 1941 to January 1943, Dédée ran the line. During that time, she personally made over 24 round trips across the Pyrenees.[7] However, in January 1943, a Spanish migrant laborer in France betrayed her to the Gestapo. She was eventually sent to Ravensbruck concentration camp and then to Mauthausen, from whence she emerged at the end of the war. The Germans did not execute her outright, as they had her father. One theory was that she survived because the Germans refused to believe that a young woman could organize and lead such an effective organization! Another theory was the Luftwaffe Secret Police "lost" her in a concentration camp to spite their rivals in the Gestapo. Even though the Germans imprisoned her body, her spirit continued to inspire members of the line.

After the Germans captured Dédée, Baron Jean Greindl (alias Nemo) took control of the line. Dédée had recruited him in June of 1942 as a helper. He used the Swedish Red Cross Canteen (Cantine Suédoise) in Brussels as cover for the line's operations. If MI9 had controlled the line, they would probably have disapproved of the cover. However, although the line was supported by MI9, it was independently controlled by its Belgian operators.

Established by the eccentric Swede Madame Scherlinck at the start of the war to care for the poor and sick children of Brussels, the Cantine Suédoise also catered to another entirely different class of *enfant*. At first, Nemo ran operations in Belgium and along the line to Paris, ably seconded by the vivacious red-haired Peggy Van Lier and Georges d'Oultremont. However, because of the relentless German pressure both Peggy and Georges were forced to flee to Spain just ahead of a Gestapo dragnet. Regardless of the mounting dangers after Dédée's arrest, Nemo ran the line in accordance with his motto "Toujours l'audace!" (Always be audacious).

From January through June of 1943, he directed the line without regard for his personal safety, even when warned that the Germans were closing in. Nemo was captured by the Luftwaffe Secret Police in June 1943 when he visited his former headquarters of the Cantine Suédoise, after having stayed away for six months. Tortured and beaten by the Gestapo, he died in an Allied bombing raid on a German barracks at d'Etterbeck on September 7, 1943. Sadly, only one bomb struck the barracks, but it scored a direct hit on the area where he was being held.

June 1943 was a bad month for the line, with over 100 arrests of helpers, guides and leaders. This was no fluke. A traitor known by the name of Jean Masson had penetrated the line, working as a trusted member for a month before betraying what he knew of the line to the Luftwaffe Secret Police. The most successful agent working for the Germans against the line, he was born Paul Desoubrie in Tourcoing, France, near the Belgian border.

Desoubrie first established his credentials by working for the Resistance in northern France. Short, blond, and nondescript, he was—on the face of it—an ideal guide. He went to work within the Comet Line on May 15, 1943. Among those he betrayed was Dédée's father, Frédéric De Jongh, who ran the line's Paris organization from July 1942 to June 1943. De Jongh revealed nothing to the Germans in spite of relentless torture and beatings. He was shot in Paris on March 28, 1944, along with several other of the line's helpers.[8]

Once they learned of the magnitude of the June disasters, the 23-year-old Baron Jean-François Nothomb, alias Franco, and Count Antoine d'Ursel, alias Jacques Cartier, took control of the line. Franco controlled the line around Paris and Cartier was responsible for the Brussels operation. Forced into hiding by Masson's efforts, Cartier nevertheless managed to recruit helpers sufficient to keep the line functioning in

Belgium. Always just a step ahead of the Gestapo, he was finally forced to flee to Paris in December of 1943.

With Paris too hot for him, Cartier was persuaded by Franco and Tante Go to cross into Spain with a group of *enfants*. Unfortunately, Cartier drowned along with one of the *enfants* while crossing the Bidassoa River which was in spate. The Germans displayed their bodies in the courtyard of the church in the village of Biriatu as an object lesson. The Basque villagers demonstrated their contempt for the Germans by covering the bodies with garlands of flowers. The Germans then took the bodies away. No one ever found out where they were buried.[9]

The full management of the line from Brussels to Paris now devolved on Franco. His alias came from a nickname Dédée had bestowed on him—Franquito. When the alias Franco first appeared in British diplomatic message traffic, it caused quite a stir at Whitehall as some thought it referred to the Spanish dictator Francisco Franco! In addition to shepherding the line, Franco also acted as a guide from Paris to Anglet.

During one trip, Franco was escorting three American airmen via bicycle. One of them had never ridden a bicycle before. After several falls, the airman finally got the hang of it enough to wobble slowly along. Unfortunately, he couldn't seem to keep to the right side of the road. When two German officers approached, the poor airman so lost his composure that he wobbled right into them. Before the dust had settled, the quick-thinking Franco was off his bicycle, helping the Germans to their feet, and apologizing profusely. Franco pulled an empty cognac bottle from his pocket and said, "Look what this fellow has drunk! All in one gulp!"[10] He then began to berate the hapless airman. The result was that the Germans cycled away laughing at Franco's stream of exaggerated verbal abuse.

In the fall of 1943, Franco went to Gibraltar to meet with the governor, Lieutenant General Sir Neil Mason-MacFarlane. He thanked Franco for his work, pledged further support, and suggested Franco go to England to avoid arrest. He declined to leave and went back to work. After several more highly successful trips, Franco was betrayed by Desoubrie in Paris on January 18, 1944. He was imprisoned in a series of concentration camps but emerged at the end of the war. Always a religious man, Franco become a Catholic priest. True to his character, Franco prayed with Desoubrie before his execution as a traitor in Lille at end of the war.[11]

In a little over a month, Desoubrie had compromised a large portion of the line. Like a snake shedding his skin, he shed the identity of Jean Masson for that of Pierre Boulin. Desoubrie then went to work trying to shut the damaged line down permanently. That he failed was largely due to his exposure as a traitor in March of 1944 by Lily Dumont, alias Michou. Petite and innocent in appearance, Michou was often taken for a teenager. This often stood her in good stead while working as a guide. When several line members were arrested by the Germans in a short period of time, Tante Go suspected treachery, as did Michou. One of those arrested was her friend and family dentist, Martine.

Despite the risks, Michou went to Fresnes prison south of Paris where Martine was being held. Standing outside, she called to her, asking for the traitor's identity. Martine shouted in reply, "It is Pierre! It is Pierre!" Before Michou could leave, she was detained by a *gendarme*. Taken to the prison commandant, Michou went through her prepared story that explained her behavior as an innocent inquiry after a family dentist. Released with a warning not to come back to the prison, Michou lost no time in notifying Tante Go. Soon the remaining line members were on the alert. Desoubrie would claim no more victims from the Comet Line.

Tante Go took over the line in February of 1944. She got her nickname from her recently deceased dog, Gogo. Appropriately, one of the early recognition phrases used within her line was, "Gogo est mort." (Gogo is dead). She and her husband Frederic, alias l'Oncle (the Uncle), had fled from Belgium at the start of the war, winding up near the France–Spain border in Anglet.

In addition to her work as a smuggler of *enfants*, Tante Go was the premier black marketeer in her corner of France. She took great care to provide excellent goods at very reasonable prices to senior officers of the Wehrmacht, Gestapo, and Luftwaffe Secret Police. Buying black market goods meant a quick trip to the Russian Front for any German so unfortunate as to be caught. Therefore, on the several occasions where she was detained, Tante Go merely had to mention the name of one of her senior officer clients to secure a quick release.

During the build up to D-Day, the nature of the line changed. The Allied bombing offensive against the French transportation system was in full swing. Allied bombers and fighter bombers kept up a steady drumbeat of attacks against railways, marshalling yards, bridges, and viaducts. After D-Day, the French Resistance mounted attacks against the railways as well. Railway movement became unreliable and downright hazardous. Therefore, MI9 conceived a plan code-named *Sherwood*. Instead of being brought out of the country, *enfants* would be kept in camps in wooded and hilly areas off the main highways.

After D-Day, Tante Go adjusted the line's operations to conform to *Sherwood*. However, the line continued to bring a trickle of *enfants* through to Spain and freedom until the Allied breakout from Normandy in August of 1944. Unable to focus on helping *enfants*, the line began to concentrate on gathering intelligence. In July, Tante Go made three border crossings carrying intelligence to the British Consul at San Sebastian.

When Dédée was captured by the Germans, Tante Go had hatched several plans to free her, none of which succeeded. However, in July 1944 Tante Go managed to liberate a key member of the line who had fallen into German hands. A month after D-Day, at 3 a.m., Florentino Goicoechea crossed the Bidassoa River heading for his hometown of Urrigne. Still on the French side of the border, he was ambushed by a German patrol. Severely wounded in the leg, he hid the papers he was carrying under a boulder. He then commenced to roll down the hill, away from the boulder. With the bones in his leg shattered into over 100 pieces, it was agonizing. The Germans found him and questioned him, but he refused to speak a word. They eventually took him to a civilian hospital in Bayonne, where Tante Go located him within 24 hours.

On the pretense of visiting a young man injured in a recent Allied bombardment, she whispered to Florentino in Spanish, "Two o'clock." At 2 p.m. that afternoon, three men who appeared to be Gestapo agents armed with the proper documents arrived at the hospital. They informed the Sisters of Mercy that Florentino was being moved. Despite the Sisters' protests, the men loaded a silent Florentino into a waiting ambulance and drove off.

Once they were away from the hospital, the three faux Gestapo men burst into laughter and produced a bottle of cognac. The leader of the group was well known to Florentino. It was l'Oncle, Tante Go's husband. It was he who had produced the forged transfer order and requisition for one of Bayonne's municipal ambulances![12] Tante Go and her helpers persevered in the face of every difficulty until the Germans evacuated Anglet in August 1944. By September, France and Belgium were in Allied hands, along with a portion of Holland. The Comet Line was out of a job.

CHAPTER 8

The Rome Escape Line

The Rome Escape Line had its origins in the chaos of the Italian surrender in September of 1943, shortly before the Allies landed at Salerno. Prior to their surrender, the Italians had held around 80,000 Allied prisoners. Of that number roughly 42,000 were British, 26,000 were Commonwealth, and 1,300 were American. The remaining 10,000 plus were a mix of Free French, Yugoslavs, and Greeks. Due to a monumental staff screw-up or Field Marshal Sir Bernard Law Montgomery's miscalculation,[1] the prisoners had been ordered to remain in place.

While it is impossible to be certain, it seems the theory was that in the aftermath of the surrender rapidly advancing Allied columns would liberate the camps. Such a plan failed to take into consideration two factors. The first was geography, with the boot of Italy being ideal defensive territory, difficult to traverse when opposed. The second was the swift German reaction. As soon as the Italians threw in the towel, the Germans rushed southward with every formation they could muster. Italian opposition to the German advance was ineffectual at best, nonexistent at the worst.

Showing considerable initiative, over 50,000 Allied prisoners absconded from the mostly unguarded camps and headed for the hills. Around 30,000 were not so fortunate. They were rounded up by the Germans and shipped off to Germany. Of the prisoners who managed to escape, many headed for Switzerland. Over 1,800 of those who made it were assisted by Giuseppe Bacciagaluppi, his English wife, and a network of over 350 agents, of whom 20 died.[2] Many other prisoners simply went to ground with Italian families. Several thousand headed for the larger cities, particularly Rome.

To address the problem of so many escapers at large, MI9 and MIS-X set up "A Force."[3] Initially headquartered in Bari, A Force quickly set to work via a subordinate unit led by Lt. Col. Anthony C. Simonds, a veteran of the Special Operations Executive (SOE) who had transferred to MI9. Designated SIMCOL (Simonds' Column), the hastily organized unit's purpose was to bring out escapers either through the lines, via agent networks or by sea. Surprisingly, many of the escapers contacted by SIMCOL refused to budge. Most of them felt that Allied troops would soon be there to liberate them and didn't want to risk crossing German-held territory. Some were comfortably ensconced with Italian peasant families and preferred to stay put, regardless. In one case, out of a group of 1,300 escapers around Sulmona only 23 agreed to come back to Allied control.[4]

Those Allied POWs who gravitated to Rome and the surrounding countryside came under the wing of what came to be known as "The Rome Escape Line." Unlike the Comet Line which was run entirely by Belgians with MI9 financial and logistical support, the Rome Escape Line eventually came under the control of MI9. Brought to life by an Irish priest, the Right Reverend Monsignor Hugh O'Flaherty, and an escaped British officer, Major (later Lt. Col.) Sam I. Derry, the line had its headquarters within the Vatican's German College!

Sam I. Derry was a soldier's soldier. He fought in France during 1940 and was evacuated at Dunkirk. Posted to North Africa, he earned the Military Cross near Sidi Barrani, Egypt, in November of 1941 when his battery repelled the attack of 28 enemy tanks, destroying seven in the process. He was captured in February 1942 when his artillery battery was overrun by a unit of the German Afrika Korps west of Derna, Libya.[5] Soon after capture, Derry made a break for freedom, sped down a wadi by a hail of rifle fire.

Over the next few days, he managed to evade across 18 miles of desert before rejoining the Eighth Army. He fought in Operation *Crusader*, in the Battle of Gazala, and in numerous rear-guard actions before being recaptured almost 800 miles away, near El Alamein, Egypt on June 23, 1942.[6]

Ironically, he was taken prisoner by the same unit that had captured him at Derna. Recognizing him as a successful escaper, the Germans guarded Derry closely. He was flown out with a load of prisoners to an airfield at Lecce, in southern Italy. From there he was taken to camp PG 21[7] near Chieti. Located in central Italy, 124 miles east-northeast of Rome, Chieti was (and is) the capital of Chieti province in the Abruzzo region.

PG 21 was a large camp, with over 1,200 officers and their batmen (soldier servants). It was there that Derry learned the tricks of the trade as a prisoner of war, eventually becoming the head of the escape committee when the entire escape committee was shipped off as a body to Germany. Under his guidance, several successful escapes took place. Unfortunately, after the Italian surrender the Germans took control of Chieti before the Allies. So, in September 1943 Derry found himself on a train with over a thousand other prisoners, headed for Germany.

Determined to escape, Derry waited for an opening. He saw it when escorted to the bathroom by a guard. When he emerged from the bathroom, Derry employed a rugby move to evade the surprised guard. Without hesitation, he leapt from the moving train, landing awfully hard on the stony soil. Badly bruised yet miraculously having avoided being shot by the German soldiers atop the train, he gingerly limped for the hills where a sympathetic farmer and his wife offered him shelter in a haystack. Working industriously from his haystack headquarters, in less than a week Derry contacted 47 other prisoners secreted in caves and on farms throughout the area. Taking command without hesitation, Derry remembered from an MI9 briefing that his safest bet would be to contact a priest for help with the needs of his men. He contacted a local priest who hurried off with a note pleading for funds signed, "S. I. Derry, Major." Much to his surprise, the priest returned with 4,000 lire and a note asking him to come to Rome if he wished to receive more help. With some trepidation, Derry headed for Rome on a creaking wagonload of cabbages. Fortunately, he only had to burrow into the fetid pile of vegetable matter once when the cart arrived at a checkpoint on the outskirts of the Eternal City. In a short time, he found himself standing in Vatican Square in the presence of Monsignor Hugh O'Flaherty.

To the monsignor, Derry seemed the answer to a prayer. Even prior to the Italian surrender, a Council of Three consisting of the monsignor, Count Sarsfield Salazar of the Swiss Legation, and John May (butler to the British Minister to the Holy See) had been aiding escaped prisoners. Shortly before the arrival of Derry's note, the growing number of escaped prisoners in the Rome area had led them to conclude that they needed a senior officer to run the organization. They agreed that Derry seemed a perfect solution.

Soon after arriving at the German College, Derry met the British Minister to the Vatican, Sir Francis D'Arcy Godolphin Osborne. Once vetted by Osborne, Derry was given an authentic Vatican credential which identified him as Patrick Derry, an Irish journalist. While the credential would not stand up to deep scrutiny, it was sufficient to get Derry past the normal security measures in Rome. He was fully in charge of the Rome Escape Line by December 4, 1943.

Fortunately, he didn't labor alone. There were several British officers interned in the Vatican who did much of the paperwork, such as building card indexes on the escaped prisoners and their hosts. When not being worked on, these indexes were always kept buried in cookie tins in the Vatican gardens as a security precaution. It was from these records that the line produced a list of over 2,000 escaped prisoners which was subsequently microfilmed through the good offices of John May. It was smuggled out of Rome in a loaf of bread by Peter Tumiati, an MI9 agent.

What the line also needed were people capable of doing the footwork to procure supplies and safe houses. The first requirement was met chiefly by the resourceful John May, who seemed to know every source of black-market goods in Rome and its environs. The second found its fulfillment in the mid-December arrival of three former Chieti "alumni." Two were artillery subalterns—John Furman and Bill Simpson. Both were well known to Derry from Chieti. The third was Joe Pollack, a private of Cypriot origin who spoke fluent Italian. At first, Derry was suspicious of Pollack because he thought he might be responsible for the betrayal of the Chieti escape committee—a suspicion that he later learned was groundless. Together, Derry and his three helpers—whom he called his billeting officers—began the difficult task of hiding or in some cases evacuating the thousands of Allied escapees in the Rome area.

However, before the line could find its feet, disaster struck. One of the line's earliest Italian helpers, a young woman named Iride, was scooped up by the Gestapo in a raid shortly after New Year's Day, 1944. The Germans were seeking to destroy an Italian Communist resistance organization that had become increasingly active in Rome. What they found instead was one of the line's transit flats, where prisoners were billeted temporarily before more permanent arrangements could be made.

The Germans used Iride as bait to lure Joe Pollack to the flat. Despite his feeling it might be a trap, Pollack went and was taken. The Italian cook at the flat knew of two other locations, which he betrayed under pressure to the Germans. As a result, John Furman and 11 other prisoners were recaptured. Bill Simpson narrowly escaped recapture himself, warned away by an Italian porter just as he was ready to enter a building where the Germans lay in wait.

Although down to one billeting officer, Derry took immediate action to limit the damage. He ordered the evacuation of all billets known to the captured Italian helpers. More importantly, he reorganized the billeting and supply system so no Italian helper knew of more than three to four locations where prisoners were hidden. He also established a new transit billet in the basement of a block of apartments near the Vatican. In addition, he arranged for a small shop near the Vatican to serve as a place to meet and verify the identity of new arrivals. This would prevent the introduction of enemy agents into the line.

Although security was now much tighter, the Germans had somehow gotten wind of the monsignor's involvement in helping escapers. They brought pressure to bear on the Vatican Secretariat, which as a result warned O'Flaherty to remain in the Vatican on pain of immediate arrest. Undaunted by the new restrictions, the monsignor employed fellow priests as helpers. German pressure had also forced Derry to move from the German College to the British Legation in the Vatican as a precaution. He had his fake credentials buried in the garden and adopted the name of "Toni." With security thus tightened even further, the line continued to operate.

In a Fascist state, anonymous denunciations made to the secret police were an ever-present danger. However, the line had developed security to a degree where the blows aimed by the Germans often landed on empty air. An amusing example was that of Mrs. Chevalier and her five "boys." Mrs. Chevalier was a diminutive native of Malta who lived in a tiny apartment with her six daughters. Not long after the Italian surrender in September 1943, she had taken in five escaped British prisoners whom she called affectionately "my boys." Incredibly, she managed to care for her family and all five escapees in a single-room apartment with a tiny kitchen.

Warned of a raid by a young Italian boy who worked at the German headquarters, the five escapees evacuated the apartment and fled to other pre-arranged quarters. Minutes later when the Germans arrived, they quickly surveyed the single room and after a cursory search concluded that no one other than Mrs. Chevalier and her daughters could possibly fit into the apartment. They asked Mrs. Chevalier if she had seen any strangers in the area. Strongly suspecting that her next-door neighbors who were ardent Fascists had denounced her, she neatly turned the tables on them. She told the German officer in charge, "There have been some strangers coming to this building—but they all went next door."[8] The Germans went next door and proceeded to thoroughly wreck the apartment!

With the line reorganized and security tightened, Derry settled in for the long haul. A false dawn occurred when the Allies landed at Anzio on January 22, 1944, just 39 road miles south of Rome. However, the timidity of the Allied commander, US Major General John P. Lucas, and the swift, preplanned German counterattack directed by the able Field Marshal Kesselring, kept the American and British forces from advancing inland and seizing the high ground around the beachhead. The Germans delivered two violent counterattacks during February which nearly drove the Allied defenders into the sea. Even though they held on, their forces were penned up in the bridgehead by stiff German resistance. As Winston Churchill ruefully noted, "I had hoped we were hurling a wildcat into the shore, but all we got was a stranded whale."[9] After four long months, the British and American forces finally broke out on May 23, 1944. US forces from the beachhead entered Rome on June 4, 1944.[10]

Derry worried that the landings would cause many of the prisoners in hiding to head for the beachhead. He felt that, in the heat of battle, the Germans would simply shoot them out of hand. Fortunately, only a few tried, some of whom were successful. By mid-February when it became clear that the forces at Anzio weren't getting to Rome any time soon, that particular danger passed. Much to his surprise and relief, on February 14, 1944, Derry got a note from John Furman that he was back in Rome. It transpired that along with a Lieutenant Johnstone, Furman had escaped by leaping from a heavily guarded train headed for Germany after breaking a small two-foot hole in the rear of the boxcar with an iron bar he had smuggled in.

Although he was only a few miles from the Swiss border, Furman obtained two bicycles and pedaled with Johnstone at his side about 500 miles, all the way to Rome![11] Shortly thereafter, Joe Pollack showed up, having escaped from a railway station during an Allied bombing raid. He was suffering from pneumonia and tuberculosis but categorically refused to be evacuated to Switzerland. Pollack stayed and continued to help as best he could. The return of Furman and Pollack seemed at the time to be the reversal of the string of bad luck that had dogged the line. For a while, that luck held.

Then disaster struck again on March 22, 1944, in the aftermath of the detonation of a bomb hidden in a rubbish cart by Italian Communists. The attack killed 32 German soldiers outright and wounded many more. In response, the Germans and their Fascist helpers clamped down hard by instituting a tight curfew, increasing security checks, and conducting raids throughout the city. Furthermore, they took 320 prisoners at random from the city jails, transported them to the Ardeatine Caves outside Rome, and machine gunned them before blowing the cave entrances shut. Six of those killed were helpers of the line. The Ardeatine Caves massacre had one positive effect: it turned most Italians firmly against the Germans.

To make things worse, the Germans brought in additional security troops and formed an Italian unit of Fascist neo-Gestapo with wide-ranging powers who they unleashed on the hapless inhabitants of Rome. Just as things seemed to be spiraling out of control, the line had a bit of luck.

An Italian known only as Giuseppe who worked in the Questura, the headquarters of the SS and the Fascist Carabinieri, approached John May. Giuseppe offered to sell him copies of the daily Questura Routine Orders. These orders listed all the scheduled raids for the day. While they didn't cover the occasional denunciation by fascist sympathizers to the secret police, they were a priceless intelligence windfall. They allowed the line to dodge most of the blows aimed from the Questura through a series of often hurried but nonetheless successful evacuations.[12] Giuseppe was also able to make it clear that many of the raids attributed by the organization to bad luck were the result of denunciations. Through him Derry also learned that the Germans were using false priests to infiltrate the line, with some success. The line used this information to warn its helpers, no doubt avoiding more severe problems.

Despite the line's newly found source of intelligence, Bill Simpson was arrested on April 18. At first, no one in the line could find out what had happened. Eventually, they found that he was incarcerated in the forbidding *Regina Coeli* (Queen of Heaven) prison under the name of William O'Flynn—the name on his Vatican identity card. The Germans had checked with the Vatican, which denied any knowledge of him. In a tight spot, Simpson managed to persuade the head of the Fascist security forces in Rome that he and several other prisoners should be left behind when the Germans evacuated Rome. As a quid pro quo, Simpson would ensure that the Allied forces guaranteed the security of his family. As the Allies entered Rome, the Italian guards deserted their posts with alacrity, leaving the doors to the prison and all of the cells open. Simpson and the others simply walked out to freedom.

But before that day, Derry still had to, as he put it, "thrust and parry" constantly. With many of the priests who had helped the organization confined to the Vatican by their superiors, John Furman was the only billeting officer consistently left at liberty. Having been warned that the Fascists were looking for him, the diminutive Furman shaved his mustache, dyed his hair black, changed how he parted his hair, and became a typical Italian in appearance.

Throughout April and into May, the line continued to care for an increasing number of escapees and evaders. Most of the evaders were downed aircrew. Of the over 3,000 personnel cared for by the line, only around 200 were in Rome. The rest were dispersed in the rural areas nearby. For a number of reasons, it was far easier to feed and secure those outside the city. Finally, on May 23 the Allies broke out of the Anzio beachhead and began to push towards Rome. By May 30, the Allies had breached the Caesar Line, the last line of defense below Rome, and the German evacuation went into full gear. Finally, on June 4, 1944, troops of the US Fifth Army liberated Rome.

For Derry, Furman, Simpson and Pollack it wasn't over. They formed the core of a unit which recognized those who had helped the line as well as serving as a clearing house for all of the denunciations against Fascist sympathizers who had aided attacks against the line. Their microfilmed records buried in the Vatican gardens and the *Questura* lists were very helpful in that regard. The Rome Escape Line had done a magnificent job in very trying circumstances. When the Allies liberated Rome, the organization had 3,925 escapers and evaders on their rolls. This included 1,695 British, 896 South Africans, 429 Russians, 425 Greeks, and 185 Americans, with the rest hailing from more than 20 other countries. By any measure, the line was a resounding success.

CHAPTER 9

The Shelburne Line

The Shelburne Line was a creature of MI9 whose mission was to evacuate evaders and escapers from Brittany in France by sea to England or by foot across the Pyrenees into Spain. Brittany is bordered by the English Channel to the north, Normandy to the northeast, Pays de la Loire to the southeast, the Bay of Biscay to the south, and the Celtic Sea and the Atlantic Ocean to the west. At the time, it was a culturally distinct region where outsiders were quickly noticed. Mostly rural, it provided an ideal spot to assemble and hide downed aircrew and others. The Germans had not emplaced beach defenses to the degree they had from Normandy northwards. Also, it was close enough to make an overnight run from England to Brittany and back in a Motor Gun Boat (MGB). Finally, there were multiple routes through rural areas in the Pays de la Loire which could be used to move escapers and evaders south towards Spain.

The line had its roots in an earlier MI9 escape line code named Oaktree established by two MI9 agents, the lead agent a White Russian named Vladimir Bouryschkine who adopted the *nom de guerre* of Val Williams and a French-Canadian radio operator named Ray LaBrosse.[1] To establish the line, they dropped just outside Paris without benefit of a reception committee. Williams went first to Paris, where he recruited a lawyer named Francis Campinchi to head the Paris end of the line. Campinchi had experience working in escape lines, as he had worked with the Pat line before it was taken down by the Gestapo. Williams then travelled to Brittany, where he met with local Resistance groups to organize routes, security, and safe houses. The chief Resistance point of contact at the

Brittany end of the line was Françoise Le Cornec. Unfortunately, Williams was not very security conscious, despite his training. His indiscretions led to his capture and the compromise of many of the helpers the line had recruited.

Williams subsequently escaped and went into hiding in Paris. He was later evacuated through the Shelburne Line and returned to England to sit out the war. Ray LaBrosse was another matter. A former sergeant in the Canadian Army Signal Corps, he was tough and highly security conscious. After he escaped the Gestapo dragnet that had scooped up his boss, he found himself with a defective wireless set, no codes, no money, and 27 evaders to care for. LaBrosse did not despair. Instead, he managed to get all 27 evaders and himself across the Pyrenees to Spain. Flown back from Madrid to London, he volunteered to go back. While receiving additional training, LaBrosse linked up with his new boss from the Fusiliers Mont Royal, Sergeant Major Lucien Dumais who was equally tough and security minded as LaBrosse.

Thus began the Shelburne Line, which would function smoothly from October 1943 through August of 1944, never losing an evader or escaper who had entered the line. Unlike the Comet Line, which referred to evaders and escapers as *enfants*, the Shelburne Line referred to them as "parcels." The logic behind the nickname was that the evaders had to be re-wrapped in a new identity and sent to a new address.

Lucien Dumais had first enlisted in the Canadian Territorial Reserves in 1934. He was an excellent shot, a quick learner, as well as physically and mentally tough. When the war broke out, he shipped to England where he underwent commando training. He was with the Canadian 2nd Division as they hit the beaches in the disastrous Dieppe raid on the morning of August 19, 1942. He survived the battle unwounded but missed being evacuated by the boats sent to retrieve the survivors because he was wearing a heavy pack and was a poor swimmer. After nearly drowning in an attempt to reach an evacuation boat, Dumais barely made it back to shore. He took charge of defending some wounded who were sheltered in the lee of a burning Landing Craft Tank (LCT). Out of ammunition and with the wounded desperately needing medical attention, Dumais surrendered.

The Germans had captured Dumais, but not for long. Along with two others, he escaped two days later from a moving train near Rouen. Using his wits and guided by his escape training, Dumais managed to contact the Resistance and was fed into the Pat Line. He was evacuated along with 34 others by a fishing boat, the *Sea Wolf*, to Gibraltar, and was back in London by late October 1942. Once there he was debriefed by Major Jimmy Langley of MI9. He so impressed Langley that he was offered a job, which he declined. He explained, "I had had my fill of being lost behind enemy lines, and was in no mood to resume that tense, hunted life..."[2] By mid-1943 he had changed his mind, mostly due to the arrival of an officious and untested lieutenant fresh from Canada as the commander of his unit. Unable to endure his clueless superior, Dumais decided to volunteer for work with MI9. Although Langley had moved on, Major Airey Neave—who had escaped from Colditz in 1941—became Dumais' boss. It was during training that Dumais and LaBrosse met. They took to each other immediately. Even before they departed for France as part of a flight of three Lysander aircraft—a small, high-wing monoplane used for infiltrating and exfiltrating agents—they had built a strong bond of trust.

They landed north of Paris, quickly making their way to the city. From the beginning, Dumais and LaBrosse stuck to their training by using assumed names and never showing their false identity papers to anyone in their organization. They also took care not to reveal that Dumais was carrying 500,000 francs while Ray was holding 250,000. They spent the money carefully, first being sure to repay the debts racked up by the remnant of the Oaktree Line in caring for the "parcels" scattered about Paris and Brittany. Together, they scouted out multiple sites from which LaBrosse could operate his radio set.

Ever mindful of the German radio direction-finding vans prowling around Paris, LaBrosse took care never to transmit from the same location twice in a row. He also kept his transmissions short, broke down the wireless set immediately after each message, and moved immediately. Dumais located a spare room in an elderly lady's flat where he and LaBrosse could store their weapons, money, and other gear. By making a spare key, they were able to access the room when she was out without her knowledge. In this, Dumais was guided by the old axiom that you can't spill what you don't know. They also found a local printer who was able to reproduce high-quality German identity documents on short notice.

Within a few days, they were ready to commence operations, but not before Dumais laid down 10 rules to maintain overall security within the line and to avoid the introduction of false evaders by the Germans. The rules were:[3]

1. All agents were to keep their addresses secret.
2. Chiefs were to meet their helpers only when necessary, and they were never to give information that was not absolutely essential.
3. Everyone would work through accommodation addresses.[4]
4. Agents were to avoid friendly meetings together.
5. Contacts between guides and evaders would be made by pre-arranged signals only.
6. Evaders had to be passed down the line without their guides meeting each other.
7. No one was to talk about his chief, or even admit to having one.
8. The head of the network was to remain totally unknown.
9. Evaders were not to be told of the existence of any network.
10. All evaders were to be interrogated as soon as they came under the network's control.[5]

Through Campinchi, Dumais connected with a doctor named Le Balch who had recently set up a practice in Plouézec, a town in Brittany about 20 miles from Plouha where Dumais would eventually carry out the Shelburne seaborne evacuations. Travelling by local trains to Brittany with LaBrosse, Dumais met with Le Balch to select a site for the seaborne evacuations for which the code word was "Bonaparte." Shortly after, he met with Françoise Le Cornec, the local Resistance leader who had worked with Oaktree and would now play a large part in Shelburne. They formed an instant rapport as both men were professional and cautious.

They selected a beach near Plouha locally known as Sous-Kéruzeau to evacuate the "parcels." It is now the Plage Bonaparte, in honor of its wartime history. Located at the foot of a 100-foot cliff, the beach could be reached via a gully known as the Anse de Cochat at low tide.

At high tide it could only be accessed by sliding down the 70-degree cliffs. It was a small sandy beach, well suited for the operation.[6]

Once Dumais settled the details for the upcoming operation with Le Cornec, LaBrosse sent a message to London to inform them the line was operational. MI9 scheduled the first operation for the night of January 29, 1944. That night, the Resistance cell led by Le Cornec assembled 19 "parcels" in a small stone farmhouse roughly a mile from the beach. It was owned by a friend of Le Cornec named Alphonse Gicquel, a local farmer. They eagerly waited by the radio, tuned to the BBC for the message "Bonjour tout le monde à la maison d'Alphonse."[7] When it came, they proceeded to the beach with the 13 US and four RAF airmen, plus two Frenchmen on the run from the Gestapo.

After a tense wait, several small boats from the British Motor Gun Boat (MGB) 503 appeared to take delivery of the "parcels." An excellent choice for the job, MGB 503 was 117 feet in length with a 20-foot beam and a draft of only 4 feet 4 inches. Driven by three Davey Paxman diesel engines, it could make 28 knots, allowing it to make the round trip from England to Brittany during the hours of darkness. Mounting a 2-pounder pom-pom aft, two twin .5-inch machine guns in powered turrets on each side of the bridge, an additional .303 caliber light machine gun on the bridge, two 21-inch torpedo tubes, and 12 depth charges, it had the armament necessary to slug it out with any Germans who could keep up with it.[8] After an exchange of recognition signals, the small boats lowered by MGB 503 quietly grounded on the beach. There was a flurry of hushed activity as the 19 passengers embarked and the Resistance reception party unloaded six large cases of supplies. This night became a template for all future operations—parcels out, supplies in.

After they unloaded the last case, the reception party lugged them up the cliffs to the stone farmhouse. Dumais opened them in front of the members of the reception party, which he realized was "a silly mistake."[9] Besides containing "weapons, ammunition, a wireless set, chocolate, cigarettes, whiskey, and many other items" they also contained four million francs in "worn ten thousand franc notes, pressed (not ironed) into tight bundles…"[10] The sight of the money caused quite a stir among those in the farmhouse. Dumais kept the wireless set for use by LaBrosse when in Brittany. It would prevent his having to carry the set from Paris for each operation. He gave Le Cornec the weapons and ammunition, as well as sharing out some of the luxury items. He also paid everyone amounts that he and Le Cornec had previously agreed upon. Dumais suspected that it was not as much as they would have liked. He never opened any supply cases in front of a reception party again.

On the way back to Paris, Dumais was carrying two suitcases, one of them containing the four million francs. When he arrived, he ran straight into the arms of the police who were conducting a snap inspection of all persons and their luggage. As those with luggage queued up, Dumais did some quick thinking. He got in line in front of a young *gendarme* who didn't look very experienced. When the gendarme asked what was in the case, Dumais said jokingly "mortars and machine guns." Not amused, the gendarme ordered him to open it, telling Dumais they were looking for food. When he came to the money, Dumais told him it was Resistance money. That seemed to satisfy the young man who snapped the case shut and said, "Go on. Clear out." Dumais did so with alacrity.[11]

The Germans made several attempts to penetrate the line, all of which were detected before any damage was done. However, Dumais had another problem that threatened the line—an internal one. Val Williams. He was awaiting evacuation and had been indiscreet, boasting in a tavern that he had a ticket back to England. When word reached Dumais, he confronted Williams, pointed his .45 caliber automatic pistol at him and swore that if Williams didn't keep his mouth shut, he would shoot him without hesitation. Apparently, Williams believed him. Shortly afterwards, on the night of February 25, 1944, the line carried out Bonaparte II. Williams was one of the 20 "parcels" dispatched to England.

As the number of airmen within the line began to grow, Dumais sought to establish a land evasion route across the Pyrenees to Spain. A young civil servant named Jean Mettling who had worked with Oaktree knew a few Spanish smugglers who were willing to do so for a price. Dumais decided to meet their price, pay in advance, and give them the same amount as a bonus once the line had wireless confirmation from Madrid that the "parcels" had arrived safely. Within a few days, a steady stream of evaders began to flow safely across the border to freedom.

However, even with the addition of the land route, evaders began to pile up in Paris.

At one point, Dr. Campinchi had over 75 "parcels" in his care. To solve this problem, Dumais contacted London and asked for operations on March 15, 19, and 23. Not surprisingly, London asked for a repeat of the message. On those three nights MGB 503 arrived and took off a total of 75 people, although not without incident. On the night of the 15th there had been an alert in the area during which the MGB had been forced to wait until close to dawn to take off the evaders. Still, their luck held, and the Germans did not detect them. As part of the general preparation of the Atlantic Wall, the Germans laid a minefield along the top of the cliff. However, the local Resistance had observed the entire process. Each time the line conducted an operation, they would mark the location of the mines with white cloth. When they withdrew from the beach, they would remove the cloths.

Despite Dumais' emphasis on security, the line was not free from problems. First and foremost, the Germans constantly tried to introduce false evaders or helpers into the line. The normal security precautions of the line were sufficient to weed out the false evaders. However, one of the false helpers who tried to infiltrate Shelburne was Roger Le Neveu. Also known as Roger Le Légionnaire, he was a traitor and Gestapo agent who had been instrumental in the collapse of both the Pat and Oaktree Lines.[12] In April of 1944, when Dumais learned that Neveu was targeting his operation, he decided to kill him.

After having the local Resistance surveil Neveu, Dumais found what he believed was an opportunity. Neveu kept his car stored in a shed near the house in the town of Blois where he was staying with an apprentice whom he was grooming to be a Gestapo agent. The shed was accessible, so Dumais sent Jean Mettling to place an explosive device in the car. It took Jean several days of patient effort to plant the device, but he finally succeeded. The next morning the apprentice got into the car to drive into town. The explosion killed him, wrecked the car, and sent Neveu fleeing from Brittany—never to return. His flight only saved him for a short while. The Maquis caught Neveu during the liberation and disposed of him.

Another persistent problem was overly talkative members of the line. Jean Mettling played a key role in plugging such security leaks. Born in Alsace, a province of France which had been under German rule from 1870 to 1919, Jean spoke French—as did most Alsatians—with a slight German accent. When someone was being loose lipped they would be warned. If they continued with loose talk, Dumais would dispatch Jean to start making inquiries about that person. Jean knew from experience how Gestapo agents behaved, how they dressed, and the sort of questions they would ask. This was usually enough to send the blabbermouth fleeing for the hills.

When that tactic did not work, Dumais would summon the person, pay them a hefty bonus, and say that the line was shutting down operations because of all the recent Gestapo activity. Thereafter, no one from the line would have any "official" dealings with them. As a result, Dumais never had to resort to violence against members of the line.

The Normandy landings resulted in tightened security but did not entirely stop the flow of "parcels" by sea or by land. As soon as the landings took place London instructed Dumais and LaBrosse to leave Paris for Brittany immediately. Because of the successful Allied and Resistance attacks against the rail lines, Dumais and Ray set off on bicycles. They were separated during an Allied air attack near Rennes. Ray made it to Brittany without incident.

Dumais had his bicycle appropriated by some German troops. With typical sangfroid, Dumais went to the local military police headquarters and reported the theft. Although he didn't get his bicycle back, he did get an authorization to ride in a German transport to St. Brieuc in Brittany. When he showed up, his friends were surprised to see him so soon. They presumed Dumais had been forced to walk. When asked how he had managed it, Dumais replied, "By courtesy of the Wehrmacht, the Luftwaffe, the Feldgendarmerie, and the Gestapo!"[13]

After D-Day, things began to heat up in Brittany, partially due to the arrival of Special Operations Executive (SOE) teams and Special Air Service (SAS) units who teamed with the local Resistance to harry the Germans. Nevertheless, a sea-lift operation went off without a hitch on July 12. The final seaborne operation took place on July 24, 1944, despite the Germans torching the Gicquel farmhouse that very night. The final operation landed 15 cases of weapons and ammunition and took off the final five "parcels." By August 9, American troops had liberated the area but MGB 503 made a final trip to pick up an MI6 agent, two French agents and any stragglers. Shelburne was officially out of business.

Lucien Dumais donned his uniform and continued to work in the area, helping the liberating troops to sort out friend from foe. When Paris was liberated, he returned to his Paris apartment where he was promptly arrested on suspicion of being an imposter and a black marketeer! Once that was sorted out, Dumais settled in to assist in ensuring that all the line's helpers received proper recognition and that traitors received retribution. Shelburne had been a tremendous success. Thanks primarily to its high standard of security, it was never successfully penetrated and never lost a "parcel" under its control. In less than 10 months of operation, the line assisted 307 Allied evaders in making a Home Run by either land or sea, an impressive record indeed.[14]

CHAPTER 10

The Indragiri River Line

The Indragiri River Line was a unique evasion and escape line established when the fall of Singapore became a possibility. In its short life from February 13 to March 17, 1942, it allowed 2,586 military personnel to avoid capture, along with an estimated 4,000–7,000 civilians.[1] The planning for the line began as the Japanese 25th Army commanded by General Tomoyuke Yamashita marched southward on the Malay Peninsula, pushing the British and Commonwealth forces of Malaya Command steadily back. Malaya Command consisted of 10 infantry brigades. Two brigades each were allotted to the 9th and 10th Indian Divisions (forming III Indian Corps) and the 8th Australian Division. Two brigades manned the Singapore defenses, one (the 28th) was the III Indian Corps reserve, and one (the 12th) was the Malaya Command reserve.

While they had a full complement of engineers and artillery, they had no tanks. They also had many critical shortages of weaponry and other equipment. Lieutenant General Percival had requested tank units to reinforce Malaya Command but was turned down by the War Office. It was a decision that would have a definite impact on the campaign. While the Royal Air Force fought valiantly to support Malaya Command, they lost control of the air almost from the campaign's onset.[2] Using simple tactics, the Japanese drove southward with scarcely a pause. Each time the road-bound British and Commonwealth troops would make a stand the Japanese would send a unit through the jungle and around their flank. The Japanese would then establish a roadblock in the rear of the bypassed unit. With almost clockwork regularity, the British and Commonwealth troops would fall back—only to repeat the process.

Many books have discussed the disastrous Malay Campaign and the subsequent fall of Singapore.[3] The majority put a large share of the blame on the British commander, Lieutenant General Arthur E. Percival. As Richard Frank noted in *Tower of Skulls*, "Events proved that as a staff officer Percival had few peers: as a senior commander he had few inferiors."[4] However, Geoffrey Brooke, an evader from Singapore whose story is illustrative of those who escaped before the surrender, had another view. He wrote, "The whole, bad business, the climax of which was the greatest disaster to befall British arms, and even greater in its blow to British influence in the Far East, had its foundations in successive governments failing to provide for the adequate defence of Singapore."[5] In truth, it was a combination of both factors.

As the numerically inferior but qualitatively superior Japanese 25th Army drove Malaya Command southward,[6] an assessment of Singapore's defenses led many to realize that its scant defenses were primarily oriented away from the Japanese rapidly approaching the Straits of Johore. The Japanese 25th Army was composed of four infantry divisions, the 5th, 18th, 56th, and the Imperial Guards. They were reckoned among the best units in the Japanese Army. For the Malayan campaign Yamashita chose to leave the 56th Division behind and free up transport for supplies. The 18th was short a brigade, which was detailed to the Borneo campaign. As a result, Yamashita had less than three divisions, but they were well-trained combat veterans. He also had plenty of artillery and—critically—three tank regiments with 56 medium and 74 light tanks. Additionally, the 25th Army enjoyed air superiority during the entire campaign. Contrary to some accounts, the 30,000 troops of the 25th Army had received no special jungle training. They had, however, received an excellent 70-page pamphlet full of practical tactics and techniques for jungle warfare entitled *Read This Alone—And the War Can Be Won*.[7]

Against the approaching Japanese the British fielded (on paper) two Australian Brigades of the 8th Division, the British 18th Division, and the Indian III Corps, a total of roughly 80,000 troops. Contrary to popular belief, the Singapore costal artillery was able to pivot and fire across the straits of Johore. However, because of its flat trajectory, it was of limited value in stemming the onrushing Japanese tide. Worried that the "Gibraltar of the Far East" might not hold against the oncoming Japanese advance, near the end of January 1942 the War Council in Singapore decided to develop a means to evacuate as many people as possible if Singapore fell. That job landed in the capable hands of Lieutenant Colonel Alan Warren, Royal Marines, who was part of the Oriental Mission of the Special Operations Executive (SOE).[8] He had not a moment to spare. Although he did not know it, Lt. General Percival would surrender Singapore to the Japanese on February 15, 1942.

The line laid out by Lt. Col. Warren and his subordinates took advantage of the many small islands south of Singapore. On a map they form a reversed "L" which stretches south from Singapore and frames the mouths of the Indragiri and Djambi Rivers on Sumatra. The islands of the Riau Archipelago run southeast from Singapore, where they meet those of the Lingga Archipelago stretching southwest towards Sumatra.[9] Although the Indragiri was the primary escape route, the Djambi formed a reliable, if somewhat lengthier secondary route. From Singapore, following the islands it is approximately 150 miles to the mouth of the Indragiri and roughly another 250 miles further across Sumatra. Taking the Djambi route added at least 80 miles to the total distance.

Wasting no time, Lt. Col. Warren set off for Sumatra on February 3 where he first set up a base of operations at Bagansiapiapi, 60 miles across the Straits of Molucca from Kelang in Malaysia. He eventually traversed 200 miles across Sumatra to set up at Padang, the major Indian Ocean port and terminus of the Indragiri Line. As Warren made for Bagansiapiapi, Major Jock Campbell[10] and Captain Ivan Lyon[11] headed south in the 50-ton craft *Hongchuan* to lay out the escape route.[12] Lyon concentrated on establishing food dumps and arranging guides along the way, while Campbell coordinated the physical infrastructure for the line. Lyon established food dumps on Durian Island off the Soegi Strait and at Priggi Raja[13] at the Indragiri's mouth.

Another SOE member, Basil Goodfellow, established a food dump at Sambu Island 10 miles southwest of Singapore where there was a Royal Dutch Shell refinery. Lyon also negotiated with the headmen of a number of coastal villages (*kampongs*) to guide boats to the dumps at Durian and Priggi Raja as well as to give evaders directions for the next leg of their journey. Campbell was busy as well. He set up the first Indragiri waystation at Tembilahan near the river's mouth although it took until February 18 to find Captain Ernest Gordon to take permanent command. He followed the setup of Tembilahan by establishing another site at the town of Rengat which stood 100 miles upriver and was the head of navigation for ocean-going vessels.

Small craft could proceed upriver 70 miles to Taluk, where Campbell established a temporary rest camp. Thirty miles west of Rengat, Campbell also secured the Ayer Molek rubber plantation as a rest camp on February 15.[14] He was fortunate in persuading Lieutenant Colonel F. J. Dillon, an elderly Indian Army Service Corps officer, to take command. In the days that followed, Dillon would prove an able administrator and a steadying influence on those passing through the camp. Dillon (later a brigadier) was a remarkable character. He was a battery commander on the Western Front at age 19 during World War I. He subsequently served on the Northwest Frontier of India until 1935. He was awarded the Military Cross and was Mentioned in Dispatches seven times. After the war broke out, he was the quartermaster general for the 18th Division when it arrived in Singapore two weeks before the fall.[15] Based on his experience as a logistician, Dillon persuaded Campbell that evaders should move by road or rail to Padang, whether from Rengat or Taluk.

All along the line the Dutch officials and ordinary people of the towns were extremely helpful in securing lodging, transportation, food, and other supplies. By February 9, the line had begun to operate. Interestingly enough, by that time there were already 60 intrepid officers and men who had evaded the Japanese on Malaya, crossed over to Sumatra, and made their way south several hundred miles across the island to Padang. By the day Singapore fell, hundreds of evaders were already flowing through in the line. A flood tide of many hundreds more was soon to follow as those who left Singapore in anything that would float made the hazardous trip across Japanese-dominated waters.

The evacuation began in earnest in the early morning hours of Friday, February 13, 1942, forever known as "Black Friday." Around

44 unescorted ships headed southward but only one or two made it to safety. They took the shortest route to Java and perhaps Australia beyond through the Banka Strait. Unfortunately, they did not know until it was too late that a Japanese task force under Vice-Admiral Jisaburō Ozawa consisting of one aircraft carrier, three cruisers, and several destroyers lay athwart their escape route.[16] The Japanese task force was supporting operations against Allied forces in Sumatra and Java as well as their surrounding waters, but it was not above sinking any shipping that came within range.[17]

However, some smaller craft made it to the mouth of the Indragiri by laying low during the day and dodging from island to island. Not all small craft were so lucky. One such ship was the *Kung Wo*, an old 5,000-ton Chinese Yangtze river steamer which was capable of a surprising 14 knots.[18] Aboard her was newly promoted Lieutenant Geoffrey Brooke, a Royal Navy officer who had survived the sinking of the battleship HMS *Prince of Wales* by the Japanese on December 10, 1941.[19] The others aboard included 120 naval personnel and 20 non-naval passengers, among them several correspondents.

The *Kung Wo* cast off from Keppel Harbor just before midnight on February 12. They headed for open water, passing straight through a minefield on a course for the Banka Strait. At 7.30 a.m. on the 13th, they were 80 miles south of Singapore, steaming southward, when two Japanese bombers attacked. They scored three hits, bringing *Kung Wo* to a dead stop. Realizing that the Japanese would be back, the three ships' lifeboats began to shuttle people and provisions to nearby Dankau Island. At first, things were chaotic but Brooke and his fellow officer from the HMS *Prince Of Wales*, Lieutenant Commander Anthony Terry, quickly restored order.

Since the ship was settling, Brooke helped in making several rafts in case the lifeboat shuttle service wasn't fast enough. He also had the crew and passengers fill every possible receptacle with water. With this done, all but a few of the *Kung Wo*'s crew were ashore with four days of food and an adequate supply of water. They spent the night on the beach, tormented by voracious swarms of mosquitoes and continually startled by land crabs which scuttled over their recumbent forms. They were relieved to see that the island had plenty of fresh water.

When morning arrived, so did two other ships fleeing from Singapore, the *Kuala* and the *Tien Kuan*. They were both auxiliary naval vessels of around 600 tons that anchored off Pompong Island. Shortly after their arrival a Dutch motor launch and a small *tonkan* (steam launch) appeared. The *Kung Wo* had by then settled in the water, with only her masts showing. Those marooned on Dankau Island quickly came up with a plan. Lieutenant Terry would lead the launch and *tonkan* to Sumatra, each towing a lifeboat. This would bring half of those on the island to safety. Then Terry would return the next night or as soon as possible for the rest. With the number of people reduced by half, the rations would stretch to eight days. It seemed a good plan.

Brooke was fortunate that he had one of the senior officers of the Singapore fire brigade with his group. Fluent in Malay and Chinese, he would prove an invaluable asset. Unfortunately, the *Kuala* and *Tien Kuan* were sunk by the Japanese off Pompong Island the next day, marooning 350 military and 50 civilians on an island with very little water. This would complicate the evacuation plans, as the resources which would have rescued the 60-odd survivors of the *Kung Wo* were diverted to rescue the 400 from the *Kuala* and *Tien Kuan*. Lieutenant Terry returned to Dankau on the night of the 16th and took 20 more men off, promising to return as soon as possible. But his luck ran out. Brooke never saw him again.

The morning of their sixth day on the island, a man in a *kolek* (canoe) rowed up to their island. They negotiated with him to provide transportation to Sumatra. They gave him some cash and valuables to hire junks, which he set off to do. The next morning a somewhat larger sailing *kolek* arrived with three khaki-clad Europeans, one of whom proved to be Sub-Lieutenant Sjovald Cunyngham-Brown, Malayan Royal Naval Volunteer Reserve.

Cunyngham-Brown advised Brooke to make for Singkep, an island about 80 miles south where there were several hundred British soldiers and sailors under the care of the Dutch district commissioner who was in touch with the headquarters in Batavia (present day Jakarta) on Java 400 miles distant. Cunyngham-Brown felt that the chance of being picked up by a rescue ship was good. He also brought news that there were four junks anchored close by. After discussing it with the other officers, Brooke decided to head for Singkep.

Without further delay, he shoved off with Cunyngham-Brown to select the junk for his group on Dankau and send the others to Pompong. On arrival, Brooke selected the smallest, about 40 feet in length and 15 feet wide. It had two masts and a large hold amidships in which the passengers could conceal themselves from inquisitive aircraft. It took some negotiating, but the three members of the crew finally agreed to help.

They arrived around sunset, embarked everyone, and set sail for Singkep. In the early afternoon, the junk dropped anchor at the town of Dabosingkep on the southwestern shore of the island. Brooke went ashore where he conferred with Commander Alexander, Royal Navy and the other senior officers to determine the best course of action. Since the Dutch had destroyed their radio prematurely, there was no current information about the situation to the south. Additionally, Japanese air activity from a close by, newly established seaplane base made any long-distance sailing risky.

These factors helped them to opt for the Indragiri River whose estuary was a scant 50 miles away. Before Brooke's group could get going, they had to settle a dispute with their junk's crew who were adamant about being paid off and heading home. What turned the trick was a box of legal opium given to Brooke by the Dutch authorities. Box in hand, Brooke and his fellow evaders were heading for the Indragiri by late afternoon. Around midnight, they anchored near a *kampong* on a small island roughly 30 miles from the Indragiri mouth. Brooke didn't want to risk covering the last stretch in daylight. The people of the *kampong* fed and entertained them as honored guests during the day. When darkness fell, their junk sprinted for the Indragiri. Before first light, it dropped anchor in the near some fishing stakes in the mouth of the Indragiri. The hope was that this would make them appear to be innocent fishermen.

Once it was light enough to proceed, they sailed up ever-narrowing river until they arrived at Priggi Raja. It was there that they first learned of the line when the headman produced an order signed by Major Campbell. The headman also informed Brooke that he would provide a steam launch to tow the junk upriver. With the steam launch puffing industriously as it towed their junk, Brooke and his men arrived at Tembilahan shortly before midnight.

Here they were met by a Captain Gordon who explained the layout of the rest of the route. The next morning, they paid off their junk and proceeded to Ayer Molek by way of Rengat. Brooke formed a high impression of Lt. Col. Dillon, who managed to maintain the order demanded by the Dutch authorities—at one point issuing an order that any looters would be shot on sight. After a painful five-day delay because of a lack of transportation, Brooke and his party moved on to Padang. There Brooke was met by Lt. Col. Warren, who informed him that the Vice Consul had burned the code books necessary for communicating with rescue ships, so he assessed their chances of reaching friendly lines as 50/50.

Ten ships had taken off evaders so far, but he did not know how any ship had fared. What he did not know was that nine ships had made it to safety. The only ship sunk was the *Rosenboom*, with the loss of 200 military and 300 civilian passengers and crew.[20] Although disappointed there was no ship to board, Brooke was relieved to learn that Lieutenant Commander Terry had gotten away on an earlier ship. What he did not learn until much later was that it was *Rosenboom*, sunk with all hands. Brooke returned to tell his troops the situation, making a point of being absolutely honest. He then spent some time assessing the town and picking up a few personal items. It was late afternoon when he was summoned to meet with Lt. Col. Warren. To his surprise, Warren informed him that he was one of eight personnel selected to escape that night as he felt they had much to contribute to the war effort. They were to sail on a *prauw* that was moored up the coast. A *prauw* is a coastal fishing vessel, not normally used on the open ocean as it has no keel.

The *Sederhana Djohanis* was such a ship. Brooke described her as "a sailing ketch with masts of about 50ft and 25ft, carrying a very large head of sail (with main, mizzen, fore, and jib). She was roughly 45ft at the waterline, with a beam of 16ft and draught of 4ft; with no keel the result was very saucer-shaped. There was a tremendous bowsprit."[21] At first, Brooke flatly refused to go on the grounds that he had a responsibility to his men, even in captivity. However, Warren made it an order, while adding that the Japanese would segregate the officers from the men. This last bit of information persuaded Brooke, who traveled north with his seven other companions to their rendezvous with the *Sederhana Djohanis* (roughly translated as Lucky John).[22] Sixteen of the 18 crew were SOE, British Army, Royal Marines, or Royal Navy. Most of them were seasoned yachtsmen. The other two were a Malay orderly and a Chinese protégé of one of the officers.

They set sail for Ceylon on March 9, 1942, with three Sumatran fishermen along for the first leg of the journey to give them all a crash course in handling a *prauw*.[23] The lessons went well and by March 14 they had managed to travel 180 miles north along the coast of Sumatra before striking west for Ceylon, 1,000 miles away. Battling contrary winds, they slowly made their way 300 miles westward until in the early hours of March 18 the winds shifted in their favor. The dawn brought with it a Japanese air patrol which flew overhead but did not attack. As quickly as the wind had risen, it promptly died for several days, and it was March 24 before their *prauw* began to make some headway. At last, on March 28, the northeast monsoon winds arrived and the "Lucky John" began to make some real progress. The same day they were strafed by a Japanese bomber who—fortunately—had extremely poor aim. In five separate attacks he did little damage to the "Lucky John" and caused no casualties among the crew.

On Easter Day, 1942, they were buzzed by a Japanese carrier aircraft while only 250 miles from their goal. They were troubled. Had Ceylon fallen? Was it under attack? In fact, a Japanese raiding force of five carriers and four battleships under Admiral Chūichi Nagumo[24] of Pearl Harbor fame were busy hitting both Colombo and Trincomalee harbors.[25] Altogether the British lost over 110,000 tons of merchant shipping as well as the aircraft carrier *Hermes* and two cruisers, *Dorsetshire* and *Cornwall*.[26] Ignorant of the true state of affairs, the crew of the *Sederhana Djohanis* sailed on until they were less than 80 miles from Ceylon. There, on April 14, 1942, they encountered the tanker *Anglo-Canadian* bound for Bombay[27] in the aftermath of Nagumo's raid. She took them aboard, sank the *Sederhana Djohanis* with gunfire, and brought them safely to Bombay after their 1,600-mile journey. The last evaders from the Indragiri Line were back in friendly hands.

CHAPTER II

China Escape Lines

As mentioned in Chapter 2, the British Army Aid Group (BAAG) was responsible for much of the escape and evasion activity in China during the early years of the war. As the war progressed, the American Air Ground Aid Section (AGAS) began to shoulder an increasing portion of the work for a number of reasons. First was that the Allied powers had agreed that America had the primary responsibility for China as a theater of war.[1]

The second, very practical reason was that the American 14th Air Force was based in China which put them in striking range of the Japanese home islands. Crews of damaged bombers—primarily B-29s—returning to their mainland China bases were often forced to ditch in areas that were under nominal Japanese control. Their recovery was a top priority for both BAAG and AGAS. Their recovery was less difficult than it might seem, because for most of the war the Japanese only exerted firm control over the rail lines and cities. The control of the countryside was more sporadic, exercised by patrols or from the air.

This allowed either Communist or Nationalist guerillas to operate in those areas with comparative freedom.[2] Thus, BAAG and AGAS had a widely spread network of armed force available to rescue downed aircrews across much of occupied China. The Japanese Army's brutal treatment of Chinese civilians also ensured that almost all Chinese civilians would be willing helpers.

The BAAG was the Allied first escape organization to operate in China. Its commander throughout the war, Lt. Col. Sir Lindsey Ride, dated its formal existence from June 1942. That was when he set up his headquarters roughly 390 miles northwest of Hong Kong in Kweilin[3] after Headquarters in New Delhi, India provided BAAG an approved War Establishment.[4]

Roughly equivalent to an American Table of Organization and Equipment, it gave BAAG the official standing to request personnel, equipment, and supplies. It also outlined their mission. On July 19, 1942, BAAG established an advanced headquarters in the Nationalist Government-controlled town of Waichow, 43 miles north of Hong Kong.[5] The officer in charge, Lieutenant Douglas Clague, Royal Artillery had been a recent prisoner in Hong Kong, who received a Military Cross (MC) for his daring escape. Initially reluctant to accept the job, he spent 18 months commanding the post before moving on. He was subsequently awarded an Order of the British Empire (OBE) for his sterling performance. Lieutenant Clague eventually ended the war as a lieutenant colonel. His final mission was parachuting into Bangkok, Thailand on the last day of the war to establish contact with the POWs there.[6]

From Waichow BAAG agents could more easily maintain contact with the nine POW camps in and around Hong Kong. Seven camps were on Kowloon: Lai Chi Kek, Sham Shui Po, La Salle School, Argyle Street Barracks, Ma Tau Chung Prison, Kings Park, and Whitfield Barracks. The two camps on Hong Kong proper were the Military Hospital and North Point.[7] Once Waichow was operational, Ride directed the setting up of four medical aid posts as close to Hong Kong as possible to assist escaping prisoners of war and civilians, many of whom he knew would be in poor physical shape. He located two posts near Waichow, with the other two near Macao.[8]

By 1945 BAAG had further subdivided southern Kwangtung Province into six areas, each with a BAAG manned post that was a collection point for escapers or evaders. The areas were designated 1 through 5 and East. Area 1 was northwest of Hong Kong with Area 5 as its southern border and Tsingyuen as its headquarters. Area 2 was west of Area 1 with its headquarters at Szewui. Area 3 was south of Area 2, with Shaping as its headquarters. Area 4 lay west of Area 3 with its headquarters at Samfou.

Area 5 encompassed Kowloon, Hong Kong, and the land roughly 40 miles inland. The headquarters for Area 5 was Weichow. Additionally, Area 5 had two other manned posts: Frigate, which commanded a view of Mirs Bay, and Post Y, which had a view of Kowloon, Hong Kong Harbor, and Kai Tek Airport. BAAG East, headquartered at Ho Yuen, had responsibility for the rest of Kwangtung Province.[9] A network of agents throughout the province provided transportation, food, and shelter to move people to safety.

By September 1942, BAAG acquired a junk that ran trips from Hong Kong every two weeks throughout most of the war. It was instrumental in spiriting away two prominent Hong Kong Bankers, T. J. J. Fenwick, and J. A. D. Morrison, in October 1942. The junk was run by BAAG agents 19, 46, and 48 with two relatives of agent 19 filling out the crew. It was based in Ngam Tau Sha, a cape on the eastern coast of Hong Kong (Kowloon) across from Shelter Island.[10]

BAAG was truly a unique organization. Nominally controlled by a headquarters thousands of miles away in New Delhi, India it had personnel scattered in posts across thousands of square miles of China.[11] In spite of all obstacles, BAAG succeeded, in part because every post followed these simple yet effective standing orders:

(i) Absolute frankness with the Chinese officials concerning our work;
(ii) Nothing to be left undone which would raise British prestige; nothing to be done to lower it;
(iii) Maximum medical attention to all guerillas, soldiers and officials in the area;
(iv) Distribution of authentic war news to all official Chinese bodies and foreigners in the area;
(v) Maximum help within our limited means to the Chinese Forces and their full access to our intelligence reports concerning the enemy.12

Unlike most Allied escape organizations, BAAG actively collected intelligence for purposes other than escapes.[13] It was, in fact, used as cover for Special Operations Executive (SOE) intelligence operations with the understanding that Lt. Col. Ride could veto any operations which seemed likely to jeopardize BAAG's work.[14] Although this seemed to fly in the face of good security procedures, BAAG had developed separate networks for collecting intelligence while others focused on aiding prisoners or on collecting escapers or evaders.

BAAG collected its intelligence under the baleful eye of General Tai Li, the Nationalist Army Chief of Intelligence. He was an Anglophobe who made little attempt to hide his feelings. As a result, he kept BAAG on a short leash, requiring them to use Chinese ciphers and radio operators for all their communications. None the less, BAAG agents continued to provide useful intelligence, particularly on the port of Hong Kong and the ships therein.[15] Their weekly Kweilin Intelligence Summary (KWIZ) was "eagerly read by the limited circles it reached."[16]

BAAG developed a network of Chinese agents who ran in and out of Hong Kong. They gathered intelligence, smuggled medical supplies to the camps and brought supplies as well as escapers or civilian refugees out as needed.[17] At times, they even brought tailored uniforms out of Hong Kong to those British officers concerned with presenting a good appearance. David Lam was one such agent, a Chinese man born in Hong Kong in 1923. He was a former medical student, like many of Ride's agents.[18]

Lam spoke English, Mandarin, Cantonese, and Hakka. He worked for BAAG from October 12, 1942, to November 30, 1944, when he went to work for AGAS. A letter of reference stated that "He has been engaged in work of a responsible and confidential nature and has proved himself a reliable and trustworthy employee and has carried out his duties with initiative and resolution."[19] BAAG was blessed with many such men and women, who were known only by a number.[20] Not all agents made it. Some were captured by the Japanese and endured torture and grisly executions. It is a testament to the courage and resolution of the Chinese people that someone always stepped up and took the place of the lost agents.

BAAG also set out to win the hearts and minds of the guerilla organizations in the hinterlands. As Ride put it, "We set up hospitals in our areas where any Chinese could get treatment both medical and surgical equal to that available in any big modern hospital." These establishments treated over 30,000 patients a year. Additionally, BAAG brought in rice to areas of famine, feeding over 6,000 people per day. It also provided inoculations against the twin scourges of smallpox and cholera. On top of all that, it provided three million dollars in financial aid to destitute

General view of Hanowa prisoner of war camp # 6 in Honshu, Japan, 14 September 1945. (NARA, 204835814)

Colditz Castle, April 1945. POWs hung out American, British, and French flags during the liberation to avoid artillery fire. (Wikimedia Commons)

Aerial view of Stalag Luft III, German prisoner of war camp for air force personnel, at Sagen, Germany. (NARA, 204901409)

Aerial view of German prison of war camp Stalag 7A near Moosburg, Bavaria, Germany, where thousands of USAF prisoners of war were imprisoned along with thousands of Allied prisoners of various nationalities. (NARA, 204901412)

American prisoners of war celebrate the 4th of July in the Japanese prison camp of Casisange in Malaybalay, on Mindanao, Philippine Islands. (NARA, 531352)

Prisoners on the Bataan death march from Bataan to the Camp O'Donnell POW camp, with their hands tied behind their backs, April 1942. (NARA, 532548)

British soldiers of the Royal Signal Corps, that owned and operated the only radio in prisoner of war camp #13. Yokohama, Japan, September 1945. (NARA, 204835212)

Japanese brutality in Singapore. When Allied troops entered Singapore they found among Japanese records a set of atrocity pictures portraying the inhuman treatment accorded Sikh prisoners. In this picture, blindfolded prisoners, with a target on their heart, sit in a row waiting to be shot. (NARA, 148727274)

Signs on the rooftops of this prisoner of war camp in Tokyo–Yokohama–Area No. 15 (Omori) left no doubt of their identity for our B-29 airmen, or the gratitude of the starving prisoners. (NARA, 204835779)

A Boeing B-29 passes over an Allied prisoner of war camp near Nagasaki, Japan. (NARA, 204835167)

Whereas a normal diet for one man averages 3,500 calories a day, the Japanese allowed only 600 or less a day to veterans of Corregidor and Bataan held prisoner at Bilibid Prison, Manila, Philippine Islands. (NARA, 204951939)

Clothes, food and other supplies dropped by air are being gathered here by Allied prisoners of war at the Omori prisoner of war camp near Tokyo. (NARA, 6200936)

Taken after the liberation of Moosburg Prisoner of War Camp, Germany, by the US 14th Armored Division. (NARA, 205003110)

Photograph of American prisoners using improvised litters to carry comrades who fell on the march from Bataan. (NARA, 535565)

American prisoners held at Bilibid Prison, Manila, Philippine Islands stole a food tin from the Japanese and recorded in it information about daily menus and issue of food, various tortures practiced, death lists of U.S. servicemen, and other information about their captivity. (NARA, 204951005)

Emaciated Australian and Dutch prisoners of war, suffering from beriberi, at Tarsau in Thailand in 1943. The hut they are in is typical of the construction along the Thai-Burma Railway. (Wikimedia Commons)

Gaunt Allied prisoners of war at Omori camp near Yokohama cheer rescuers from the U.S. Navy. (NARA, 520992)

American and British prisoners of war freed by swift Allied advances are being flown back from the front in Douglas C-47 cargo planes of the 9th Troop Carrier Command. (NARA, 204901264)

Trucks on Yokohama, Japan, loaded with released prisoners of war. September 1945. (NARA, 204835179)

After months in a German prison camp, S/Sgt Lester Miller (left) and 2nd Lt. Glen Harrington accept much-missed goodies from Red Cross worker Jane Goodell after disembarking from the prisoner of war exchange ship *Atlantis* at Liverpool, England. 26 October 1943. (NARA, 204884659)

Ordinary rations which each internee received daily at the Hanowa prisoner of war camp #6 in Honshu, Japan. 14 September 1945. The total caloric value of this food was less than 900. (NARA, 204835781)

Capt. Tex McCrary, a member of the 324th Bomb Squadron, 91st Bomb Group, signs for an escape kit before take-off on a mission from Bassingbourne, England on 24 June 1943. (NARA, 204883519)

Charts showing escape aids and foreign currency adorn the wall of the briefing room at Headquarters, 1st Bomb Division, based in England. (NARA, 204882329)

Printed on durable silk, this Office of Strategic Services (OSS) escape and evasion map didn't rustle at night and could be folded up very compactly to be more easily concealed. The map was printed with waterproof dyes so the colors would not run if it got wet. (Wikimedia Commons)

Working a tin-can forge, two ex-prisoners demonstrate how minute quantities of fuel were burned at full efficiency in order to have occasional hot meals. (NARA, 204901312)

The McCracken brothers, Melton (left) and Harry (right), reunited at Moosburg. The file photo misidentifies the brothers as James and Thomas respectively. (NARA, 204841097)

While he was held in Bilibid Prison, Manila, Philippine Islands with other veterans of Corregidor and Bataan, Lt. Homer Hutchinson built a radio set with parts he secretly took from the Japanese. The set was concealed in the seat of a stool. (NARA, 204951032)

Carl Mydans was a prominent photographer for *Life* magazine who spent time interned by the Japanese along with his wife, first in Manila, then in Shanghai. He is shown here photographing personnel loading onto the transport SS *General William A. Mann*. (NARA, 138926278)

Members of the "Walker's Club." Members were forced down behind Japanese lines and spent one to seven weeks returning to their bases. All had narrow escapes from Japanese patrols, and one man led 31 Indian prisoners in a daring escape. (NARA, 204831526)

Happy "Blister Clubbers" (airmen who were shot down into enemy-held territory), awaiting transportation to the U.S., display a varied collection of German souvenirs they obtained from prisoners after they made their home runs. (NARA, 204893556)

During World War II many Allied airmen were helped to safety by the French Resistance, known as the Maquis. This October 1944 photo is of a group of airmen with some Maquis at a French town on the Swiss border in the process of being repatriated. (NARA, 204894688)

Pictured is the USS *Quail's* 36-foot motor launch, in which 18 men of her crew sailed from Manila Bay to Darwin, Australia, to escape the Japanese, May–June 1942. (NH 96691, Naval History and Heritage Command).

Chinese.[21] The program worked, building a strong positive incentive for the Chinese to help Allied evaders and escapers.

Their escape work was hindered to a degree by a lack of escape-mindedness in the Hong Kong camps. This attitude had its origins in the fact that many senior British officers in the camps discouraged escape attempts. Brutal punishments inflicted by the Japanese for escape attempts—successful or not—also contributed to the inertia.

Still, BAAG brought out over 1,000 people, both military and civilian. This included over 100 Europeans and over 550 overseas Chinese, as well as over 400 Indians, of whom 150 were soldiers.[22] BAAG employed separate networks to handle military and civilians. The military networks terminated eventually in Kunming. The civilian escape networks went through the neutral Portuguese colony of Macao, which had a Japanese military presence in the form of the *Kempetai*.[23]

However, the principal BAAG agent in Macao was able to find sufficient opportunities to move small groups of civilian escapees through the colony. Code named Phoenix, he was an enterprising Chinese businessman with a visceral hatred of the Japanese. It was he who made possible one of BAAG's greatest coups, the spiriting away of key technicians known as *mateys*—almost all Europeans—from the Hong Kong dockyard. Their escape forced the Japanese to bring technicians from mainland Japan just to keep the port open. The *mateys* also brought with them a wealth of intelligence about the ships using the port.[24]

In addition, BAAG managed to rescue 39 American aircrew before AGAS went into operation.[25] Lt. Col. Ride observed that, "our network was such that any escaper or evader coming into it had a nearly 100% chance of reaching safety."[26] After the war he claimed that BAAG only lost two downed aircrew and that was solely due to their being too badly wounded to move. The BAAG network was so efficient that it plucked one pilot from the very outskirts of Hong Kong, within sight of Kai Tek Airport!

By 1943, the number of escapees from the Hong Kong POW camps had dwindled to a trickle. However, BAAG still had a role to play in escape and evasion. It provided a model and helped AGAS stand up operations. As mentioned in Chapter 2, MIS-X's First Lieutenant Barclay Preston

Schoyer arrived in July 1942 with orders to set up an escape and evasion organization whose primary, but not exclusive, focus would be the rescue of downed aircrew. After meeting with Lt. Col. Ride in Kweilin, Schoyer travelled to Kunming to get permission from the Chinese Nationalist leader Chiang Kai-shek to establish what would come to be known as AGAS and to secure his cooperation. He succeeded on both counts. In late October 1942, Lt. Col. A. R. Wichtrich[27] arrived in Kunming to take command of AGAS, accompanied by Captain Maxwell Becker, the son of a missionary. Like Schoyer, Becker was fluent in Mandarin.

The pair set out to find a suitable headquarters as close as possible to that of the 14th Air Force. It was during their search that Lt. Col. Wichtrich decided on the name of his new organization. He wanted an innocuous sounding name, "So I took a cue from MI9, the British intelligence agency whose British Army Aid Group was involved in similar escape and evasion efforts. I decided to call our group Air Ground Aid Section, or AGAS, and that was what our operation was known by, even today."[28]

After establishing themselves in a single office in Hostel #1, a combined Chinese and American headquarters, Wichtrich and Maxwell linked up with the newly promoted Captain Schoyer. Together, they began planning for the networks needed to recover downed aircrew. Wichtrich noted, "From Kunming we would send a liaison officer or team of officers (with a radio operator and an interpreter, if necessary) out into safe areas to establish a base of operations."[29] In practice, the usual field team was an officer and an enlisted radio operator with a jeep and a jeep-mounted radio.

Wichtrich, Maxwell, and Schoyer quickly agreed that security, both physical and communications, was of paramount importance. They were conscious of the terrible physical risks the field teams and the Chinese agents they employed would run. The Japanese were a highly competent enemy who would have no mercy on those they captured. Fortunately, no AGAS field team was ever captured, although there was no shortage of close calls. Unfortunately, the same could not be said of their brave Chinese agents.

To minimize the chance of detection, the field teams kept their coded radio transmissions short. They also had a ring of guerillas or Nationalist troops deployed around the transmission site as local security. Once they completed the transmission, the team rapidly broke down the antenna and quickly moved by the jeep to another area, similarly secured by Chinese troops. The local security at the transmission site would disperse after erasing any sign that the AGAS team had been there. It was an eminently workable system. Evaders were either brought to the team or the team went to collect them. Once the evaders were safely in hand, they would be taken to a makeshift airstrip and flown out by an aircraft stationed at Kunming.

Not long after his arrival, Wichtrich set Maxwell and Schoyer to work establishing the AGAS network. In this they were aided by Lt. Col. Ride and other BAAG personnel. Indeed, had it not been for the mentorship and assistance of BAAG, the AGAS would have had a much rockier start. The AGAS also benefited from the tireless humanitarian work of BAAG among the Chinese civilian population. With Schoyer and Maxwell in the field, Wichtrich set to work establishing a proper headquarters. First, he roughed out his personnel requirements and sent them off to MIS-X at Fort Hunt. Then he set to work on getting suitable facilities. He managed to persuade the Chinese government to build him a walled brick compound with sufficient room for a motor pool holding a few jeeps and a truck, a kitchen, a large dining room, sufficient office space for the staff, sleeping quarters, and a radio room which housed 20 radio operators, all Chinese.

To a man, they were former Yangtze riverboat radio operators who had a well-deserved reputation for being incredibly skilled at plucking faint transmissions from the ether.[30] Captain Kurt New and Sergeants Jones, Young, and Taylor provided oversight for radio room operations. Captain New was also the codes officer, as such he was prepared to protect the security of the codes with his life. Shortly after the headquarters was finished, Major Monroe Hagood arrived as the AGAS executive officer. With a staffed and secure headquarters, AGAS could now begin full-blown operations.

AGAS' first mission was to rescue a group of missionaries and their families from Hainan Island. Although the 14th Air Force had no aircraft capable of making the rescue, Wichtrich reasoned that the Navy might. After a flurry of messages, the Navy agreed to furnish a PBY Catalina Flying Boat to make the pickup. The missionaries had scouted out a secluded cove where the PBY could land without being observed by the Japanese. The rescue went as planned, much to Wichtrich's relief. The PBY continued to work with AGAS by shuttling fuel to some Chinese junks which provided weather reports and observed both Japanese troop deployments and shipping. So, the Hainan Island rescue was AGAS' entry into the intelligence business as well.

In addition to aiding downed aircrew of the 14th Air Force, AGAS found itself supporting the 20th Air Force charged with bringing supplies from India to China across the Himalayas (or the Hump as the pilots called it). It did so by establishing contact with the Lisu tribe of Yunnan province.[31] Their tribal territory was directly athwart the aerial supply route from India to China. Although there were no Japanese troops anywhere near the flight route, the terrain and climate made setting up some sort of aid for crashed aircrew essential. Unfortunately, the Chinese were fighting the Lisu to subjugate them. As of 2005, there were 729,000 Lisu in China, mostly concentrated in northwestern Yunnan Province. The remainder are sprinkled across the rest of Yunnan Province and in the Xichang and Yanbian counties in Sichuan Province. There are also Lisu communities in Myanmar and in northern Thailand.[32] This dispersal pattern made the Lisu ideal candidates for running rescue networks.

For the sake of the aircrew flying over the Hump, Wichtrich felt it was important to establish a good working relationship with the Lisu. It took two weeks in total of walking through the rugged terrain of Yunnan, but Wichtrich contacted the tribe and convinced them to help. He also established a payment scale for services rendered in the only currency the Lisu would accept—raw silver.[33] Not long after establishing safe areas in Lisu territory, AGAS set up additional ones among the Shan-speaking peoples of Burma. IN 1944, AGAS established similar safe areas in much of what was then French Indochina, primarily to rescue downed naval aviators.[34]

Shortly after their arrival in mid-1943, Wichtrich dispatched Captain Henry Whittlesey and Master Sergeant Robert Clarke to north China to work with the Chinese Communists. After two weeks of travel across rugged terrain on dirt roads, they arrived at their destination of Yan'an and met with Chou En-lai. They obviously made a good impression, as the Chinese Communists gave them unstinting support. Within a week of their arrival, they recovered a B-29 crew. Unfortunately, Captain Whittlesey had too much fighting spirit to stick to his two jobs—aiding escapers and evaders and gathering intelligence. He went out on a combat patrol with the Chinese Communists and became the only military fatality that AGAS suffered during the war. Master Sergeant Clarke remained in contact with the Chinese Communists for the rest of the war, ensuring that AGAS' work continued unabated.

AGAS provided indirect aid to prisoners as well. Initially, it was on a small scale due primarily to a lack of funds., but Lt. Col. Winfrey came up with the plan to make a deal with Chiang Kai-shek's government, the Kuomintang, for Chinese currency. It involved printing two million dollars' worth of Chinese yuan in the US, backed by funds from the US Treasury. It took State Department involvement, but by October 1944 Lt. Col. Robley Winfrey had delivered the funds into Lt. Col. Wichtrich's hands in Kunming.[35]

After delivering the money, Winfrey stayed on with AGAS until the end of the war. Since it lacked a direct connection with Hong Kong where the largest number of Allied POWs was concentrated, AGAS funneled much of the money through BAAG. Chinese agents employed by BAAG paid the money to the farmers who provided produce or gave the money directly to the prisoners themselves. These agents also brought in desperately needed medical supplies. At least three them were captured, viciously tortured, and executed by the Japanese. Despite their deaths—or perhaps because of them—the flow of aid to the prisoners in the Hong Kong camps never ceased.

After the Japanese surrendered, the Commander US Forces in China, Lieutenant General Albert Wedemeyer, put AGAS to work securing American prisoners of war in Shanghai, Formosa (Taiwan), Saigon, and Hong Kong. Wichtrich had Major Hagood write up a manifesto which AGAS had dropped on POW camps and airfields nearby. Stating that the war was over, it addressed itself to the Japanese general officers in the area. The manifesto made it clear that the Allies would hold them responsible for the safety of the POWs. It further explained that unarmed transport aircraft would arrive with unarmed personnel on a mission of mercy. It went on to say that they would take steps to care for and evacuate the prisoners as soon as possible. They executed their plans without incident.[36]

No better summary of AGAS' work could be given than the one given by Lt. Col. Wichtrich in *MIS-X Top Secret*: "AGAS was in existence from December 1, 1943, to September 2, 1945. It had 39 sub-headquarters scattered throughout the China theater, from Saigon to the Gobi Desert. AGAS was responsible for the rescue of 898 American airmen. All American POWs in China, Indochina, and Formosa now known as Taiwan were released by AGAS officers."[37] By September 23, 1945, the organization had ceased to exist, with all of the files destroyed and the personnel reassigned—their mission complete.

CHAPTER 12

Colditz to England—Small Group Assisted

Most escapers or evaders received some help, either from their POW camp organization or from individuals along the way. However, many were unassisted by any formal escape organization. The largest number of escapes and evasions were early in the war or in the Pacific Theater. Escapes or evasions came in different sizes. Anything less than half-a-dozen escapees or evaders is a small event; anything greater than this classes as a large event. This chapter tells the story of the assisted escape by Airey Neave and a companion from Colditz Castle in Germany. The following chapter sets forth the tale of the unassisted escape of Lieutenant Edgar Whitcomb from the island of Corregidor in the Philippines.

Airey Neave arrived in France in February of 1940 with the British Expeditionary Force as part of a searchlight unit composed mostly of World War I veterans. His unit took part in the fighting around Arras in May 1940, where the Germans received a temporary check before pushing the BEF into a large pocket around Dunkirk and a much smaller one around Calais. It was to Calais that Neave's unit withdrew. Leading an ad hoc group of British soldiers as infantry, Neave was wounded during street fighting on May 24. Evacuated to a makeshift hospital, he was captured by the jubilant Germans when Calais fell on May 26.

Once he recovered sufficiently to walk without aid, he marched along with other prisoners to Germany. Passing from one transit camp to another, Neave wound up in August 1940 at Oflag IXA/H outside the town of Spangenberg, in central Germany. The camp was at first entirely housed in the castle itself. However, the Germans soon built a more conventional barbed-wire enclosure below the castle, to which they moved Neave and many others. Neave passed the time quietly until February 1941, when he and many others were transferred to Stalag[1] XX A/H at Thorn, Poland. The main *Stalag* was built outside an old Polish fortress, complete with moat, on the Vistula River. However, the officers were held in dank, musty, and dark vaulted ammunition chambers within the fortress itself. It was shortly after his arrival at the dismal accommodations of Thorn that Neave became determined to escape.

He teamed up with a flying officer from the Royal Air Force named Norman Forbes, who spoke fluent German. Through the already-growing escape organization within the camp, they obtained papers and bartered for some clothing. They also accumulated enough food to take them to the demarcation line between German- and Soviet-occupied Poland. It consisted largely of a few bars of chocolate, tinned sardines, and condensed milk. Since the Soviet Union was neutral at the time, their plan was to slip across the border and be repatriated, as international law allowed for escaped prisoners.

After the first night's travel, Neave's feet were a bloody mess. That same day their meager supply of chocolate gave out. Neave lamented, "Sardines and condensed milk! No one who has ever been reduced to such a diet is likely to forget it."[2] As they went on, they dodged Wehrmacht patrols, suspicious Germans who had been transplanted onto Polish farms, and the ever-present and suspicious Hitler Youth. Whenever they stopped at a Polish home, they were always cared for even though the Poles gave them aid at the risk of their lives.

Despite all the hazards encountered, they nearly made it. On the fourth day they were caught by German border guards within sight of their goal. Once the Germans positively identified them as escaped prisoners, Neave and Forbes were sent back to Stalag XX A/H. On their arrival, they were both thrown into tiny, filthy, makeshift solitary confinement cells. While in their adjacent cells, Neave and Forbes did a thorough postmortem of their escape attempt.

Neave concluded that, "We had attempted to cross this wild, cheerless land at too fast a pace and without method." He observed that, "Loneliness and physical stress undermine the most resolute. He must conserve his forces by lying up for long periods where he can keep warm, if only in a haystack or thicket."[3] Within a few days of his release from solitary confinement, a guard awakened Neave and told him to be ready to move. It was shortly afterwards that Neave learned his destination: Oflag IVC—Colditz.

On arrival in Colditz in August of 1941, Neave immediately set about planning his next escape. He observed that although the camp was based in a medieval castle that had three of its walls resting on sheer cliffs, the fourth wall fronted on a dry moat. He realized that if a prisoner could gain the dry moat, he stood a good chance of getting free. His first scheme for escape, although ingenious, did not work out well. Using a uniform he had bartered for and some dye, he put together what in normal daylight looked like a passable Wehrmacht uniform of an Infantry *Gefreiter*.[4]

His plan was to wait until the guard changed and simply walk out the front gate. Unfortunately for Neave, the main gate was brightly illuminated by arc lighting. His ersatz Wehrmacht uniform showed up as a distinctive blue-green instead of the regulation field gray. Quickly apprehended, Neave was placed in solitary confinement for 28 days although this didn't actually happen until October. The camp security officer, Hauptmann Priem, made an announcement following Neave's failed attempt at evening roll call: "Gefreiter [Private] Neave is to be sent to the Russian Front."[5] Everyone except Neave enjoyed a good laugh. Like any good escaper, he was already thinking about his next chance at a Home Run.

It came in the form of a scheme concocted by Pat Reid and "Hank" Wardle—two inveterate explorers of Colditz Castle and members of the escape committee. They had found a torturous but concealed way through the castle that would allow the escapers to emerge in the hallway outside the Officers' Mess. They reasoned that an escaper, dressed as a Wehrmacht officer, could time their exit from the hallway for when it was empty. Then they could emerge from the Officers' Mess without bumping into any of the German officers running the camp. This would allow them to head straight for the main gate without arousing suspicion.

The escape committee picked four prisoners, two Dutch and two English, to escape in two teams at 24-hour intervals. Neave was paired with Lieutenant Toni Luteyn, formerly of the Netherlands East Indies Army. Aided by the various sub-committees of the Colditz escape organization, the escapers were soon equipped with very passable German uniforms. This was possible because the Dutch uniform resembled the German closely in color. Additionally, the escape organization produced decorations, epaulettes, and other accoutrements from painted linoleum, cardboard, and wood.

It took time, but by late December all was in readiness for their 400-mile journey to Switzerland. They had originally planned to escape right after a Christmas performance of a farce written by Neave entitled "The Mystery of Wombat College." Due to logistical issues, their departure was pushed back to January 5, 1942. That night, they crept through the passages of the castle, with Wardle leading the way and Pat Reid picking locks to gain access to passages the Germans thought inaccessible.

After a few tense moments with the last lock, they emerged into the passageway near the Officers' Mess. Neave and Luteyn boldly stepped off through the corridor, into the Officers' Mess, and out into the night where the snow was falling thick and fast. They passed through the gate without incident. Clear of the camp, they buried their uniforms, transforming into a pair of Dutch electrical workers. Using their compasses, they headed for the small town of Leisnig, 6 miles away, to take an early workman's train.

They would head to Leipzig based on a railway timetable obtained by the Dutch through bribery. The trip to Leipzig was without incident, except for Neave falling asleep and muttering in English. He was kicked awake by Luteyn, and they were fortunate that no one noticed. At 6 a.m. on January 6, they arrived in Leipzig and discovered that no trains were leaving for Ulm, the next leg of their journey, until 10:30 p.m.

While figuring out how to safely pass the time, Neave committed a blunder which could have resulted in the failure of their escape attempt. Absentmindedly, he took some Red Cross chocolate out of his pocket and began to nibble at it. Since chocolate hadn't been seen in Germany since early 1940, it drew unwanted attention. As Neave put it, "To sit eating this forbidden delicacy in the waiting room of a great station made one not only an object of envy but deep suspicion."[6] He and Luteyn quickly left the waiting room and wandered around town, going to two different cinemas and several restaurants for coffee.

They returned to the station in time to catch the train to Ulm, where they found themselves in a compartment with an unusually gregarious SS officer. Oddly enough, he saved them from some possible embarrassment when the military police boarded the train at a stop near Ulm. Before they could ask Neave and Luteyn for their papers, the SS officer said dismissively, "These are foreign workers (*Fremdarbeiter*), Dutch."[7] This seemed to satisfy the *Feldgendarmes*, so they moved on.

At 9 a.m. on the second day of their escape, the train bearing Neave and Luteyn arrived in Ulm. They went to the ticketing office, where Luteyn tried to buy two tickets to Singen on the Swiss border. This aroused the suspicion of the railway clerk, who summoned a railway policeman to question them. After a short consultation with his lieutenant, the policeman announced they would have to go to the local Labor Office and have their credentials verified. Staying calm, they flattered the policeman with compliments about Ulm. In the short walk to the Labor Office, they built sufficient rapport with the policeman that he allowed them to enter the office building unaccompanied. Relieved at their good fortune, they quickly found a way out through the rear doors. They consulted their map and left Ulm on foot for the small town of Laupheim about 15 miles away, where they boarded a local train for Stockach, a village as close to the border as they dared go.

They arrived at 9 p.m. and immediately set out on foot for Singen, about 13 miles distant. By 5 a.m. on January 8, they were still on the road to Singen when they encountered four German woodcutters who after a brief conversation sent for the police. Perceiving that the woodcutters were afraid of them, Luteyn and Neave bolted for the woods, running as fast as they could through deep snow. When they were at their last reserves of strength, they found a beekeeper's hut only a few miles from Singen that was closed up for the winter. Gaining access through a side window, they both "staggered crazily around the hut" until they found a bed with a single old blanket. They collapsed onto the bed and slept until the afternoon. When they arose, Neave and Luteyn searched the hut and found two long white beekeepers' coats as well as two shovels.

They left the hut and walked towards town, where around 5 p.m. they ran into two inquisitive Hitler Youth, both armed with truncheons. Luteyn managed to put them off with a story that they were Westphalian workers returning from work to their rooms in Singen. Since when the Dutch speak German they sound like Westphalians, the trick worked.

It was lucky for the boys that they accepted the story, because Neave and Luteyn would have killed them if they had not. They cleared Singen in the darkness and headed southeast on a compass bearing for the Swiss border. Once in the woods, they donned the white beekeepers' coats for camouflage. By 2 a.m. on January 9 they were 2 miles north of the border near Schaffhausen. Moving slowly through the deep snow and in the bitter cold, they made it to a road that ran along the border. Neave and Luteyn rested for an hour, eating their last bit of chocolate, slaking their thirst with handfuls of snow while watching a sentry patrol the road. When the sentry reached a point where he was out of sight, they surged across the road and into Switzerland. Once across the road they travelled for several miles and came to a town. But they were not entirely sure they were in Switzerland. After some cautious exploration, they found they were in the Swiss village of Ramsen.

They turned themselves in to a Swiss border guard, who celebrated with them by dancing in the snow-covered street. They were free! Neave and Luteyn had to spend several days in extremely comfortable "hotel arrest" in the center of Schaffhausen before they travelled by train to Berne. There they parted, collected by representatives of their respective governments. After he had been safely in Switzerland for several weeks, Neave sent a postcard in English to the commandant of Colditz, Oberst Prawitz. It read, "Dear Oberst, I am glad to be able to inform you that my friend and I have arrived safely for our holiday in Switzerland. We had a pleasant journey, suffering the minimum of inconvenience. I hope that you will not get sent to the Russian Front on my account. My regards to Hauptmann Priem. Yours sincerely, A. M. S. Neave, Lieutenant, Royal Artillery."[8]

Like many escapers, Neave felt conflicted even though he was back among his fellow countrymen. It took him a while to become accustomed to street traffic, for example. A doctor who examined Neave prescribed three weeks' rest in the country. He went to the town of Rosengarten, where he remained until mid-April of 1942, when he was summoned to Geneva.[9] He was instructed to leave his luggage at the Rosengarten station. In Geneva he was to meet a man wearing a dark felt hat and reading a Swiss newspaper. He met the man, who appeared to be reading the paper upside down. After an exchange of bona fides, they went for a drink. It was over a Pernod that Neave learned that he was to escape over the Swiss border the next day with Captain Hugh Woollatt, Military Cross (MC) of the Lancashire Fusiliers.[10] The agent, who referred to himself as "Robert," parted with Neave, giving him a suitcase full of clothes as well as instructions to meet with Woollatt.

A regular officer, Woollatt was "tall with a thin face and rather long dark hair, which gave him a carefree appearance, particularly when he wore a beret basque."[11] His sense of humor was an asset during their crossing of Vichy France and neutral Spain. Meeting Woollatt at the hotel, Neave was nonplussed when it came to signing the hotel registry. Woollatt laughed and suggested, "Write a false name old boy, as if you were staying here with a tart." Neave laughed and signed his name as Oscar Wilde.[12] The next day they met a man who introduced himself as Victor, who briefed them on the dangers involved in crossing Vichy France. He also provided them with papers and money for their journey.[13]

The papers allowed them to travel to Marseilles as Czech refugees. They crossed the border at 4 a.m. Once in France, they concealed themselves and waited for their contact. He arrived and introduced himself as "Louis," formerly of the Ritz Hotel in London. Neave and Woollatt were now in an escape line. As Neave observed, "The future plans had been made by others. All I had to do was obey the orders of my guides."[14]

They passed from guide to guide until they arrived by train in Marseilles. Their initial contact in Marseilles did not go well but they did have an alternative address and password, the café of a man named Gaston. After a rocky start with a naturally cautious Gaston, they were accepted into the network. While in the network at Marseilles, they met with a man named Louis Nouveau. Wealthy and privileged, Louis could have stayed clear of danger. Instead, he worked extremely hard for the Allied cause. Neave and Woollatt spent a week with Louis before being dispatched on a train for Toulouse accompanied by their guide, Francis Blanchain.[15] There they went to the Hôtel de Paris where they were given forged instructions to report to a refugee center near the Spanish border. Six days later, Neave, Woollatt and 10 other escapers left by train from Toulouse for Perpignan. The last leg of their rail journey took them to Port Vendres, a fishing port, close to the Spanish border.

When Neave detrained, a gendarme stopped him. The gendarme questioned him as to where he was going and if he were British. Neave stuck to his cover story and the obviously dubious gendarme released him with a friendly "Good luck anyway." Not much further on, Neave and Woollatt encountered and fled from some not-so-friendly *gendarmes*. After making sure they were not followed, they went to an address they had been given. It was there that they met their guide José, who would lead them on foot over the Pyrenees into neutral Spain.[16]

Neave described José as "a determined character, thin and wiry, and his eyes were always watchful."[17] José inspected their belongings, making them get rid of anything that was not absolutely necessary. The crossing was not without incident. The Pyrenees were rough going in good weather, but they had the bad luck to run into a terrible rainstorm that lasted almost their entire trip.

Eventually, after a night and a day of walking, they made it to the Spanish town of Figueres in Catalonia at 1 a.m. Without time to dry their sodden clothes, their new guide Pedro hustled them onto a train for Barcelona, 87 miles away, at 6 a.m. The journey went smoothly, as Pedro had apparently bribed the police liberally. At the station in Barcelona the British evaders were met by a "young Englishman from the British Consulate with a military moustache and a green felt hat."[18]

Neave and Woollatt were hidden at a Spanish working man's house where they waited impatiently to be taken to Gibraltar. On May 1, 1942, that time arrived. They drove in a late model Bentley to Madrid where they were guests at the Embassy for a few days. Along with several other evaders and escapers, they were loaded onto a large orange bus and driven to Gibraltar. Their papers described them as students, a description which would not have passed muster if not for the liberal bribes paid to the Spanish authorities.

At any event, they crossed over to Gibraltar with no difficulty. At last, Neave, Woollatt, and their companions had reached British territory. Neave was granted an audience with the governor of Gibraltar, who listened with some interest at his story. After two days on "the Rock" the escapers received orders to embark on a troopship for home. Airey Neave completed his Home Run on May 13, 1942, landing at Gourock, Scotland. He later went on to become one of the leading lights of MI9.

CHAPTER 13

Corregidor to the US—Single Unassisted

While Airey Neave travelled 400 miles through enemy territory to reach Switzerland, US Army Air Corps Second Lieutenant (2LT) Edgar D. "Whit" Whitcomb, a navigator of the 19th Bombardment Group, made an epic journey of over 11,000 miles to make his Home Run. His saga began when he flew as a navigator in one of the first 26 B-17 bombers of the 19th Bombardment Group to arrive at Clark Field on the Philippine island of Luzon on November 6, 1941 to begin a two-year tour of duty. Another seven bombers straggled in over the next few days. Within two weeks of their arrival, 17 of the group's bombers flew south to Del Monte Field on the island of Mindanao.

Whitcomb was at Clark Field when the Japanese attacked on December 8, 1941, destroying every B-17 there within minutes. Left without an aircraft to navigate, Whitcomb became a signals officer, a job he knew nothing about. In the weeks that followed, he spent almost all his time in a signals van and got plenty of on-the-job training. Much to his chagrin, when the 19th Bombardment Group left for Del Monte Field in late December, the signal van and its makeshift crew stayed behind to provide communications support to the few aircraft still operational.

Before the beginning of the year, along with elements of the 19th Bombardment Group headquarters, Whitcomb found himself defending the Bataan Peninsula along with thousands of other US and Filipino troops. Whitcomb's signals van was set up south of Mount Mariveles, an extinct volcano, to provide communications support to Cabcaben and Bataan Fields. Both airfields were single runways suitable only for the few fighters remaining to the defenders of Bataan. Cabcaben Airfield was located near the Bataan Peninsula's southeastern coast.

The Bataan Airfield was roughly 2.5 miles to the south on the Bataan Peninsula's east coast.[1] Whitcomb's unit would later support an airfield near the town of Mariveles as well. Although few in number, the P-40 Warhawks flown from those dirt airstrips by men such as Captain Edward Dyess extracted a toll from the Japanese as they maintained ferocious pressure against the US and Filipino defenders. In mid-March, Whitcomb came down with malaria. It was so bad that he was transferred to a nearby field hospital.

When he returned to duty, he found that he was now a liaison officer to General Fransisco, Commander of the 2nd Regular Division, Philippine Commonwealth Army.[2] He was in the job for less than a week when the final Japanese offensive cracked Bataan's defensive line on April 7, 1942. Two days later when the US and Philippine forces on the peninsula surrendered, Whitcomb and two friends, James Dey and John Renka, decided to head to Corregidor. They found a small boat and made their way to the island, which Whitcomb described as the "most heavily fortified in the world."[3]

Corregidor was a formidable obstacle to anyone attempting to enter Manila Bay. But much like the British Fortress of Singapore, its defenses faced seaward, in this case to the west. None of the massive concrete blockhouses faced north or northeast, from whence the Japanese would most likely come. Still, the defenders dug defensive positions to cover the other approaches.

When Whitcomb arrived, he was put in charge of an antiquated 75mm gun on the southeastern shore of the island at Monkey Point. It was manned by 15 veteran Filipino soldiers, which gave Whitcomb some comfort. On the evening of May 6, the Japanese began their invasion. Whitcomb found himself acting as an infantry officer, bolstering the defenses wherever he could throughout the night and into the next day. After enduring a 28-day siege, Whitcomb became a prisoner of the Japanese when the garrison surrendered at noon on May 7, 1942.

Shortly after the surrender, Whitcomb, along with many others, was marched around the island until nightfall when they were told to sit down and sleep—on a railroad. The Japanese troops which took Whitcomb prisoner were not brutal, just indifferent. The next day, along with many others, Whitcomb was put to work with hand tools to repair the bomb-damaged landing strip on the eastern end of the island. The next day after they finished work on the airstrip, they were packed along with 11,000 other prisoners into a roughly two-square-block-sized barbed-wire enclosure on the western side of the island about 8 miles across Manila Bay from the Cavite Naval Base.

As each man entered, they had a number penciled on their back. This brought home to Whitcomb that he was just a number to his captors. Several weeks passed as the Japanese alternately worked or neglected them. It was during that time that Whitcomb hatched a bold escape plan with a Marine lieutenant, Bill Harris. They would go out on a working party, conceal themselves until nightfall, and then swim the channel between the Bataan Peninsula and Corregidor at its narrowest point. Once on Luzon, they would find a boat and sail to mainland China, where they would join up with Chinese forces.

They knew any working parties were always very lightly guarded, and the Japanese didn't bother with roll calls or prisoner counts. Harris knew the area they would conceal themselves in well, as it had been his defensive sector before the surrender. As they were both good swimmers, Whitcomb and Harris believed they could do the slightly less than 3 miles in the hours of darkness. At noon on May 22, 1942, they went out on a wood-gathering party determined to make their break for freedom.

Slipping away from the other prisoners, they found an old fighting position where they concealed themselves. Luckily, they found a half-full bottle of quinine pills as well as several empties. These they used to store what little cash they had managed to conceal from the Japanese. When night fell, they set out for Bataan. The swim was not easy and the current almost beat them. But they both persevered, even on the one occasion they were separated. In the grey dawn hours of May 23, Whitcomb and Harris dragged themselves out onto dry land. They had made it.

Clad only in khaki shorts, the pair trod warily north along trails and pathways through the jungle. They came upon deserted campsites—American, Filipino, and Japanese—which eventually yielded up shirts, trousers, and shoes for them both. Relatively well clad, they made for a fisherman's hut near Cabcaben Airfield where they were fed a meal of steaming rice. The old fisherman gave them a precious gift before they left, a bolo to ease their passage through the jungle. Not wanting to put him in any danger, Whitcomb and Harris left as soon as they had finished their meal.

Moving north toward Mount Mariveles through the gathering darkness, they walked for two days, foraging as they went. However, their progress was slowed by the rough terrain. Reluctantly, they followed a ridge toward the coast where going would be easier. They encountered an abandoned US camp near the site where many of the US and Filipino troops had surrendered. It was there that Harris picked up a rifle and a bandolier of ammunition. Whitcomb declined to take one as he was a poor shot and could run much faster without one. They moved out along a jungle trail where they were fired on by an unseen Japanese patrol. Harris discarded his rifle and they both fled into the hills, unfollowed by the enemy.

After some deliberation, they decided to follow the western coast road. At first, they tried to move during the day, but the presence of Japanese patrols made them decide to move only by night. Mile by slow mile, they made their way first through the deserted town of Bagac to the outskirts of Morong. There they encountered a young boy who guided them into the town. The boy dashed their hopes of finding a boat big enough to cross over to China, explaining that the Japanese had already taken every boat of any size.

Whitcomb and Harris set out for Balayan, a town on Balayan Bay, south of Manila. When they first arrived, Whitcomb noted that, "The people were so friendly that we were suspicious."[4] The mayor met with them and told them they would be kept safe until he could get a boat ready for them capable of sailing to Australia. They were taken to a hiding place where they were visited by nearly one hundred well-wishers in the first two days. Feeling insecure with so many people knowing their hiding place, they decided to leave.

However, the landowner, Don Sixto Lopez,[5] sent an emissary to persuade them to hide with two other Americans, Marines who had escaped from Corregidor. They were T. O. "Army" Armstrong and Reid

Carlos Chamberlain. They soon became fast friends and waited—impatiently—for their boat. In the latter part of July 1942, the boat was ready, and they were surprised to see how well it was suited for long-distance travel. They were even presented with a compass. Without further ado, they shoved off into the night. However, the winds died down at night and it took them five days to travel 25 miles. Harris, Chamberlain, and Armstrong wanted to sail during daylight, but Whitcomb disagreed, feeling it would be sure to result in their capture. In the end, they split up, with Whitcomb remaining on land as his three comrades sailed off.

Left to his own devices, Whitcomb began to walk south. He soon learned from a friendly Filipino who hosted him for an evening that two American civilian mining engineers, from the Le Panto copper mine near Baguio in central Luzon, were preparing a boat to sail to Australia. After a day's search he found them—Ralph Conrad and Fred Bacon—in a small town on the shores of Balayan Bay, 15 miles east of Batangas. They hit it off instantly.

When Bacon and Conrad invited him to come along, Whitcomb accepted with alacrity. They sailed east that very night, crossing both the Batangas and the Tabayas bays before making landfall. There fortune deserted them. Whitcomb, Bacon, and Conrad fell into the hands of Filipino collaborators, who took them to jail in the nearby town of Agdangan. Whitcomb worried that the Japanese would deal harshly with Bacon and Conrad if they knew he was military. So, while in the holding cell, the three concocted a story that transformed 2nd Lieutenant Edgar Whitcomb, US Army Air Force into Robert Johnson, civilian mining engineer.

The story was paper thin, with the only touchstone to reality being that Fred Johnson (Robert Johnson's putative father), the superintendent of Le Panto mine, had flown out to the United States just days before the war began. While still in the cell, Whitcomb disposed of his dog tags and silver aviator wings but concealed a quantity of quinine pills in the seam of his clothing. They were turned over to a Japanese patrol shortly thereafter. Escorted onto a train, they were taken to the area headquarters near Legaspi, where the commandant informed them they were headed for an internment camp in Manila at Santo Tomas. What he did not tell them was that they would first be taken to the infamous Santiago Prison in Manila.

On the morning of August 14, 1942, they set off. The trip was pleasant enough but when they arrived at the prison, all three realized they could be in for a rough time. They were placed in separate cells, each of which was crammed with other prisoners. In Whitcomb's cell was Roy C. Bennett, a newspaperman who had often spoken out about the Japanese threat before the war. He proved an invaluable tutor to Whitcomb.

It was not long before a series of non-threatening interrogations began, where Whitcomb filled in the blanks of Robert Johnson. Without warning, the interrogation became brutal. The Japanese interrogator beat Whitcomb with a lead pipe, but Whitcomb stuck doggedly to his story. When returned to his cell, Whitcomb came down with an attack of malaria. Many prisoners had died from malaria because the Japanese had denied them treatment. What saved him was the quinine smuggled in the seam of his clothing.

Several days later, although he was barely recovered, the Japanese interrogated Whitcomb again for six hours. This time they concentrated on obtaining a map of a town he had supposedly hidden in along with Bacon and Conrad. The interrogator would demand, "Now you draw mappo Lusud."[6] Never having been in Lusud, Whitcomb drew what to him was a typical Filipino village in an attempt to satisfy the interrogator. Each failure earned him a savage beating. At the end of six grueling hours, he was sent back to his cell with paper and pencil to draw a "mappo Lusud."

Providentially, the guard put him in the wrong cell—with Ralph Conrad! In a whispered conversation, they exchanged what they had told the Japanese. Conrad also sketched a detailed map of Lusud. Knowing that if he didn't speak up there would be dire consequences, Whitcomb hailed an officer who returned him to the proper cell. Back in his cell, Whitcomb studied the map until he could draw it from memory. Then he destroyed it.

During the night, Frank Bacon sent him the story he had told the Japanese, written on toilet paper. There were so many discrepancies that Whitcomb seriously considered confessing.[7] However, when he presented the map at his next interrogation, the interrogator became almost friendly and returned him to his cell. The next morning, September 2, 1942, the Japanese transferred Whitcomb, Bacon, and Conrad to Santo Tomas.

When the jailer returned their belongings prior to their transfer, Whitcomb was horrified to see that Bacon and Conrad had kept a Mobile gasoline map which traced the 200-mile route that Bacon and Conrad had taken across Luzon, complete with the names and locations of their Filipino helpers. Everything the interrogator had wanted to know was on that map! They were amazed yet relieved that the Japanese had been so sloppy. Frank tucked the map away for disposal at Santo Tomas.

After inprocessing, Whitcomb went for a haircut, where he learned that there would be a ship taking a limited number of internees to Shanghai. Reasoning that it would be the perfect way to reach the Chinese mainland and head for Chungking, Whitcomb went straight to the commandant, who he described as an "old gentleman with a kindly manner and spoke very fine English."[8] Told that there was only a very small chance he could be put on the list, Whitcomb pressed his case with extreme politeness. The commandant promised that if there was a vacancy, he would place Whitcomb on the passenger manifest.

After leaving the commandant's office, he visited with Frank and Ralph to tell them about Shanghai. They both decided not to leave Santo Tomas. During the next few days Whitcomb went to work in the kitchen, where he learned that some in the camp suspected him of being a soldier and a deserter. He had just managed to put those stories to rest when the arrival of some Army nurses who had escaped from Corregidor to the southern islands almost exposed him. He managed through some quick thinking to avoid being outed as a soldier. One nurse who he knew well spread the word with the other nurses to stay quiet.

Once again, Whitcomb considered confessing but decided against it. The next day a soldier who had a racket going within camp that was shut down by the civilian administration, gave away the identity of 25 soldiers and Marines in the camp in a fit of anger.[9] They were taken away by truck, never to be seen again. That same day, Whitcomb was called to the commandant's office. Fearing the worst, he considered escaping but went anyway. To his delight the commandant informed him that after a physical examination, Whitcomb would be on the sailing list.

So, on September 12, 1942, along with 90 other American and British civilians, he found himself aboard the 2,500-ton Japanese freighter *Maya Maru* for an eight-day trip to Shanghai. During the trip he had another malaria attack but was tended to by his fellow passengers. Life on the ship was not severe, just a bit cramped. But Whitcomb observed that everyone was packed in tightly, even the Japanese soldiers. As the ship plowed northward to Shanghai, he realized he would have to find someone to aid him when they reached port.

He settled on Carl and Shelly Mydans, a young couple who worked for *Time* and *Life* magazines.[10] Once they disembarked on September 20, 1942, he approached them for help. They invited him to visit at the Palace Hotel, where they were to stay. Relieved, Whitcomb then headed for the American School where he was to stay. He was very surprised that the internees could come and go as they pleased. What worried him was the requirement to get an ID at French police headquarters that might expose him as a soldier.

That afternoon he went straight to the Mydans and told them everything. They rewarded him with $50 and an introduction to Mr. Henningsen, president of the American Association. The next day, Whitcomb met Mr. Henningsen who poured cold water on the idea of an immediate escape attempt. Whitcomb spoke no Chinese, the Nationalist Chinese forces were far away, and winter was approaching. Henningsen did promise to work on the problem, while giving Whitcomb an additional $50 and a new suit of clothes.

On Mr. Henningsen's advice, he got both a French and a Swiss ID card. He couldn't help feeling guilty for enjoying a life of relative luxury compared to what military prisoners of war suffered. He didn't have too much time to reflect because another malaria attack struck in early October. The head of the clinic, Dr. Hyla S. Watters, proposed to treat it with neosalvarsan, an anti-syphilis drug that she had observed would cure certain types of malaria. Whitcomb consented and after the treatment never had another attack of malaria.

Throughout the rest of October, he worked in the clinic, performing lab tests and waiting to hear from Mr. Henningsen. Unfortunately, in the first week of November the Japanese rounded up all prominent

American and British citizens and placed them in an internment camp, including Mr. Henningsen. With his trip to Chungking on indefinite hold, Whitcomb moved to the Palace Hotel at the Mydans' suggestion. Then their liberty came to an end. On February 1, 1943, all enemy aliens were interned in camps.

The Japanese allowed Whitcomb to be interned with the families at Chapei University camp because Dr. Watters expressed concerns about his "malaria." Whitcomb continued to work for Dr. Watters as a lab technician, all the while thinking of ways to escape. He had a few people ask him openly if he was a deserter, but his responses seemed to satisfy them. Throughout the summer, rumors swirled through the camp that they would be repatriated. In late summer the Japanese confirmed the rumors. Then news came that the Japanese had selected the entire Manila contingent for repatriation.

On September 20, 1943, they boarded the *Tia Maru*, a former French passenger ship, with several hundred other internees. They sailed to Portuguese Goa via Hong Kong, the Philippines, Saigon, and Singapore where they disembarked and boarded the Swedish liner *Gripsholm*. Whitcomb related it was "like stepping into heaven."[11] It was now mid-October 1943 and the *Gripsholm* sailed first to Port Elizabeth, South Africa, then to Rio De Janiero, Brazil, and finally to New York City, arriving on December 9, 1943. As soon as the ship docked, the FBI came on board and discreetly took him ashore. He was warned not to contact his family or anyone he knew before the war. They sent him to Washington, where he underwent a series of debriefings. Staying in the Hotel Lafayette, he reflected on how disconnected he felt: "I could not associate the conditions of scarcity and want which we suffered in the Pacific with the seeming abundance of everything in Washington."[12]

At first "a fat colonel in the intelligence service" informed him that he would most likely be interned for the duration of the war. This was to prevent the story of how he had been repatriated as a civilian from leaking out. That could have a potentially catastrophic impact on the repatriation process. Whitcomb pointed out that the Japanese never knew they had captured 2LT Edgar Whitcomb, nor had he ever been entered on a prisoner of war roll. Sanity prevailed, and he was allowed to go home for Christmas in Hayden, Indiana.

After a few days, he was itching to get back into the fight. At first, he took part in supply runs and attended the Command and General Staff College. Finally, in mid-April 1945 Captain Edgar Whitcomb received orders to the Far East Air Force. On landing at Clark Field, the 345th Bomb Group "Air Apaches" assigned him to the 499th Bombardment Squadron at San Marcellino, 35 miles southwest of Clark Field near Subic Bay. Within days he was flying combat missions in B-25 Js, strafing Japanese airfields and installations.

Because he had been to Command and General Staff College, Whitcomb was assigned to 5th Air Force staff in late July of 1945 right after the Air Apaches moved to Okinawa. In a sublime bit of closure, on August 14, 1945, Whitcomb navigated a flight for General Smith of the 5th Fighter Command to Clark Field. It was there on August 15 that he heard the news of the Japanese surrender. He ended the war where he had begun it.

CHAPTER 14

Singapore to Australia—Mass Escapes/Evasions Assisted

This chapter tells the story of the breakout of 17 British Commonwealth prisoners from a Japanese prison camp near Pasir Panjang in Singapore in February of 1942. They were led by Charles McCormac, a Royal Air Force sergeant who spent his formative years in Malaya where his father was a planter. Absorbing the culture and languages of the area, he came to speak—as well as English—fluent Malay, some Tamil, Chinese, and Japanese. He also enjoyed exploring the jungle where he learned many survival lessons. His family sent him to school in Australia where he waited until his 18th birthday to join the Royal Air Force (RAF) in 1937.

After completing his wireless operator training, he was posted to a torpedo bomber squadron flying obsolescent Vildebeest biplanes.[1] In 1939 his aircraft went down in the waters off Malaya. He survived 13 hours in the drink before being rescued by a flying boat. Little did he realize that many of his life experiences had equipped him to survive a five-month trek across 2,200 miles of land and ocean from a POW camp to freedom.

When the war opened, McCormac was stationed in Singapore at Seletar Aerodrome assigned to Headquarters of No. 205 Squadron as a wireless operator.[2] As the Japanese rolled south towards the Lion City, their aircraft began to bomb it with increasing frequency and accuracy. This led McCormac to decide to evacuate his wife Pat who was then pregnant with their first child. On January 30, 1942, she reluctantly departed on the USS *Wakefield* with over 400 other civilian evacuees. *Wakefield* was the last large ship to make it through an increasingly tight Japanese net of aircraft and naval vessels.[3] The USS *Wakefield* was the former SS *Manhattan*, a 24,000-ton luxury liner. The following description of the USS *Wakefield* comes from the Dictionary of American Naval Fighting Ships (DANFS).

> On 29 January, *Wakefield* and *West Point* arrived at Singapore to disembark troops doomed later to capture by the Japanese upon the fall of the city in the following month. On 30 January, *Wakefield* commenced fueling at Keppel Harbor for the return voyage and awaited the arrival of some 400 British women and children who were being evacuated to Ceylon. At 1100, lookouts spotted two formations of Japanese bombers, 27 planes in each, approaching the dock area at Keppel Harbor. Unhampered by antiaircraft fire or British fighter planes, the enemy bombers droned overhead and released a brief rain of bombs on the waterfront. One bomb hit 50 yards off *Wakefield*'s port quarter, and another blew up in the dock area 40 feet from the transport's bow before a third struck the ship's 'B' deck and penetrated through to 'C' deck where it exploded in the sick bay spaces. A fire broke out, but it was extinguished in less than one-half hour. Using oxygen masks, firefighting and damage control crews extricated five dead and nine wounded. Medical assistance soon came from *West Point*. Completing her fueling, *Wakefield* embarked her passengers and got underway soon thereafter, burying her dead at sea at 2200 and pushing on for Ceylon. After disembarking her passengers at Colombo, the ship found that port authorities would not cooperate in arranging for repair of her damage. *Wakefield*, therefore, promptly sailed for Bombay, India, where she was able to effect temporary repairs and embark 336 American evacuees. Steaming home via Capetown, the transport reached New York on 23 March and then proceeded to Philadelphia for permanent repairs.[4]

With only himself to care for, McCormac went looking for his squadron, which he discovered had left for Java without him. Determined to be of some use in defending Singapore, he wound up working with a mixed group of civilians and military "working on the Bukit Timnah Road, near Woodlands."[5] It was there that he met R. G. Donaldson, an Australian civilian who was to become his close friend through all that ensued. He described Donaldson as "a rugged, powerfully built fellow, a little over forty, with thinning ginger hair. His eyes were cold and intolerant, and his smile had little merriment in it."[6]

Not long after they met, McCormac tried to persuade Donaldson to escape across the straits into Malaya and join up with Chinese guerilla bands that were already operating against the Japanese occupiers. Donaldson scotched the idea with his observation that the straits were crawling with Japanese troops, watercraft, and aircraft. The morning of the surrender, McCormac and Donaldson were unaware that General Percival had given up. So, when a party of 20 Japanese soldiers led by a European civilian appeared in the open in front of them, McCormac opened fire and killed three of their soldiers. Instantly realizing he had made a serious mistake, McCormac threw down his Tommy gun and surrendered. It was a close-run thing, but he and Donaldson were eventually moved to Pasir Panjang—a camp for "troublemakers" who the Japanese had earmarked for death by mistreatment, overwork, or a combination of both.

Pasir Panjang was hellish. The prisoners, a mix of military and civilians, were systematically starved, beaten, and overworked. Some prisoners were given "the bamboo treatment" as a form of execution. These unfortunates were staked out over young bamboo shoots. As McCormac noted, "In the tropical heat bamboo grows quickly—several inches a day—and the shoots are strong enough to be neither stopped nor diverted by the live flesh of a human body."[7] Added to the everyday cruelty were the brutal interrogations by a Japanese captain named Teruchi who was a member of the Kempetai, the Japanese Army's military police. Interestingly enough, McCormac did not believe the camp commandant was a willing accomplice to the cruelties. However, when some prisoners escaped from a sea bathing outing, the commandant had 12 randomly selected prisoners bayonetted to death. In the weeks that followed, many of the prisoners were removed for interrogation. Most did not return. Those who did had almost always been savagely beaten. Six weeks after he had been taken prisoner, it was McCormac's turn for interrogation outside the camp.

Along with a truckload of other prisoners, he was taken to the YMCA building near Collyer's Quay,[8] where they were segregated and called, one by one, for interrogation. When McCormac was called back, he was interrogated, but aside from a slap across the face he was not mistreated. That changed the next day, when he was brutally interrogated by Captain Teruchi who after beating him nearly senseless slashed McCormac across the face with his sword. For some reason, the Japanese returned him to camp instead of disposing of him like so many others.

When he arrived, Donaldson cleaned him up as best he could. It was at that point they both resolved to escape. Since the Japanese had shown they would execute the remaining members of any work party from which a prisoner escaped, McCormac proposed that they recruit an entire work party. Donaldson agreed and began to cautiously sound out the European men of their work party. All but six agreed. Since the Japanese only cared about numbers and not names, six men from other parties who wanted to chance an escape switched places with the reluctant ones.

While still making their plans, they had a stroke of good fortune. It was the appearance in camp of a Portuguese Eurasian named Rodriguez, employed by the Japanese as a work party supervisor and translator. He confirmed that the prisoners at Pasir Panjang were considered dangerous and were marked for death. More importantly, he offered the use of his fishing boats as a means to escape across the Straits of Johore to Malaya. Then the escapers could join Rodriguez' brother who was with a band of Chinese and Eurasian guerillas near Kuala Lupis. Rodriguez also revealed his reason for taking such a risk—the Japanese had raped his eldest daughter and carried her off for use as a prostitute.

In a series of furtive conversations, McCormac and Rodriguez worked out the details. After the escape, McCormac would link up with Rodriguez at his home in Paya Lebar a little less than 10 miles west of the camp. Then Rodriguez would guide them to the boats which were moored slightly more than 12 miles away on the northern shore of the island. McCormac, who was very familiar with the island, realized that the distances they needed to cover meant that any breakout would have to occur shortly after dark.

Their plan was simple. Each man would arm themselves as best they could, which most of them did by finding stout pieces of wood or metal while out on a work party. Once darkness fell, McCormac would short-circuit the generator that lit the compound. With the camp plunged into darkness, they would then force open the flimsy front gate. Disposing of any guards who got in their way, they would proceed in small groups to a rendezvous point near Rodriguez' home. Like many simple plans, it worked.

During the breakout they only lost two members of their party while managing to dispose of five or six of the guards. In the brief struggle at the gate, both McCormac and Donaldson exchanged their improvised weapons for a bayonet taken from a dead guard. Within a few hours, 15 of the escapers had assembled in Paya Lebar. It was there that they hit the first snag. Because of increased Japanese security measures, Rodriguez was unable to guide them to the boats. However, he did provide them with 350 dollars in Japanese occupation currency.

McCormac was concerned that the boats were moored at Kranji Point. This was a scant 300 yards away from the heavily guarded causeway connecting Singapore and Johore Baru. Realizing there was no helping the situation, the group struck out immediately for the boats. When they were almost in sight of Kranji Point, they encountered a section-sized Japanese patrol. The normal Japanese infantry section had 10 men. It included a commander, six riflemen, and a three-man light machine gun crew.[9] They might have managed to evade contact, but one of the men at the tail of the group shouted, "Japs!". This led to a wild melee in which the escapers killed all but one of the patrol. Unfortunately, the escapers lost seven of their number in doing so. Moving swiftly, the eight survivors managed to quickly locate the boat and shove off into the Johore Straits. The boat they hurriedly selected had a single paddle in the bottom. Shoving off, they began to paddle toward the Malaysian shore.

However, at that point their luck gave out. A searchlight on the causeway began to play about the water near the boat. They were forced to stop paddling, crouch beneath the gunwales, and drift with the current which bore them relentlessly westward toward Sumatra. Several times the searchlight came to rest on the boat, but the Japanese did not fire. When morning dawned, the current had borne the boat out into the Straits of Malacca out of sight of land.

Before the eight survivors could make any progress toward Malaysia, two Japanese Zero fighters showed up and strafed the boat. When they departed only four of the escapees were left alive: McCormac, Donaldson, Skinner, and Roy. Having lost their paddle in the strafing, they could not prevent the boat drifting steadily out into the straits. However, after a day adrift, their luck changed. A Dutch flying boat spotted them, picked them up, and deposited them in a *kampong*[10] near Medan, near the northern tip of Sumatra.

Although the Dutch were unable to take the four escapers any further, they did link them up with a local village chief. He fed them and advised them to head west toward the mountains, where they might link up with a guerilla band near Lake Toga. The alternative was to traverse 500 miles of Sumatra, cross the Sunda Strait to Java, and then find a way to reach Australia. While at the *kampong*, McCormac got the chance to size up his two other fellow escapers. Roy was a tall, thin private who rarely spoke. During the time they knew him, no one in the group learned his last name or anything else about him. Skinner was another matter. He was a Welshman, "small, dark, profane and possessed of boundless energy and humor. An inveterate grumbler, he had a one-track mind and only one topic of conversation: women."[11]

After three days of rest, the group struck out southwestward for Lake Toga, 60 miles distant. They might have rested longer, but the chief of the *kampong* was worried. He felt that the Japanese would return and that the 400-guilder reward for turning in a European might be irresistible to some. He provided the group with several days of food and showed them a path which he assured them led to Lake Toga.

After only a couple of days in the jungle, McCormac realized that ascending the 60 miles into the mountains was beyond their ability. The path the *kampong* headman had shown them petered out among an unbroken series of crocodile-infested swamps that formed an impenetrable barrier to their movement. Additionally, they could find no source of potable water. Roy was also extremely sick with dysentery. Reluctantly, they decided to abandon their original plan and head toward the southern tip of the island where they might find someone to treat Roy.

Once they headed toward the coast, they hit a hard-surfaced road which they used as a navigational handrail for three days. They decided to leave the road after seeing a Japanese staff car drive by. For several weeks they plodded southward through terrain that was increasingly dry and without food. Then came three days and four nights without any food or water. They were reduced to drinking their own urine, which they strained by filling their pants legs with earth. It was bitter but slaked their thirst.

They continued south, seeking water. Fortunately, they found it on the second day of their search, guided by the movement of a group of orangutans. They also found some termites which they consumed with gusto. Shortly after, they struck a hard-surfaced road which bordered more open country and had a swiftly flowing stream alongside. They camped there for three days to rebuild their strength before striking out along the road for a week. Throughout their journey, McCormac's knowledge of the jungle as well as of the local languages and culture served the escapers well time and again.

On the eighth day, they encountered a fairly substantial *kampong* of almost 500 inhabitants. As Roy's health was steadily worsening, they decided to risk contact. Not certain that the inhabitants were friendly, McCormac entered alone. Fortunately, they were quite friendly and somewhat taken aback that a European could speak their language. Some of the inhabitants of the *kampong* were Chinese and the village headman wore the Queen Wilhelmina Medal—a sure sign of loyalty to the Allies.

It was in this village that they met Nan Seng, a Nationalist Chinese man who played a double game with the Japanese. To them, he was a supplier of rubber and a collaborator. In reality, he was part of the emerging Indonesian resistance movement. Nan Seng offered to drive them south in a few days by truck, hidden beneath sheets of raw rubber. After some discussion amongst themselves, the escapers agreed to Nan Seng's plan. For the next week, the group rested and recuperated from their two-week trek through the jungle. One of the *kampong*'s women even managed to temporarily cure Roy's dysentery.

Finally, it was time to go. Concealed beneath the smelly rubber sheets only when necessary, they set out on a four-day trip to a *kampong* just north of Palembang where they rested for the night. Then they embarked on a sampan for a short trip to a rail yard. There the sampan captain instructed them to hide beneath some sheets of raw rubber in a train car "until friends come." The train began moving and the friends came, in the form of several Javanese who offered the group cigarettes. They traveled the rest of the way atop the sheets of rubber, keeping an eye out for Japanese.

The train was bound for Oosthaven,[12] a port at the southernmost tip of Sumatra on the Sunda Strait where the group could seek passage to Java. As the train began to slow down, the Javanese advised them to leave the train and head for Oosthaven. This they did and after several days and nights of cautious travel, they found a *kampong* whose headman proudly wore the Queen Wilhelmina Medal. They introduced themselves as Eurasians who had fled from Japanese forced labor. Whether the headman bought the explanation is impossible to say. However, besides food and fresh clothing their genial host offered them female companionship in keeping with local customs. After an evening, the headman directed them to a *kampong* on the coast where he believed they could catch a fishing boat to Java. Unfortunately, as they moved south along the trail, Roy's health took a turn for the worse. His dysentery returned with the added complication of malaria, making him so sick he could not even walk.

At this point, Skinner returned from foraging for food with a girl named Li-Tong in tow. She explained that she was the niece of the headman of the *kampong* they were heading toward. She told them it was only 2 miles away, so they followed her there carrying Roy on their backs. They arrived to a lukewarm welcome from the headman. McCormac repeated the story that they were Eurasians but added the twist that they had escaped from "the Dutch Company" and had fled south. The headman was nervous that the Japanese would patrol through the *kampong* but when McCormac offered to report for labor with the Japanese and give his pay to the headman, he relented. For a week, McCormac performed manual labor on an airstrip under the supervision of a singularly uninquisitive Japanese sergeant whose only question for McCormac was about his blue eyes. McCormac replied that his father was German and that satisfied the sergeant.

The third day after their arrival, Roy died despite all the care the local women had shown him. The combination of malaria and dysentery had simply been too much. When McCormac returned from work on the fifth day, the headman remarked, "You will want to be moving on, Tuan."[13] McCormac knew from being addressed as "Tuan" that the headman realized they were Europeans. He asked for the headman's help to find a way to cross the Sunda Strait to Java. Initially, the headman was hesitant to help. However, McCormac reminded him that the Japanese might capture them and make them talk—with terrible consequences for the entire *kampong*. Faced with the possibility of Japanese reprisal for harboring Europeans, the headman agreed to try to help. It only took a few hours for the plan to coalesce. Li-Tong's father agreed to have fishermen ferry McCormac and Donaldson to Java in return for Skinner marrying Li-Tong! Not surprisingly, Skinner was all for the arrangement. At first, McCormac didn't know whether he should shake Skinner's hand or kick him.[14] At dusk, McCormac and Donaldson set out for Java.

The trip was uneventful, and they landed on a beach near a town called Merak at the northwestern tip of Java. Before shoving off for home, the fisherman went inland and brought a morose Javanese as a guide. He took them inland for a way, pointed them down a trail, and told them they would be met by someone soon. He then left with no further explanation. Within an hour they were met by an Australian who greeted them with, "What are you two fairy-like bastards doing here?"[15] With that auspicious beginning, McCormac and Donaldson came under the control of a local guerilla band led by a Dutch officer named Mansfeldt. He interrogated McCormac and Donaldson separately before he decided they could stay with his band for a while. His band consisted of around 70 men, mostly Javanese, half of whom had firearms, the rest swords.

The entire time they remained with Mansfeldt's band fell into a pattern. Mansfeldt would select a small Japanese outpost of 10–12 men several days' march away from their current camp as a target. The band would descend on the Japanese, wipe them out, and return with more rifles, ammunition, and other supplies. They would then break camp and move for three or four days before establishing another camp. This went on for about six weeks until they had come fairly close to Java's southern coast. One morning Mansfeldt introduced them to a Javanese who would be their guide on the next stage of their journey. Before bidding them farewell, Mansfeldt emphasized that they should follow their guide's orders. They left the camp and walked for several days, with scarcely a word from their guide. One evening he deposited them in a *kampong* on the coast where the headman told them they would leave by fishing boat soon.

The headman was as good as his word. Later that night they departed eastward in a fishing sampan crewed by several Javanese. They sailed east along the coast for six days, stopping each night at a friendly *kampong*. At the end of the sixth day, they put in at a *kampong* where they were met by an Australian who during their short stay never gave them his name. The news he did impart floored them. They were going to fly out to Darwin on the next resupply aircraft. Both McCormac and Donaldson had trouble wrapping their heads around the idea. Right after their arrival, the weather turned foul for two days. As soon as it cleared, they went out that evening with the Australian and several Javanese in a fishing sampan. After seven hours of anxious waiting, McCormac heard the drone of an aircraft's engines. Following an exchange of recognition signals, the flying boat landed and taxied close to the sampan. Still clad in loincloths and looking much like native Javanese, McCormac and Donaldson boarded the aircraft. As they prepared to take off, McCormac asked for the date. He was somewhat startled to hear that it was the September 16. It had been five months since their escape from Pasir Panjang. After a 12-hour flight, they set down in Darwin, free at last.

McCormac and Donaldson went their separate ways soon after their arrival. McCormac received a Distinguished Conduct Medal,[16] a commission as a squadron leader,[17] and a job teaching airmen escape and evasion. He was reunited with his wife and daughter, who had survived the trip to Ceylon aboard the *Wakefield*. At the end of the war, he was in Singapore as part of Lord Mountbatten's staff. As related later (page 155), this posting provided him with unique closure for his wartime experiences. Despite extensive research, the author was unable to find anything on the wartime fate of R. G. Donaldson of Melbourne. As for Skinner, McCormac related that he once debriefed six aircrew who were recovered after being shot down on airstrikes against the port of Telok Betong, Sumatra in 1944. They said they owed their escape to a network run by a white "Tuan." Based on their description of the man and his wife, McCormac had no doubt that the "Tuan" was Skinner.[18] This news was a heartening postscript to their terrible ordeal.

CHAPTER 15

Corregidor to Australia—Mass Escapes/Evasions Unassisted

This chapter relates the daring evasion by 18 men led by Lieutenant Commander John H. Morrill from the minesweeper USS *Quail* right after the fall of Corregidor in May of 1942. They spent 31 days in a 36-foot boat sailing through Japanese-dominated waters. It captures the dangers faced and risks taken by those who bravely struck out on their own in their bid to remain free. When they arrived in Darwin, Australia and ever after, the 17 *Quail* survivors invariably gave the credit for their escape to their commander. A humble and self-effacing man, Morrill's account of the escape always points out his mistakes and the positive contributions of others. If it were not for the accounts of his crew, his sterling leadership qualities and strength of character would escape the casual eye. In fact, he was only awarded the Navy Cross for his actions in command of *Quail* posthumously!

Born in Miller, South Dakota on January 7, 1903, Morrill grew up in Minneapolis. He entered the US Naval Academy at Annapolis, Maryland in 1920 and graduated in 1924. He spent the interwar years on nearly every class of ship the Navy had, including 10 years on S-Class submarines. He assumed command of *Quail* in June 1939. The following description of the USS *Quail* comes from the Dictionary of American Naval Fighting Ships (DANFS).

> *Quail* was a Lapwing Class minesweeper, laid down May 14 1918 by the Chester Shipbuilding Co., Chester, Pa.; launched October 6 1918; and commissioned April 29, 1919. She operated with this force clearing the North Sea of mines until November 25 1919. She operated with the Atlantic Fleet in Cuban waters during

early 1920, and then along the east coast. In September 1922, she was attached to the submarine base at Coco Solo, Canal Zone, operating in the Caribbean. She made a cruise to the east coast in late 1923, and in 1925 she was at Philadelphia for repairs. In 1927 she spent time patrolling the west coast of Nicaragua, and later joined the fleet in the Caribbean for maneuvers. From July 1928 to January 1929, she was on the east coast, operating between Virginia and Massachusetts. She returned to Coco Solo in 1929. Following duty with the control force in the Panama Canal area from 1929 to 1931, *Quail* operated out of Pearl Harbor, Hawaii, from 1931 to 1941, including in her duties a period of survey work off Alaska. With the outbreak of war with Japan *Quail* was in the Philippines.

During the defense of Corregidor, she swept a channel providing access to South Harbor, Corregidor. Her crew then went ashore to aid in the defense of that island. Damaged by enemy bombs and guns, *Quail* was scuttled 5 May 1942 by US forces to prevent her capture. Part of her crew escaped to Darwin, Australia, in a 36-foot motor launch. *Quail* received one battle star for World War II service. Like others of her class, *Quail* had a wooden hull, displaced 950 tons was 187'10" long, had a beam of 35'6" and drew 9'10". Her top speed was 14 knots. *Quail* had a crew of 78 officers and men. Her main armament was two 3-inch guns, mounted fore and aft. She had plied the Atlantic, Caribbean, and Pacific sea lanes for over 20 years.[1]

Quail was having her engines overhauled at the Cavite Naval Base[2] in the Philippines when war broke out. The Japanese attacked Cavite on December 10, 1941, with devastating effect, wrecking many of the shops and storage areas. Moored at Machera Wharf, *Quail* pitched in to defend the base, downing several attacking aircraft and towing several damaged ships to safety.[3] It was here that Morrill won the Navy Cross. His citation for the first days of the war reads:

> The President of the United States of America takes pride in presenting the Navy Cross (Posthumously) to Lieutenant Commander John Henry Morrill, United States Navy, for extraordinary heroism and distinguished service in the line of his profession as Commanding Officer of the Minesweeper U.S.S. QUAIL (AM-15), in combat against enemy Japanese forces during the bombardment of Cavite Navy Yard, Philippine Islands, on 10 December 1941. Despite the fires and frequent explosion of air flasks and war heads, Lieutenant Commander Morrill while in command of a small auxiliary craft, displayed extraordinary courage and determination in proceeding into the danger zone and towing disabled surface craft alongside docks to a safe zone. This prompt and daring action undoubtedly saved the crews from serious danger and saved the vessels aided for further war service. The conduct of Lieutenant Commander Morrill throughout this action

reflects great credit upon himself, and was in keeping with the highest traditions of the United States Naval Service. He gallantly gave his life for his country.[4]

Once Manila fell, *Quail* concentrated on sweeping mines to keep the supply lanes to Corregidor open. Corregidor is the northernmost and largest of four islands that guard the approaches to Manila Bay. Shaped like a tadpole, it housed the fortifications of Fort Mills. The other three islands which stretch southeast from Corregidor—Caballo, El Fraile, and Carabao—were home to Forts Hughes, Drum, and Frank, respectively.[5] From the time Bataan fell on April 9, 1942 until the fall of Corregidor on May 5, 1942, Morrill and *Quail* found their job increasingly difficult due to dwindling fuel supplies and the increasing tempo of Japanese attacks from both land-based artillery on Bataan and aircraft. Still, *Quail* and its crew continued to do their job, keeping the vital lifeline open while bringing down a number of Japanese aircraft. Along with *Tangier* and *Finch*, two other Lapwing Class minesweepers, they regularly fired on the morning reconnaissance plane which they nicknamed "Oscar."

After they brought down a few of the interlopers, their combined efforts soon forced "Oscar" to fly higher, interfering with his search for targets. When not in action, Morrill would anchor *Quail* near Caballo Island, using the wrecks of other ships to conceal it. He was so successful that *Quail* was the last ship still operating when the Japanese stormed Corregidor on May 6, 1942. In the end, Morrill scuttled her on orders on May 5, 1942, to prevent the enemy from taking her as a prize. During the period between the fall of Bataan and the capture of Corregidor, *Quail's* crew was steadily diminished by drafts of officers and men to operate anti-aircraft artillery, man coast defense guns, and perform other services on Corregidor, Caballo, El Fraile, and Carabao. Thus, when it became obvious that surrender was imminent, Lieutenant Commander Morrill could only locate fewer than 25 of his officers and crew on Caballo Island.

Of those only 17 decided to join him in escaping. Among these were Donald G. Taylor, the gunnery officer,[6] Head the pharmacist's mate, Nick Cucinello, a chief petty officer, Richardson, a wizard with small engines, and J. F. Meeker, a man of ideas and action.[7] One of the men who declined to escape gave Morrill a pocket watch which would act as a ship's chronometer during their escape.[8] Morrill selected *Quail's* 36-foot diesel boat as their "gangplank to freedom."[9] Anchored in the middle of Caballo's South Harbor, it had escaped the attention of the Japanese. The day of the surrender, Morrill and several of his men used a gasoline-powered motor launch to approach the site where a tugboat, *Ranger*, was beached.

They ransacked her for supplies, coming up with four automatic weapons and six Springfield rifles, some dynamite, cases of tinned corned beef and salmon, coffee, sardines, bananas, a large can of tomato juice, and lubricating oil, as well as charts and maps. However, while they had good charts and maps for the Philippines, they found only a single large-area, small-scale map of the Western Pacific to navigate the Dutch East Indies (now Indonesia). Fortunately, Morrill and his men secured 450 gallons of diesel fuel. It was far less than they needed to get to Australia, but it was sufficient to begin their escape. When night fell, Cucinello took the gasoline-powered boat to the South Harbor dock and gathered the rest of those who were determined to escape, including two Filipino mess boys. They then went and got the diesel boat, taking her to where *Ranger* was beached. After they completed loading the boat, her gunwales were only six inches above the water. Fully loaded, they headed to the dock to pick up Head, their pharmacist's mate. With their 4-cylinder Buda[10] diesel engine purring like a kitten, they shaped their course for Australia and freedom.

The first of many problems they solved was crossing the minefields surrounding the entrance to Manila Bay. Posting two men to keep a sharp lookout for "bubbles of TNT,"[11] Morrill headed south along the coast of Luzon. Forced ashore by a rising moon and a Japanese destroyer to seaward they put into a small cove only 5 miles down the coast from Corregidor. After they camouflaged their boat, they took shelter in the nearby trees. Unfortunately, the Japanese destroyer dropped anchor across the mouth of the cove where they spent the night. It was at that time that the Filipino mess boys asked permission to leave for their village only 30 miles away. After Morrill gave permission, they gave him 100 pesos as a parting gift. After a long day of waiting, they were preparing to depart when another Japanese destroyer showed up. This time, it anchored in a cove further south.

Springing into action, Morrill and his men got underway, shielded by a cloudy night sky. Dodging Japanese destroyers and patrol boats, they managed to penetrate the Japanese picket line across the mouth of Manila Bay. Moving southward past Fortune Island at around 4 knots, Morrill decided to lighten the boat to see if they could increase their speed. Several Lewis machine guns as well as some mushroom anchors used in minesweeping went overboard, allowing the boat to pick up speed and lose sight of the picket boats to their north. The Lewis gun was a machine gun of American design and had played a significant part in World War I. Weighing close to 26 pounds, it was a crew-served weapon capable of firing 550 rounds per minute.[12] The machine guns would have been of little use if they had encountered Japanese patrol boats, so the decision to throw them overboard is understandable. As LCDR Morrill observed, "They were heavy, and we had more guns than we knew what to do with."[13]

They headed for an island just off the Kalatayan Peninsula, where they anchored for the day, stripped the boat of its heavy brass taffrail[14] and painted the hull black.[15] They were now 40 miles from Corregidor with a plan to cover 50 miles that night. Around 8 p.m., they headed south through the Verde Island Passage, evading two Japanese patrol boats at the 10-mile-wide head of the passage. When they reached the narrowest point of the passage near Marikaban Island,[16] they successively evaded two lines of patrol boats, two destroyers, and two submarines. This was no small feat, considering their boat was held fast in a tidal current for three interminable hours. Free of the current and shielded by cloud cover, they made their way to Point Puñas[17] on Luzon before making landfall at the town of Digas.[18] It was there that they met friendly Filipinos who led them to a secure anchorage, fresh water, and supplies of fresh fruits and vegetables. After a day's rest, a bath, and a good feed, they headed out, skirting Marinduque Island on its north side. On May 10 they arrived at the Bondoc Peninsula on the southern tip of Luzon where they encountered friendly Filipinos once again. This was fortunate as they had to strip the engine down for maintenance.

The first night of their stay a prosperous local farmer looked after them, giving them food and shelter. He also gave them his precious stock of lubricating oil which he kept for his tractor because he had already experienced Japanese behavior in Manila. He told Morrill, "They will take everything… They will take the tractor and the plows, the electric wires, the pumps, even the machetes."[19] The rest of the man's story only reinforced Morrill's determination to escape. To lengthen the odds of a successful escape, with local help they installed a mast, a boom, and rigging.[20] Along with shedding the taffrail and painting the ship black, the sail made the boat look even more like a native fishing vessel. This would stand them in good stead several times during the rest of their journey. The night before they left, they slept in the boat to practice for the many nights they might be forced to do so in the open sea. As Morrill observed, "There's an art to sleeping on a bare floor or deck. When you get used to it, no feather bed is more comfortable."[21]

It wasn't until the evening of May 13 that they were able to shove off west of Masbate Island across the Sibuyan Sea passing the northern tip of Cebu Island for Leyte Island. Morrill chose to take the somewhat longer route because he knew that the Sibuyan Sea was full of reefs and other obstructions, making it unlikely that they would encounter any large vessels.[22] The first night the seas became choppy and rain poured down in buckets. It took some furious bailing, but they managed to keep the boat afloat.

Shortly after the rain ceased near the northern tip of Cebu Island, they encountered a Japanese tanker. Everyone but Taylor, who was of dark complexion, crawled under a tarp. The tanker passed them at around 3,000 yards but showed no interest. They made landfall on Tabango Bay,[23] Leyte Island at 11 a.m. on May 15.[24] They were welcomed once again by a wealthy landowner who fed them and gave them the news that the Japanese were on Leyte in force. A Chinese merchant sold them lubricating oil, diesel fuel, manila sail line, and canned goods. They also exchanged their khaki clothing for what Morrill described as a "grey-green prison suit combination."[25] With that, they departed.

Having been warned not to stop anywhere on Leyte, Morrill directed their course south through the Surigao Straits. During their passage through the straits they encountered rough seas and foul weather, but they had prepared by taking down the mast and securing loose gear and their diesel fuel drums. Having traversed the Camotes Sea without much trouble, they entered the Pacific Ocean.

Skirting down the eastern coast of Mindanao, they briefly landed at Port Lamon on the night of May 17.[26] There they took on more diesel and supplies, provided by friendly Filipinos. They were mill workers turned farmers as the result of a typhoon which had destroyed their mill. Despite being short of food, the Filipinos offered to feed them. Since his crew had ample food supplies, Morrill refused, politely but firmly. He did, however, take some lumber to deck over the boat and install sideboards to make her more seaworthy. They also fabricated a sextant which was accurate to half a degree.[27]

The next night, impelled by the presence of Japanese patrol boats, they continued their trek southward into the unknown waters of the Dutch East Indies, with just enough fuel to reach Australia in perfect conditions. Of course, Morrill was experienced enough to realize that perfect conditions were a pipe dream. It was a relief when the Filipinos swam a drum of diesel to them as they were already departing. Morrill chose to shape his course over coral reefs, as the boat only drew four feet of water while the Japanese patrol boats would draw at least twice that. His decision proved to be sound and soon they were in open water, clear of any marauding patrol boats.

On May 22 they passed the island of Morotai, the northernmost of the Maluku Islands. They narrowly avoided an encounter with a 40-foot steam launch flying a Japanese merchant flag. They headed south to Halmahera, 60 miles away, which they reached in the afternoon. However, after the encounter with the steam launch, Morrill decided to continue on to Sajafi, another 60 miles to the south. They encountered some local inhabitants, with whom they bartered for some coconuts and bananas. They also managed to lay on a supply of fresh water. It was during their short sojourn at Sajafi that Morrill observed, "We all felt that some power, stronger than circumstance, had been looking out for us."[28]

After six days at sea, they passed Pisang Island, north of Timor, in the morning hours of May 24.[29] They came to Teeor where there was a good-sized settlement. Uncertain of the locals' allegiance, Morrill and crew headed for a small unpopulated island 9 miles distant. There, the engine died. With a dead battery, they had to wrap ropes around the propeller shaft to start it. The inhabitants of the islands they passed were neither interested in helping Americans nor were they hostile. Had Morrill and his men been Dutch, the story might have been different. The Indonesian people hated the Dutch almost as much as they hated the Japanese.

Morrill was forced to barter for supplies, as the islanders would take neither American nor Philippine currency. They limped south to Keoor, the easternmost island in the Dutch East Indies. A schoolteacher assured them that the Japanese had already conquered New Zealand, Tasmania, and most of Australia. After questioning him closely, Morrill realized that his news source was Japanese propaganda broadcasts. Feeling uneasy about the man's loyalty, Morrill decided to put out to sea. While anchored about 500 yards off the island, Richardson fashioned an engine bearing out of lignum vitae (an extremely hard wood) driftwood.[30] When they departed, the engine was running but Richardson was concerned. He wanted to run some checks on dry land.

The island of Taam, with a predominantly Muslim population, reluctantly provided them with the time and place to finish the repairs. They departed in the early morning of June 1, heading across the Arafura Sea in the teeth of a gale. Green water crashed over the boat repeatedly and the rain squalls coming at 15-minute intervals were nearly as bad. It proved to be their worst night at sea. Morrill admitted to being "scared out of my wits."[31] However, careful boat handling in the blinding rain plus continuous bailing kept them afloat—that, plus their reliable diesel engine which kept chugging along even when immersed. Morrill shuddered to think what would have happened had they been using a gasoline engine. Without power in such a storm, they would have likely died almost within sight of their goal.

The next morning, they arrived at Moloe Island and the gale mercifully quit. Stopping briefly, they topped off their supply of fresh water and traded with the islanders for some tobacco and fruit. Since they were so close to Australia, one of the crewmen—Binkley—got to work on an American flag using an undershirt as the base. They did not want to be mistaken for an unfriendly craft. The flag was one-sided and had only 24 stars, but the entire crew was proud of it. Some of the men were concerned about putting into Darwin, based upon what the schoolteacher had said. They thought that the port might be under attack. Morrill reasoned that they had weathered plenty of bombs in the recent past, so Darwin was the place to go, bombs or no bombs. For two days they continued across the Arafura Sea, which they had nicknamed "Our Fury Sea" to commemorate the terrible storm they endured.[32] They decided that an intermediate stop before Darwin would be Melville Island, although they determined that if they found the Japanese in possession of the area they would keep on going until they reached an unoccupied territory.

As Morrill explained, "We would seize a boat bigger than ours, one we could go across the Pacific in, if we had to."[33] The night of June 3 was rough, but by morning the weather was clear and Morrill gave the orders for full speed ahead. They arrived at Melville Island, north of Darwin, in the early morning of June 4, 1942. After choosing an inlet at random, they motored inland until they met a group of islanders led by a Jesuit missionary named Brother John. They spent the better part of the day at the mission, where they slept in beds for the first time in almost a month. In the afternoon they went to another mission at the other end of the strait. They crossed over on June 5, arriving in Darwin two days after the great American victory at Midway.

In an astounding feat of seamanship, they had traversed over 2,000 miles without a proper sextant, some large-scale charts, and only a pocket watch as a chronometer. Their arrival in Darwin was a bit anticlimactic. Once they managed to convince the Australian authorities of their identities, they were without a place to stay or clothes to wear. Colonel Wortsmith of the US Army Air Corps took them under his wing, finding them billets and clothing.

Two days later, they flew out to Adelaide, Australia. Morrill commented, "It was colder than a penguin's undercarriage in that crate."[34] From there they flew on to Melbourne the next day. They spent a week at a hotel, eating everything in sight. Finally, they received news that 13 of them would report to Sidney for active duty. At a farewell dinner that evening, the men presented Morrill with a watch inscribed with "To Our Gallant Skipper From Seventeen Grateful Men." He tried to make a speech but ended up simply saying, "Well, you know how I feel about it."[35] The next morning, they split up and went their separate ways. They had made their Home Run.

CHAPTER 16

Liberation!

Liberation from captivity was an extremely emotional event for most POWs, some of whom had been behind barbed wire for five years or more. No single account could capture the complex problems involved in liberating prisoners from captivity. In the European Theater nearly all the POWs were liberated before Germany surrendered on May 7, 1945. The events surrounding the Allied capture of Colditz (Oflag IV C) on April 16, 1945[1] were exceptional, while the experiences of those liberated at Moosburg (Stalag VII A) typify the experiences of most POWs in German hands, the exception being those like the Berga survivors related earlier who were liberated while on the march. The experiences of those in Japan require a different approach. Two camps in the Philippines—Los Baños and Cabanatuan—were taken by US forces in daring operations. For continuity's sake, this work will examine the Cabanatuan rescue. After the Japanese surrender, the accounts of liberation are of a piece and emblematic of the experience of many in Japanese hands at the war's end.

As the American Army approached Colditz, the senior Allied officers made a decision. If ordered to evacuate the castle, they would refuse to go. The British Lieutenant Colonel Tod, French General Daine, and American Colonel Duke all informed their men of their decision, with which the men heartily agreed. On the morning of April 14, 1945, the "ZR order" came from the General Command at Glachau. They were ordered to destroy all papers and supplies which could not be moved

(*Zerstörüng*) and to evacuate the prisoners (*Räumung*). When the German commander Oberst Prawitt summoned Todd, Daine, and Duke to his office he was met with a flat refusal to move. Prawitt was a bit of a martinet, but he was no fool. He knew that any attempt to move a thousand balky prisoners with only two hundred poorly trained and equipped staff would be bound to result in numerous deaths—which could be viewed as war crimes by the victorious Allies. Unwilling to take responsibility for such actions, Prawitt called his higher headquarters at Glachau to see if they would take responsibility. When Glachau refused, Prawitt eventually got permission to stay put and surrender to the Americans.[2] However, Glachau insisted that all classified material had to be destroyed. Prawitt gave orders to Hauptmann Eggers, the head of security, to burn all the files. Eggers managed to do so with some difficulty. The men initially detailed to burn the files simply piled them in the furnace and left. Eggers had to round up a second crew and burned files until midnight.[3]

In response to the changing fortunes of war Lieutenant Colonel Tod drew up a document surrendering the castle—to the former prisoners! Prawitt signed, as did all three senior Allied officers. However, although American troops were close by, exactly when they would arrive was uncertain. Also, there were SS troops and Hitler Youth in defensive positions in the town just below the castle. If they sensed that the castle was no longer under German control, they would undoubtedly act. At the very least, they would force the prisoners to move. At the worst, they would simply massacre them. This made everyone realize the importance of keeping up the appearance of German control. So, while the German guards continued their daily routine, they did so with unloaded weapons. To an outside observer, all was in order. What an outsider could not see was that the armory and all other areas within the castle were under the control of the former prisoners.

Approaching the castle from the south-west was the 3rd Battalion, 273rd Infantry Regiment of the 69th Infantry Division. Although they had only been in action for six weeks, they had seen enough combat to be classified as experienced. Supported by half-a-dozen Sherman tanks, they were tasked with securing the area around Colditz and liberating the prisoners held in the castle. On the morning of April 15, elements of the battalion entered the town. They came under heavy sniper and machine gun fire from SS, Hitler Youth, and Home Guard troops deployed in well-selected defensive positions. So, the Americans deployed and began the slow process of forcing the Germans out of the town. It was not easy, particularly in the case of the battle-hardened SS troops. When night fell, the battalion had not gained full control of the town. Undeterred, they set their sights on a final push the next morning to evict the enemy. When morning dawned, it turned out that the Germans had withdrawn in the night. The troops of 3rd Battalion headed for the castle.[4]

While the fighting was going on in the town, around mid-day the castle was struck by several rounds of varying calibers. One of the prisoners, who was sitting in his room, was knocked to the floor by the blast. To make it clear to the approaching friendly troops that the castle had friendly occupants, hastily made British, French, and American flags were draped from the upper story windows. They must have worked as the firing ceased. Still, to be safe all occupants of the castle headed for the cellars. If the castle had caught fire, there were plans to move to a nearby park, but these fortunately were not executed.[5]

At around 10 a.m. on the morning of April 16, a patrol warily picked its way to the castle. They were greeted at the guardhouse by two former prisoners. When they entered the courtyard, they were greeted by the sight of the Germans, in formation and ready to surrender (again). The 3rd Battalion commander arrived shortly after the lead patrol to handle the surrender. While this was going on, the members of the patrol spread out through the castle, where they met jubilant ex-prisoners who shook their hands, hugged them, and kissed them on the cheek. The liberated prisoners broke out their hidden stashes of Red Cross food and insisted on preparing a meal for their liberators. The celebrations went on well into the night. Two days later, the former prisoners were on their way home. The British went by plane to England, the French overland to their homes, and the Americans by land to Le Havre where they caught ships to the USA.[6]

The prisoners at Moosburg (Stalag VII A) had a different experience. Originally designed to hold 15,000 prisoners, Moosburg had ballooned to around 110,000 occupants because of the evacuation of other *Stalags* further east in the path of the Soviet Army's advance.[7] Some of the men in the compound were originally from Stalag Luft III. Located northeast of Munich, Stalag VII A lay in the sector of advance for the 14th Armored Division which was seeking to seize a crossing site on the Isar River. Combat Command A under Brigadier General Charles Karlstad was in the lead as they approached Moosburg. The Germans attempted to use the camp as a bargaining chip to allow them to withdraw unmolested in the face of the American advance. The existence of the camp came as a surprise to Karlstad, but he refused the offer. Instead, the troops of the 47th Tank Battalion with some attached infantrymen from the 395th Infantry Regiment in support barreled toward the camp with BG Karlstad in the lead. They arrived on April 29 and after a brief battle, secured the compound.[8]

The prisoners knew that liberation was upon them for certain when a Sherman tank crashed through the barbed wire and rolled into the camp. "Immediately the tank was surrounded as Kriegies [prisoners] rushed to welcome their liberators, and within seconds it was invisible. Men stood on top and everywhere there was an inch of space. Wild cheers, and the sound of men laughing and crying, were the only anthem needed when the Nazi flag came down and the Stars and Stripes were raised."[9] Shortly after the camp was liberated, the US Third Army commander, General George S. Patton, arrived to see the camp and speak to the prisoners. After delivering a short but colorful speech, he departed amid cheers.

Before Patton's speech, an unlikely reunion took place between two brothers, Melton and Harry McCracken. The Germans had captured Melton in May of 1944. When he learned of his brother's capture, Harry vowed to be the one who liberated him. Harry was so confident of success that he ordered a set of clothing for Melton and took it wherever he went. As a medic attached to the 395th Infantry Regiment, his jeep was one of the first vehicles to follow the lead Sherman tank through the wire. After inquiring with the Senior American Officer if there were any McCrackens in the camp, Harry was told there were several. But the officer hastened to add that in all the pandemonium of the liberation, it might be best to wait and inquire later. Somewhat disheartened, Harry turned to leave, and his eyes lit upon a familiar figure framed in a nearby doorway. It was his brother, Melton! They celebrated that day and, in the evening, Melton got his new set of clothes.[10]

As the realization of being free men again sunk in, some of the former prisoners found Eisenhower's "stay put" order too much to bear. So, they struck out on their own, hitchhiking to Paris or other big cities as waypoints in their journey home. Most former prisoners stayed in place, however. They followed the path home of those who were in Colditz. The Americans in particular had plenty of time to decompress and put on weight as they went from rest camp to oceangoing ship. By the time all of them got home, the atomic bombs had been dropped and the war was over. They could get on with the task of rebuilding their lives in peace.

By the beginning of 1945, the Japanese Imperial Army and Navy were on the back foot in both Asia and the Pacific. The prisoners languishing in their hands were haunted by the specter of being massacred if they stood a chance of being liberated. Indeed, on December 14, 1944, the Japanese had already murdered 139 US prisoners of war at the Puerto Princesa Camp on Palawan in the Philippines. The Japanese had forced them into air raid shelters before setting them alight with gasoline. The guards shot those trying to escape their infernos. Only 11 escaped to tell the tale.

When the forces led by General Douglas MacArthur landed at Lingayen Gulf on January 9, 1945, only 511 prisoners of war were left in Cabanatuan. Although MacArthur's forces were only 65 miles northwest of the camp, they were headed south to capture Manila. Inside the camp something bewildering happened two days prior to the landings at Lingayen. The entire Japanese guard force at Cabanatuan mustered and marched away, leaving behind loads of food, clothing, and other useful items. The prisoners made haste to bring as much of it as they could under their control. It is well that they did, because soon the camp was used a rest stop for Japanese forces retreating along the road north from Manila. Often, they had tanks with them, a worrying presence.

Fortunately for the prisoners, Philippine guerilla captain Juan Pajota had been watching the camp closely for many months. He had intensified his surveillance after Margaret Utinsky fled Manila to avoid arrest by the Japanese. Major Bob Lapham, the senior US guerilla leader, and Captain

Pajota tried to come up with a plan for evacuating the prisoners using guerilla forces, but the logistical requirements were insurmountable. They had no means to care for the sick, move 500-plus people, or conceal them for any length of time. On January 26, 1945, the lead elements of General Walter Krueger's Sixth Army arrived at Gumbia, a barrio 25 miles from the camp. Lapham set off to link up with them and make the case for a rescue attempt.

He found a willing audience in Colonel Horton White, the Sixth Army Intelligence Officer (G2). Lapham convinced Col. White that the Japanese would kill the prisoners if rescue seemed imminent. At the current rate of advance that meant the Sixth Army needed to rescue the prisoners by January 29. Col. White determined to make a rescue attempt and selected the man and the unit to do it—Lieutenant Colonel Henry Mucci and his 6th Ranger Battalion, supported by two teams of Alamo scouts and Captain Pajota's guerillas. Mucci—a West Point graduate—directed Captain Bob Prince to produce a plan and lead the operation. Prince devised a plan that was both simple and executable. The Alamo scouts would perform reconnaissance along the route and to make sure of conditions at and around the camp. The Rangers would hit the compound, eliminate any threats to the prisoners, and evacuate the prisoners to a point from which US vehicles could transport them to friendly lines. Captain Pajota's guerillas would establish ambushes and roadblocks to prevent the approximately 9,000 Japanese in the vicinity from interfering with the Rangers during the rescue. They later helped provide carabao-drawn carts to get the prisoners away from the immediate vicinity of the camp.[11]

H-Hour for the raid was 7:30 p.m. on January 29—54 hours from the time initial orders were issued. To allow them to operate in their usual stealthy and thorough manner, two teams of Alamo Scouts pushed off 24 hours ahead of the Rangers. Led by Lieutenants Tom Rounsaville and Bill Nellist, the 13 men infiltrated Japanese territory and arrived at the camp undetected. They then made observations about the strength and disposition of the enemy, as well as the strengths and weaknesses of the perimeter fence and gate. Their reconnaissance complete, they settled in to await the arrival of the Rangers. It is interesting to note that enemy action did not claim the life of a single Alamo Scout during the unit's existence.

As the 121 Rangers in the raiding force crossed into enemy territory, they moved quietly yet quickly through the darkness. Accompanied by 80 Filipino guerillas, their goal was Balincarin, a barrio 5 miles north of their target which they reached at daybreak on January 29. After a 12-hour, 25-mile trek through the bush, the Rangers were tired. Mucci let them rest until 4 p.m. and then pushed on to Platero, a barrio 2 miles away.[12] When they reached Platero, Mucci received the latest intelligence from the Alamo Scouts and guerillas on the situation around the target—and it was not good. First, the terrain around the camp was flat and featureless, requiring a stealthy crawl for hundreds of yards to get into assault positions. Second, a force of six to eight hundred Japanese had stopped and bivouacked near the camp on their way north to join General Yamashita's command in northern Luzon. There were also around 5,000 Japanese troops digging in near Cabanatuan City, preparing to contest the advance of the Sixth Army. Based on this intelligence, Mucci prudently decided to postpone the operation by 24 hours.[13]

On the afternoon of the 30th the Rangers and the Filipino guerillas set out from Platero for their objectives. To reach them they had to cross the Pampanga River, which fortunately was at low stage and could be forded. Once across, the guerillas under Captains Joson and Pajota went to the right and left of the line of march respectively to take up blocking positions along the road. Never having worked with them before, Mucci was concerned the guerillas might not be able to hold the Japanese long enough to let the Rangers strike, free the prisoners, and exfiltrate. He need not have worried.

The Rangers had to make a long, slow approach to the compound, crawling across rice paddies and open fields for nearly 1,000 yards.[14] A platoon from Fox Company had split off earlier and circled around the camp where they would be out of sight of the main force. Therefore, they would initiate the attack by opening fire on the Japanese guard force barracks at 7:30 p.m. In their final approach they were aided by a P-61 "Black Widow" night fighter that buzzed the compound to distract the guards. It did more than distract—it terrified them to the point where they seemed able to notice nothing else.[15]

Captain Pajota and his 91 guerillas moved silently into their ambush positions near the Cebu River. Armed with bolt-action rifles, Browning Automatic Rifles (BAR), and .30 caliber water-cooled machine guns, they were spoiling for a fight. They succeeded in laying 20 land mines on the approaches to the bridge, as well as planting a demolition charge on the bridge set to detonate at 7:45 p.m. Captain Joson and his 75 men were disposed in a similar ambush on the road to Cabanatuan City. He hoped the guerillas sent by Captain Pajota had succeeded in severing the telephone lines from the camp. Otherwise, he would face an over-whelming force very quickly.[16] Since Captain Eduardo Joson's unit was closest to the largest enemy force, it was given a Ranger bazooka team. This was in addition to the bazooka the Rangers had given each guerilla unit, along with a 20-minute crash course on their use. One hundred fifty unarmed guerillas were busy assembling a train of 25 carabao-drawn carts to transport those prisoners who could not walk.[17]

As with most military operations, things did not go exactly according to plan. As the platoon from Fox Company was almost in place, a guard apparently spotted three of the Rangers getting into position. The guard called out but did not fire. Instead, he kept calling for help—which fortunately did not come. At 7:44 p.m. the platoon opened fire on the barracks, decimating the unprepared Japanese troops. The other Rangers quickly gained access to the compound through the front and back gates, systematically eliminating all resistance. Specially designated teams began to fan out and search for prisoners.

When the gunfire shattered the stillness of the night, many prisoners thought the Japanese had begun a massacre. Some didn't know what to think. The sight of American troops filled them with a mixture of emotions. At first, the uniforms and weapons were strange and caused some confusion. But the realization that these were Americans come to rescue them brought joy to their hearts. As one of the prisoners recalled, "Then we heard a voice call out in an unmistakable Southern drawl, 'Y'all are free! Head fer the front gate!' No Jap could sound like that, we decided."[18] Although emaciated and sick, the prisoners followed orders and streamed toward the front gate where they were quickly organized. Rangers carried those unable to walk. It was during the withdrawal from the compound that the Rangers suffered their only fatality, the battalion surgeon, Captain Jimmy Fisher. The Rangers were in the compound for 28 minutes from start to finish, killing 250 enemy troops and freeing 511 prisoners. Captain Prince fired the signal to withdraw, which was seen by both Pajota and Joson. With the Alamo Scouts in the lead, the Rangers headed for the Pampanga River where the carabao carts were waiting. Joson's force was able to pull out unmolested, as the Japanese in Cabanatuan City had no apparent inkling of the raid on the camp.

As the raid was taking place Juan Pajota's demolitions blew a 30-foot gap in the Cebu River bridge, denying its use to tanks or vehicles. For 30 minutes a firefight raged as Pajota's unit first hit the encamped Japanese and then turned back successive attacks. The guerilla bazooka team managed to hit a moving truck full of soldiers as it attempted to cross the bridge, as well as destroying several parked trucks concealed beneath the trees. Pajota extracted his men from the ambush site cautiously when the Japanese stopped attacking.

Before Pajota withdrew, the Rangers and those they had rescued reached the river. They found a dozen carts waiting into which they loaded the wounded and those unable to walk. The column pushed on for Platero, where they took a 30-minute stop to allow the former prisoners some rest, assess the situation, and organize the column accordingly. At Platero they also found 38 additional carabao carts waiting, so they now had sufficient cartage to carry several hundred of the weaker ex-prisoners. The column headed for Gumbia, moving along trails in the light of a nearly full moon. Overhead, a dozen P-61 fighters prowled the skies as a protective umbrella. As the sun came up, the mile-long column encountered a barrio filled with Communist Huk guerillas. Although anti-Japanese, they were also fiercely anti-American and often fought bloody battles with pro-American guerilla bands. When it seemed like they would block the column's progress, Mucci threatened to call artillery fire and level the barrio. It was a bluff, but it worked.[19] At 8 a.m., Mucci finally established radio contact with Sixth Army to receive some good news. The Americans had advanced a further 15 miles over the past three days. Even better, Sixth Army directed them to a link-up point in the town of Talavera, only 10 miles away. With a force grown to 71 carabao-drawn carts, they could now carry all the freed prisoners—even if it was at the plodding pace of a carabao. By the afternoon, they crossed into friendly lines, where they were met by ambulances and trucks to speed them to the rear.[20] The gallant men of the Alamo Scouts, the 6th Ranger Battalion, and the Philippine guerillas had brought them from captivity to freedom in a daring operation that will long be remembered.

By late summer of 1945, no one who was a prisoner of the Japanese doubted that they would be massacred if the home islands—Honshu, Kyushu, Shikoku, or Hokkaido—were invaded. Most of the works by those who had been prisoners of the Japanese record at least one instance of being warned by the Japanese that they would be killed rather than liberated. Indeed, the Imperial War Ministry issued an order on August 1, 1944, on the "final disposition" of prisoners of war. It stated that prisoners were to be prevented from falling into enemy hands by any means possible and became known as the "Kill All" order.[21] It was cited as the reason for the Puerto Princesa massacre in the IMTFE trials. The Japanese operation plan for the defense of the island of Kyushu had as one of its tasks the elimination of any prisoners of war in the event of an invasion.

So, it came as quite a relief to the POWs scattered in camps across Asia and Japan when the war ended. Their experiences of the process of liberation were similar in a large degree. Usually, the first sign was that they were no longer made to work. Lieutenant Tom Wade recalled that after the Emperor Hirohito's broadcast announcing the end of the war (surrender was never mentioned), "Hours later one foreman whispered that the Emperor had announced there was to be no more fighting. Other *hanchos* (foremen) confirmed this. The men returned from work jubilant."[22] In Saigon, survivors of USS *Houston* and the 131st Field Artillery noticed that "the guards no longer cared if they worked or not."[23] The 29 men of USS *Houston* left behind in Changi noted the same behavior. Although resting from their labors convinced most prisoners that the war was truly over, a few harbored suspicions.

Those lingering doubts were blown away like rain clouds before a strong wind when the Japanese—usually through a senior officer—announced that "to avoid further bloodshed, the Emperor has made peace."[24] In some places, this did not happen. Instead, particularly in Japan, many (or all) of the guards would simply leave. As Harold Poole, a survivor of the Bataan death march imprisoned in Japan, noted, "They just dropped like a wet rag. We told them to run and they ran."[25] Not every guard left his post at every camp in Japan, but those like Sergeant Mutsuhiro Watanabe who had mistreated prisoners fled. Imperial Army Headquarters had in fact issued a warning for all involved in disciplining prisoners to flee. In the occupied areas of Thailand, Burma, Singapore, Malaya, Indochina, China, and Indonesia, the guards remained but showed no interest in their former charges. In fact, many of the junior enlisted who had not done anything but stand guard tried to be friendly.

Most of the prisoners had little interest in their former captors. As Lieutenant Tom Wade put it, "We took no revenge. We were so glad that after three years to be able to ignore them, to forget them, that we gave them not a glance, not a word, not a blow."[26] This was not true of all prisoners. Some took revenge on the worst of their tormenters. It might be as mild as defecating in a pair of boots, or forcing them to scrub outhouses, or it could escalate to a savage beating. In very few cases was anyone killed.[27] The reasons it did not escalate were simple. Most of the worst offenders had already fled by the time of surrender. Also, the former prisoners were now free men and had full stomachs for the first time in years. For the vast majority, they were focused on going home, not on revenge.

Sometime in the process, air drops of food, clothing, and medicine would take place—much to the delight of the sick and starving prisoners. Instructed by the Japanese to paint PW in large letters on their barracks, the prisoners were soon amazed at the cornucopia of food, clothing, medicine, and personal comfort items that fell from the skies. The supplies were brought by B-29 bombers which each dropped 40 loaded 55-gallon drums with parachutes attached from their bomb bays. They had to fly at 165 miles per hour with their wheels down to increase drag and plant the supplies most accurately. From the surrender on August 15 to mid-September, over 63,000 supply drums were dropped to 150 camps in Thailand, Southeast Asia, Manchuria, Korea, and Japan by the Army Air Force and the Navy.[28] Harold Poole observed, "We had American food again, and all we could eat! It was like heaven."[29]

At long last, British, Australian, or US forces would arrive to complete the process of liberation. Japan saw the first prisoners liberated by the US Navy on August 30 at Omori. One of the prisoners, Frank Fujita, was so excited by the sight of Navy torpedo boats approaching the dock that he leaped into the water to swim out and meet them. Unfortunately, he overestimated his ability to swim and after only a short distance began to founder. Luckily, the sailors in one of the boats fished him out of the water. Since he had a shaved head, they were forced to pull him aboard by his ears![30] In Singapore, on August 19 the prisoners at Changi began to demand the release of Red Cross parcels and prisoners held in solitary confinement at the Outram Road Jail. The Japanese complied without a word. Three of the prisoners—Seaman First Class Melfred "Gus" Forsman, Captain William "Ike" Parker, and Major Winthrop "Windy" Rogers—who were released thought the Japanese were going to shoot them. They tried to run away but, due to their weakened state, they merely stumbled along for a few yards. Then they realized that the guards were not shooting, merely following them with their weapons slung on their shoulders and puzzled looks on their faces.[31] They returned to an issue of Red Cross parcels and the freedom to go into Singapore at will. Then B-24 Liberator bombers began delivering a flood of supplies by parachute. The former prisoners began to eat well. Almost as an anticlimax, the Royal Navy steamed in and completed the release of the prisoners at Changi in early September. In Southeast Asia the US Office of Strategic Services (OSS) and the British Special Operations Executive (SOE) teamed up to take control of and evacuate the former prisoners in their areas, flying them out of Phet Buri and Bangkok, Thailand. Most of the evacuees flew to Rangoon and then on to Calcutta where they boarded ships for home.

One of the most unique stories of liberation is told by Lieutenant Tom Wade. Rather than sending troops to liberate the camp, someone in MacArthur's Headquarters decided that the most expeditious means of evacuation was self-liberation. So, based on instructions from headquarters, they boarded a passenger train to Yokoyama—unescorted. When Wade and his comrades arrived they were greeted by a sight which made their collective jaws drop. "Before me in immaculate khaki uniform and cap stood an American girl with a magazine cover smile, faultless make-up and peroxide blonde hair. After three and a half years in prison camp, I had been liberated by the great American blonde!"[32]

CHAPTER 17

Conclusion

After six long and bloody years, World War II came to a close. In Europe it ended on May 8, 1945, with the unconditional surrender of the German Armed Forces, the disintegration of the Nazi regime, and the occupation by the victorious Allies of the smoking ruins of the "Thousand Year Reich." In the Pacific it ended on August 14, 1945, in the shadow of two atomic bombs and the Soviet invasion of Manchuria. The Japanese Emperor Hirohito made his broadcast to the Empire of Japan declaring a cessation of hostilities on August 14. He made no formal mention of surrender or defeat. The distinguished historian and author Richard Frank notes in his book *Downfall* that even though surrender was not mentioned, "spasms of insubordination and insurrection still flared within the Homeland."[1] While the Japanese Armed Forces surrendered unconditionally and Allied troops occupied Japan, the emperor was left in place as the titular head of Japan despite his involvement in the infamous Unit 731.

To both Germany and Japan, the Allies dealt out a measure of retribution for their violations of international law in general and to prisoners of war in particular. The intelligence collected by MI9 and MIS-X, resistance members, and from POW debriefings helped provide the prosecutors at the International Military Tribunal (IMT) at Nuremburg and the International Military Tribunal for the Far East (IMTFE) with solid cases. Some of the worst offenders were caught and dealt with. However, there were many that were punished lightly—or not at all. It is difficult to say what percentage of those who committed crimes were caught, tried, and punished. In a macabre echo of the Rome Escape Line, many of the Nazis who escaped justice did so through an escape line run through the Vatican. For the Japanese, the advent of the Korean War and the treaty signed in 1952 returning sovereignty to Japan resulted in the release of the last war criminal in 1958. Indeed, in 1979 the Japanese memorialized the seven worst war criminals at their most sacred war memorial—the Yasukuni Shrine.[2] As of 2004, the Japanese did not teach the truth about World War II.[3] The Germans, on the other hand, took every effort to erase the memory of the Nazi war criminals, without attempting to erase history.

Formerly occupied countries such as France, Belgium, Holland, the Philippines, and China gave short shrift to their citizens who had collaborated with the Germans or Japanese. This included those who had aided the enemy in attacking escape lines or who had betrayed Allied evaders. In most cases the punishment was execution, many times summarily. It may be fashionable now to deplore such actions when removed from the depraved inhumanity of the murderers and torturers of Allied POWs, evaders, and their helpers. However, such a view is wrong. As observed by George MacDonald Frazier in *Quartered Safe Out Here, A Recollection of the War in Burma*, "You cannot, you must not, judge the past by the present; you must see it in its own terms and values, if you are to have any inkling of it. You may not like what you see, but do not on that account fall into the error of trying to adjust it to suit your own vision of what it ought to have been."[4]

During the war, the odds of making a Home Run varied among theaters and depended on a number of factors. These included enemy vigilance, the individual's will to escape, the tools at hand, the availability of help along the way, and luck. What MI9 and MIS-X strove to do was reduce the need for luck to the minimum. They succeeded in helping 35,000 servicemen escape or elude the clutches of the Germans and Japanese. In Europe, an Allied airman shot down over France, Belgium, Holland, or Luxembourg had a 50 percent chance of evading capture. The chances for escape from a POW camp in Europe were far lower. In the certain parts of the Pacific, the Coastwatchers provided the same service as an escape line.[5] For those in Japanese hands, escape from a POW camp was extremely rare. In some cases, such as for the Allied POWs transported in the Hell Ships to Japan, escape was literally impossible.

Once the war ended, the POWs began to return home—over 19,000 American and slightly less than 140,000 British Commonwealth troops from the Pacific and over 92,000 Americans and slightly less than 170,000 British Commonwealth troops from Europe.[6] Most POWs did not return home immediately, particularly those who had been in Japanese hands. Rather, they were kept in comfortable camps for a period where they received three meals a day and saw a movie every night. They also received medical treatment for their physical ailments—although most got precious little psychological care. Some soldiers suspected they were being fattened up to avoid stirring up controversy at home. Others like Peter Iosso, a Berga survivor, felt that "The purpose of that was to make us human beings again and have us readjust to civilized life—the food, family, and friendship."[7] With the war over, politicians at home were already viewing the Soviet Union with a jaundiced eye. Many felt that a rehabilitated Germany and Japan would be necessary allies against the looming Communist threat. So, it would follow that bringing home emaciated POWs might sway public opinion against such a course of action. Or it may have been a simple manifestation of one of the oldest bureaucratic rules, "Don't rock the boat." Logistics undoubtedly played a role as well.

Whatever the cause, the POWs returned home to a country many of them hardly recognized, particularly those captured early in the war. As related by Gavan Daws in *Prisoners of the Japanese*, "They had a hole in their lives as big as three and a half years of prison camp." When first liberated, they were astounded by the strength of their military and both the quantity and quality of the new weaponry. As for the home front, "There was no end of wonders, the pictures in *Life* magazines were as extravagant as the Arabian Nights."[8]

As the returning POWs tried to pick up the threads of their lives, so did those who were members of the various escape lines. Those who had evaded arrest still had to deal with the post-traumatic stress of having spent several years in a clandestine lifestyle. Those who had been arrested and consigned to concentration camps had to cope with the horrific memories of an existence behind barbed wire in the hands of a twisted, perverted Nazi ideology. Anyone the Japanese caught aiding evaders or escapers had no such problems. They were almost invariably executed out of hand. In an interesting contrast, British law mandated a maximum sentence of two years' imprisonment and a £5,000 fine for harboring an escaped enemy soldier, sailor, or airman.

As Flint Whitlock eloquently noted in *Given Up For Dead*:

> Because the POWs did not return as a unit, like most of the other divisions, they were greeted by no parades, no welcoming speeches by dignitaries, no great civic celebrations to commemorate the Allied victory in Europe. Instead, there were quiet, tearful reunions with mothers, fathers, sisters, brothers, and wives. There was laughing and crying and prayers of thanks that those who had been given up for dead were, at long last, home safe and—outwardly at least—sound.[9]

The members of MI9 and MIS-X mostly returned to civilian life. Following the war, Brigadier General Norman Crockatt became a stock-broker and, later, the director of an oil company. He died on October 9, 1956, after a distinguished career. Airey Neave went on to become a prolific writer as well as a Member of Parliament. He was assassinated on March 20, 1979, by the Irish National Liberation Army with a car bomb. Colonel Johnston, commander of MIS-X, remained in the Army until his death on October 17, 1951, in Baltimore, Maryland. Colonel Winfrey left the army and returned to a long career in civil engineering. He passed away in 1993 after a prolonged battle with Alzheimer's.[10]

The organizers of the escape lines who survived led varied lives after the war. After her release from Ravensbruck Concentration Camp, Dédée de Jongh of the Comet Line continued to put her life on the line for others. She moved first to the Belgian Congo, then to Cameroon, next to Addis Ababa in Ethiopia, and finally to Senegal where she worked in leper hospitals. In failing health, she eventually retired to Brussels where she passed away October 13, 2007. Lieutenant Colonel Samuel Ironmonger Derry finished the war ensuring that the helpers of the Rome Escape Line were properly recognized by the Allies. He returned home to Newark, Nottinghamshire where he immersed himself in local politics, education, and Freemasonry. Derry was named Lord Lieutenant for Nottinghamshire in 1979. He died on December 3, 1996, at the age of 82. Lucien Dumais concluded the war in deep cover rooting out Nazi collaborators. By the end of the war, he had been awarded the Military Cross, the Military Medal, the Efficiency Medal, and the Freedom Medal. He came home to Canada after the war and went into business in Montreal. He returned to France in 1984 where he participated in the 40th anniversary of D-Day by dedicating a monument at Plouha. He died in 1989. After the war, Lieutenant Colonel (Sir) Lindsay Ride remained in Hong Kong. He served from 1948 to 1962 as colonel commandant of the Royal Hong Kong Defence Force and as vice-chancellor of the University of Hong Kong from 1949 to 1964. He was knighted in 1962 in recognition of his selfless work. He died on October 17, 1977, in Hong Kong and was survived by his wife, two sons and two daughters.

Most of the returning POWs just tried to get on with their lives. For many, that was made easier by loving families and supportive employers. For a significant number, their return to some semblance of normalcy was more difficult, if not impossible. Many had suffered debilitating, permanent injuries at the hands of their captors. For some, their wives or sweethearts were no longer there for them. In some cases, wives had remarried in the sincere belief that their husband was dead. In other cases, wives were unable to adjust to the stranger who had returned from overseas. Haunted by the ghosts of their imprisonment, many turned to alcohol and other addictive pastimes for solace. Some, unable to cope at all, simply ended their lives. Most of those who made the transition did so by staying busy, by living in the moment, and refusing to mentally pick over the years of their captivity. There would be bad moments, but by refusing to dwell in the past, those moments became fewer and further between.

Tom Wade, who had gone from Changi to the labor camps in Japan via South Korea, was impressed by the Americans' efficient repatriation of POWs. He was less impressed when he arrived in England. Given the choice between signing up for another year of service or immediate discharge, he opted for the latter. He noted, "I never received one talk, one leaflet, one pamphlet, any guidance or advice on how to return to civilian life in much-altered Britain after three years and seven months of prison camp and over five years of army service."[11] Yet he was not bitter towards his former jailers. Having spent much of his life in Asia, he also spoke some Japanese. He understood and appreciated Japanese culture as well and could see beyond those who had done him ill. He married, had a daughter and two sons. He passed away peacefully at the age of 94.[12]

Hans Kasten, who had been imprisoned in the Berga Concentration Camp, was typical of many who had trouble adjusting. He suffered "50 percent hearing loss, damaged eyesight, and damaged vertebrae that caused stiffness in his neck and headaches."[13] Like most POWs he was denied adequate compensation for his injuries by US government policy. The US War Crimes Acts of 1948 and 1952 gave each former POW one dollar for each day of imprisonment—provided they could prove they didn't receive the rations mandated by the Geneva Conventions. It gave an additional $1.50 per day if the prisoner could prove they had been subjected to inhumane treatment or hard labor. So American POWs got a maximum of $2.50 per day as compensation. Kasten moved to the Philippines shortly after the war. There he went to work for Mueller and Phillips, a US manufacturing company.

For the rest of his life, his failure to bring his tormentor Willi Hack to justice haunted him. He never knew that Soviet forces had captured, tried, convicted, and hanged Willi Hack in 1946. He also never knew that Hauptmann Merz and Sergeant Metz had cheated the hangman. Captured by the Americans, at their trials they both lied, claiming that they had done everything in their power to help the prisoners. Since no prisoner in their charge was ever called to testify, they both served only short terms in prison. Kasten married four times but, haunted by his time as a POW, was never able to build a solid relationship. He remained in the Philippines until his death in 2007. His remains were later interred in Arlington National Cemetery in 2008.

Louis Zamperini was similarly haunted by his memories of repeated beatings and torture by the Japanese prison guard named Mutsuhiro Watanabe, nicknamed "The Bird." He attempted to drown those memories in alcohol. As Laura Hillenbrand notes in *Unbroken*, "No one could reach Louie, because he had never really come home. In prison camp, he'd been beaten into dehumanized obedience to a world order in which The Bird was absolute sovereign, and it was under that world order that he still lived."[14] He felt his only redemption from his living nightmare would be to personally kill The Bird. Then, he went to two Billy Graham Crusade meetings. He stormed out of the first and had nearly done so from the second. Instead, he walked the aisle and gave up his hatred. The dreams of his tortures at The Bird's hand never troubled him again. In 1997, Zamperini penned a letter of forgiveness to Watanabe. It was never answered. Watanabe died in 2003, still maintaining he had done nothing wrong.

Charles McCormac's story brought a different sort of closure. After his epic escape from Singapore, he subsequently returned to duty. His final assignment during the war was serving under Lord Louis Mountbatten on the IMTFE in Singapore. He witnessed the trial and execution by hanging of Captain Teruchi for his crimes against POWs during the war. When the trial was over, McCormac asked Lord Mountbatten for Teruchi's sword. Puzzled, Mountbatten asked him why. When McCormac briefly related the story of his torture at Teruchi's hands Mountbatten agreed, saying, "It's yours." As he noted in *You'll Die in Singapore*, "The sword is locked away now, safe from the inquisitive fingers of our three children; but sometimes when I am alone I will take it out and think of things that cannot easily be forgotten."[15] He lived quietly in Australia until his passing in 1985 at the age of 70.

Edgar Whitcomb enjoyed a long life, passing away in 2016 at the age of 98. After his return from the war, he studied law. He went into politics and became the 43rd Governor of Indiana, 1969–1973. At 72 years of age, he embarked on a leisurely 10-year solo sail around the world. His wife Mary would fly to various ports of call to meet him, where they would sometimes stay for months at a time. Then he would sail to the next port and repeat the process. After his return from circumnavigating the globe, he retired to a small cabin in Rome in southern Indiana where he lived out the rest of his days.[16] He was survived by his wife, three daughters, one son, and "many grandchildren and great-grandchildren."[17]

Not all POWs hated all their captors. Indeed, among both the Germans and the Japanese there were those who were merciful and concerned with the prisoners' welfare. Hans Joachim Scharff, the Luftwaffe interrogator at the Dulag Luft in Oberursel, Germany, was an exceptional case. He was so well regarded that several US Army Air Corps veteran associations invited him to their reunions. Reinhold Eggers, the security officer at Colditz from February 1944 to April 1945, was also invited to numerous Colditz inmate reunions. In the foreword to the Dutch edition of Eggers' book, *Colditz, the German Viewpoint*, Lieutenant Damiaen J. van Doorninck, a former Dutch POW, wrote, "This man was our opponent, but nevertheless he earned our respect by his correct attitude, self-control and total lack of rancour despite all the harassment we gave him."[18]

At Stalag IX B, there was a guard named Schmidt who had always been kind to the prisoners. When the camp was liberated, the prisoners vouched for Schmidt. He was given a parole and allowed to go home to his farm.[19] Kuta Schugota, known as "Smiley" by the prisoners at Palawan and who had never mistreated a prisoner, gave evidence of the atrocities committed during his time as a guard.[20] At Camp O'Donnell there was a Sergeant Nakamura nicknamed "the Bull" by the prisoners who was in charge of a work detail. He never mistreated the prisoners, nor allowed their mistreatment by anyone else. As a result, the prisoners respected him.[21]

Although the events in this book took place over 75 years ago, they still speak to us. They demonstrate that mankind is capable of great good and of great evil. They also show that even in the most difficult situations, leadership, courage, and quick thinking can spring forth from surprising sources. Although most of those who took part in these events are gone, I dedicate this book to their memory.

Endnotes

Chapter 1

1 Ian Dear, *Escape and Evasion: POW breakouts in World War II* (London: Rigel Publications, 2004), 35–49.

2 M. R. D. Foot and J. M. Langley, *MI9: Escape and Evasion 1939–1945* (Boston, MA: Little, Brown and Company, 1980), 220–2.

3 Richard Vinen, *The Unfree French: Life Under the Occupation* (London: Allen Lane, 2006), 198.

4 Ibid., 189.

5 I have chosen the MI9 figures because the American figures lack a means of verification. If the MIS-X figures are used, the number of escapers and evaders could be as high as 40,000. Foot and Langley, *MI9: Escape and Evasion 1939–1945*, 315.

6 MI9 was actually established in 1939. However, its distribution of escape aids didn't begin until 1941. See: Clayton Hutton, *Official Secret*. New York, NY: Crown Publishers, 1961.

7 International Committee of the Red Cross. "Convention (IV) respecting the Laws and Customs of War on Land and its annex: Regulations concerning the Laws and Customs of War on Land. The Hague, 18 October 1907," Accessed September 7, 2019, https://ihl-databases.icrc.org/applic/ihl/ihl.nsf/Treaty.umentId=4D47F92DF3966A7EC12563CD002D6788&action=openDocument.

8 International Committee of the Red Cross, "Convention relative to the Treatment of Prisoners of War. Geneva 27 July 1929," accessed September 7, 2019, https://ihl-databases.icrc.org/applic/ihl/ihl.nsf/Treaty. Treaty.xsp?action=openDocument&documentId=0BDEDDD046FDEBA9C12563CD002D69B1.

9 1929 Geneva Convention, Section II, Art. 11. "The food ration of prisoners of war shall be equivalent in quantity and quality to that of the depot troops."

10 Tom Henling Wade, *Prisoner of the Japanese: From Changi to Tokyo* (Nashville, TN: Kangaroo Press, 2011. Kindle), location 1549.

11 Jerry Sage, *Sage: The Man the Nazis Couldn't Hold* (Wayne, PA: Miles Standish Press, 1986), 113–5.

12 Nazi is a shortened form of the German *Nationalsozialistische Deutsche Arbeiterpartei* or in English, National Socialist German Worker's Party. See: Britannica, "Nazi Party," https://www.britannica.com/topic/Nazi-Party.

13 Dear, *Escape and Evasion*, 61–8. There was a U-Boat rating who managed to escape to the US in 1940, but he was detained for the entire war and thus never made a "home run."

14 Just before he ended his life, Hitler ordered the execution of all Allied prisoners of war still in German hands. Thankfully, the orders were never relayed.

15 The SS or *Schutzstaffel*, German for "Protective Echelon," first came into existence in 1925. They initially served as Adolf Hitler's personal bodyguards. They later added a ground combat organization called the Waffen SS. Their power in Germany increased even as the overall fortunes of their country waned. At the end of the war, they were deemed to be a criminal organization. See: History.com, "The SS," https://www.history.com/topics/world-war-ii/ss.

16 *Arbeitsdienstlager* translates to "work camp."

17 The SS rank of Obersturbannführer was equivalent to that of lieutenant colonel in the US Army. See: Wikipedia, "Obersturbannführer," https://en.wikipedia.org/wiki/Obersturmbannf%C3%BChrer.

18 The 1929 Geneva Convention, Section V, Art. 54 states, "Imprisonment is the most severe disciplinary punishment which may be inflicted on a prisoner of war. The duration of any single punishment shall not exceed thirty days."

19 Wikipedia, "Houston Stewart Chamberlain," https://en.wikipedia.org/wiki/Houston_Stewart_Chamberlain.

20 Richard B. Frank, *Tower of Skulls: A History of the Asia-Pacific War: July 1937–May 1942* (New York, NY: W. W. Norton and Company, 2020), 57.

21 The 1907 Hague Convention, Section II, Article 4, states, "Prisoners of war are in the power of the hostile Government, but not of the individuals or corps who capture them. *They must be humanely treated.*" Italics added for emphasis.

22 The 1907 Hague Convention, Section II, Article 8, states that "Prisoners of war shall be subject to the laws, regulations, and orders in force in the army of the State in whose power they are. Any act of insubordination justifies the adoption towards them of such measures of severity as may be considered necessary. Escaped prisoners who are retaken before being able to rejoin their own army or before leaving the territory occupied by the army which captured them are liable to disciplinary punishment."

23 Numerous sources point to the physical discipline meted out by superiors. These include: Meirion Harries and Susie Harries, *Soldiers of the Sun: The Rise and Fall of the Imperial Japanese Army* (New York, NY: Random House, 1991); Frank, *Tower of Skulls*; Gavan Daws, *Prisoners of the Japanese: POWs of World War II in the Pacific* (New York, NY: William Morrow and Company, Inc., 1994); Jack Coggins, *The Fighting Man: An Illustrated History of the World's Greatest Fighting Forces* (Garden City, NY: Doubleday & Company, Inc., 1966); and Wade, *Prisoner of the Japanese*.

24 Harries and Harries, *Soldiers of the Sun*, 18–20.

25 Dear, *Escape and Evasion*, 158–70.

26 Daws, *Prisoners of the Japanese*, 360.

27 "Guests of the Third Reich, Global Conflict, War Crimes, Berga and Malmedy," https://guestsofthethirdreich.org/global-conflict/.

28 The Soviet mortality rate in German hands approached 60 percent. See: Henry Chancellor, *Colditz: The Untold Story of World War II's Greatest Escapes* (New York, NY: HarperCollins Publishers, Inc., 2001), 127–8.

29 Daws, *Prisoners of the Japanese*, 336.

30 Wade, *Prisoner of the Japanese*, location 3586.

Chapter 2

1   Foot and Langley, MI9: Escape and Evasion 1939–1945, 26. Endnotes

2   Ibid., 25.

3   Hutton, *Official Secret*, 9–14.

4   Ibid., 6.

5   WO 208/3242, transcribed by https://www.arcre.com/mi9.

6   Ibid., 26.

7   Foot and Langley, *MI9: Escape and Evasion 1939–1945*, 42–3.

8   Lloyd R. Shoemaker, *The Escape Factory: The Story of MIS-X, the Super-Secret U.S. Agency Behind World War II's Greatest Escapes* (New York, NY: St. Martin's Press, 1990), 7–11.

9   Records Group 332, Washington National Records Center, Suitland, MD.

10 Shoemaker, *The Escape Factory*, 12.

11 "Uncle Sam's General Mercantile" (or Merc) was the nickname given by the men of MIS-X to the Shop. See: Shoemaker, *The Escape Factory*, 29–35.

12 Present-day Sri Lanka.

13 Foot and Langley, *MI9: Escape and Evasion 1939–1945*, 274.

14 *MI9: Escape and Evasion 1939–1945* features a statistical table which, by the authors' admission, is an approximation for a number of reasons. See: Foot and Langley, *MI9: Escape and Evasion 1939–1945*, appendix 1, 313–5.

Chapter 3

1   Hutton, *Official Secret*, 95–6.

2   Shoemaker, *The Escape Factory*, 36.

3   Hutton, *Official Secret*, 51–4.

4   Sage, *Sage: The Man the Nazis Couldn't Hold*, 255.

5   Daws, *Prisoners of the Japanese*, 113.

6   Business Insider, "Here's how many days a person can survive without water," https:// www.businessinsider.com/how-many-days-can-you-survive-without-water-2014-5.

7   Airey Neave, *Saturday at MI9*. London: Biteback Publishing Ltd., 2013, location 1030. Kindle.

8   Hutton, *Official Secret*, 37–45.

9   Ibid., location 1030.

10 Foot and Langley, *MI9: Escape and Evasion 1939–1945*, 249.

11 Ibid., 247–8.

12 Stephen L. Moore, *As Good As Dead: The Daring Escape of American POWs From a Japanese Death Camp* (New York, NY: Caliber, 2016), 202–28.

13 Foot and Langley, *MI9: Escape and Evasion 1939–1945*, 276.

14 Paul Brickhill, *The Great Escape* (New York, NY: W. W. Norton & Co., 1950), 165.

15 Shoemaker, *The Escape Factory*, 57, 67.

16 *Kommandantur* translates to "Headquarters."

17 Airey Neave, *Saturday at MI9* (Barnsley: Pen & Sword Books Ltd., 2010. Kindle), location 2173.

18 Airey Neave, *Little Cyclone* (London: Biteback Publishing Ltd., 2013. Kindle), location 1460.

Chapter 4

1   For a detailed survey of Japanese brutal mistreatment of Allied POWs, see: Baron Edward Frederick Langley Russell, *The Knights of Bushido: A history of Japanese war crimes during World War II* (New York: Skyhorse Publishing, 2008. Kindle).

2   Brickhill, *The Great Escape*, 231.

3   Foot and Langley, *MI9: Escape and Evasion 1939–1945*, 119.

4   Arthur A. Durand, *Stalag Luft III: The Secret Story* (Baton Rouge, LA: Louisiana State University Press, 1988), 272–3.

5   Ibid., 255.

6   Sage, *Sage: The Man the Nazis Couldn't Hold*, 105–6.

7   Foot and Langley, *MI9: Escape and Evasion 1939–1945*, 93–4.

8   Chancellor, *Colditz*, 113.

9   Ibid., 280–5.

10 Sage, *Sage: The Man the Nazis Couldn't Hold*, 152.

11 Ibid., 255.

12 Ibid., 239.

13 Foot and Langley, *MI9: Escape and Evasion 1939–1945*, 94–6.

14 Shoemaker, *The Escape Factory*, 20.

15 Ibid., 20–2.

16 Reinhold Eggers, *Colditz: The German Viewpoint* (London: New English Library, 1973), 106.

17 Shoemaker, *The Escape Factory*, 57, 66, 84, 139.

18 Sage, *Sage: The Man the Nazis Couldn't Hold*, 130.
19 Hutton, *Official Secret*, 89–90.
20 Eric Williams, *The Wooden Horse* (New York, NY: Harper & Brothers Publishers, 1949), 245.
21 Mark Felton, *Operation Swallow: American Soldiers' Remarkable Escape from Berga Concentration Camp* (New York, NY: Center Street, The Hachette Book Group, 2019. Kindle), 200–13.

Chapter 5

1 Kenneth W. Simmons, *Kriegie: Prisoner of War* (New York, NY: Nelson, 2019. Kindle), location 1143.
2 *Oflag* is an abbreviation for Officer's Camp. See: Durand, *Stalag Luft III*, 103.
3 Chancellor, *Colditz*, 10.
4 Eggers, *Colditz*, 20–1.
5 Chancellor, *Colditz*, 380–1.
6 Oberstleutnant is the equivalent to lieutenant colonel in the US and British Armies. See: Military Wikia, "Oberstleutnant," https://military-history.fandom.com/wiki/Army_officer_ranks.
7 Chancellor, *Colditz*, 17.
8 Ibid., 180.
9 Withholding food and firewood was a violation of the Geneva Conventions. See: Felton, *Operation Swallow*, 158.
10 Ibid., 108–9.
11 Flint Whitlock, *Given Up For Dead: American GI's in the Nazi Concentration Camp at Berga* (New York, NY: Basic Books, A Member of the Perseus Books Group, 2005. Kindle), 90.
12 Ibid., 98.
13 Ibid., 98.
14 Ibid., 89.
15 Ibid., 119.
16 Felton, *Operation Swallow*, 162–3.
17 The number of prisoners sent to Berga has been quoted as high as 363. However, I have chosen to use the number of 350 provided by Hans Kasten, who was the Man of Confidence at Berga. See: Felton, *Operation Swallow*, 167.
18 Ibid., 257.
19 Durand, *Stalag Luft III*, 56.
20 Ibid., 61.
21 Ibid., 68–9.
22 Further details on Colonel Hubert "Hub" Zemke may be found at: National Aviation Hall of Fame, Hubert "Hub" Zemke, https://web.archive.org/web/20070707020916/

http://nationalaviation.blade6.donet.com/components/content_manager_v02/view_nahf/ htdocs/menu_ps.asp?NodeId=-2009132779&Group_ID=1134656385&Parent_ID=-1.
23 Raymond F. Toliver, *The Interrogator: The Story of Hans Joachim Scharff, Master Interrogator of the Luftwaffe* (Atglen, PA: Shiffer Publishing Ltd., 1997), 181.
24 Simmons, *Kriegie*, location 672.
25 Ibid., location 956–88.
26 Durand, *Stalag Luft III*, 330.
27 Whitlock, *Given Up For Dead*, 167–8.
28 Ibid., 189–95.

Chapter 6

1 History.com, "How Japan Took Control of Korea," https://www.history.com/ news/japan-colonization-korea.
2 COFEPOW.com, "The Loyal Regiment," https://www.cofepow.org.uk/ armed-forces-stories-list/the-loyal-regiment.
3 Wade, *Prisoner of the Japanese*, location 1187–234.
4 Ibid., location 1689.
5 Peter Brune, *Descent Into Hell, The Fall of Singapore—Pudu and Changi—the Thai–Burma Railway* (Sydney, Melbourne, Auckland, London: Allen & Unwin, 2014. Kindle), location 8801.
6 Ibid., locations 8687–700.
7 For details see: Singapore War Crimes Trials, "Fukuei Shimpei," https://www. singaporewarcrimestrials.com/case-summaries/detail/007.
8 By August 1943 all officers above the rank of colonel were shipped off to Japan. See: Brune, *Descent into Hell*, location 8417.
9 Wade, *Prisoner of the Japanese*, location 1008.
10 James D. Hornfischer, *Ship of Ghosts: The Story of the USS Houston, FDR's Legendary Lost Cruiser, and the Epic Saga of Her Survivors* (Annapolis, MD: US Naval Institute, 2006. Kindle), locations 3814–70.
11 FEPOW.family, "Nong Pladuc," https://www.fepow.family/Articles/Death_ Railway/html/nong_pladuc.htm.
12 War History Online, "Horror Of The Death Railway, Japan's Project For WW2 Prisoners Of War," https://www.warhistoryonline.com/instant-articles/death-railway-japan-pow-project.html. See also: Brune, *Descent into Hell*, location 9078.
13 Hornfischer, *Ship of Ghosts*, location 6907.
14 The Southern Army received the authority to proceed with the railway in the summer of 1942. See: Hornfischer, *Ship of Ghosts*, location 6943.
15 This webpage included a moving "Last Post" Memorial Ceremony video. His two sons served in the Australian Army. The eldest was captured in Singapore and survived the war. The youngest fell in New Guinea in 1945. See: Australian War Memorial, "The Last Post Ceremony commemorating the service of (NX35005)

Brigadier Arthur Leslie Varley, 22nd Infantry Brigade, Second World War," https://www.awm.gov.au/collection/C2094320.

16 Brigadier General Varley's diaries may be found at Australian War Memorial, "Transcript of the Diary of Arthur Leslie Varley, 1942–1944," https://www.awm.gov.au/collection/C2668108?image=253.

17 Brune, *Descent into Hell*, location 9163.

18 Australian War Memorial, "Brigadier Arthur Varley," https://www.awm.gov.au/collection/ART26425.

19 Lieutenant Colonel Ramsay's records of his captivity are preserved at the Australian War Memorial, as PDF documents, https://www.awm.gov.au/collection/P10679787.

20 D. C. S. Sissons, *The Australian War Crimes Trials and Investigations (1942–51)*. 2007, Open Computing Facility Berkeley, "Australian War Crimes Trials," https://www.ocf.berkeley.edu/~changmin/documents/Sissons%20Final%20War%20Crimes%20Text%2018-3-06.pdf.

21 H. Robert Charles, *Last Man Out: Surviving the Burma-Thailand Death Railway: A Memoir* (St. Paul, MN: Zenith Press, 2006. Kindle), location 1987.

22 Ibid., locations 1560–74.

23 Hornfischer, *Ship of Ghosts*, locations 3463–95.

24 Charles, *Last Man Out*, location 779.

25 Ibid., location 2622.

26 Mansell.com, "Tokyo Main Camp, Omori," http://www.mansell.com/pow_resources/camplists/tokyo/omori/omori.html.

27 Wade, *Prisoner of the Japanese*, locations 1721–32.

28 Ibid., location 2076.

29 Ibid., locations 2031–65.

30 Laura Hillenbrand, *Unbroken: A World War II Story of Survival, Resilience, and Redemption* (New York, NY: Random House, 2010), 233–4.

31 Ibid., 235–8.

32 Wade, *Prisoner of the Japanese*, location 3579.

33 Hillenbrand, *Unbroken*, 242–3.

34 Sidney Stewart, *Give Us This Day* (New York, NY: W. W. Norton & Company, 1999), 124–6.

35 William B. Breuer, *The Great Raid On Cabanatuan: Rescuing the Doomed Ghosts of Bataan and Corregidor* (New York, NY: John Wiley & Sons, Inc., 1994. Kindle), location 28.

36 Ibid., 57–8.

37 Defenders of the Philippines, "Margaret Utinsky," https://web.archive.org/web/20171029081142/http://philippine-defenders.lib.wv.us/html/utinsky_margaret_bio.html.

38 Theresa Kaminski, *Angels of the Underground: The American Women Who Resisted the Japanese in the Philippines in World War II* (New York, NY: Oxford University Press, 2016), 208–9.
39 Breuer, *The Great Raid On Cabanatuan*, locations 70–8.
40 James W. Parkinson and Lee Benson, *Soldier Slaves: Abandoned by the White House, Courts, and Congress* (Annapolis, MD: Naval Institute Press, 2006), 122–4.

Chapter 7

1   Neave, *Little Cyclone*, locations 155–83.
2   Ibid., location 2319.
3   Dachau was not a single camp. It was a sprawling complex of subcamps that contained over 67,000 prisoners. Troops from the US 42nd and 45th Infantry Divisions and the US 20th Armored Division all played a part in liberating the camps on April 29, 1945. See: United States Holocaust Museum, "Liberation of Dachau," https://www.ushmm.org/learn/timeline-of-events/1942-1945/liberation-of-dachau.
4   Literally, "field gendarme." The *Feldgendarmerie* were the uniformed military police units of the Wehrmacht. See: Military Wikia, "Feldgendarmerie," https://military.wikia.org/wiki/Feldgendarmerie.
5   Neave, *Little Cyclone*, locations 470–81.
6   In the early days of the line, the journey from Brussels to Bayonne was done without a halt in Paris. See: Ibid., location 535.
7   Neave, *Little Cyclone*, location 1455.
8   Ibid., location 2428.
9   Peter Eisner, *The Freedom Line: The Brave Men and Women Who Rescued Allied Airmen from the Nazis During World War II* (New York, NY: HarperCollins Publishers, Inc., 2004), 222.
10 Neave, *Little Cyclone*, location 2010.
11 Ibid., location 908.
12 Ibid., location 2294.

Chapter 8

1   Foot and Langley, *MI9: Escape and Evasion 1939–1945*, 152–3.
2   Dear, *Escape and Evasion*, 119.
3   Camp 59 Survivors, "I.S.9 History—Operations in Italy, Part 3," https://camp59survivors.com/2014/03/08/i-s-9-history-operations-in-italy-part-3/.
4   Dear, *Escape and Evasion*, 119–20.
5   BBC News, "Nottinghamshire town honours a war hero who saved 4,000 lives," https://www.bbc.com/news/uk-england-nottinghamshire-23189450.

6   Carol A. Bryan, "Lieutenant-Colonel Sam Derry, Newark-On-Trent most decorated war hero, holder of the Military Cross and Distinguished Service Order," accessed March 9, 2020, https://newarkcemeteryuk.wordpress.com/2012/05/22/lieutenant-colonel-sam-derry-of-newark-on-trent/.
7   "PG" is the Italian abbreviation for prisoner of war. See: Sam L. Derry, *The Rome Escape Line* (New York, NY: W. W. Norton & Company, Inc., 1960), 13.
8   Ibid., 121.
9   Walking the Battlefields, "The Anzio Bridgehead (Jan to Jun 1944)" http://www.walkingthebattlefields.com/2019/11/the-anzio-bridgehead-jan-to-jun-1944.html.
10 B. H. Liddell Hart, *History of the Second World War* (New York, NY: G. P. Putnam & Sons, 1970), 526–36.
11 Derry, *The Rome Escape Line*, 131–4.
12 Dear, *Escape and Evasion*, 131.

Chapter 9

1   I have chosen to spell his name LaBrosse (French), although some sources list him as Labrosse (Anglicized).
2   Lucien Dumais, *The Man Who Went Back* (London: Futura Publications, 1975), 96.
3   Dear, *Escape and Evasion*, 153.
4   An address that a person or company uses to receive letters, packages, etc. that is not where they live or do business. See: Cambridge Dictionary, "Accommodation address," https://dictionary.cambridge.org/us/dictionary/english/accommodation-address.
5   The quickest means of sorting out false evaders from real was by asking Americans about baseball and the English about cricket. See: Dumais, *The Man Who Went Back*, 135.
6   Dear, *Escape and Evasion*, 153.
7   "Hello to everyone at Alphonse's house."
8   Angus Konstam, *British Motor Gun Boat 1939–45* (Oxford and Long Island City, NY: Osprey Publishing Ltd., 2010. Kindle), location 699.
9   Dumais, *The Man Who Went Back*, 152.
10 Ibid., 152.
11 Ibid., 156–7.
12 Dear, *Escape and Evasion*, 152.
13 Dumais, *The Man Who Went Back*, 195.
14 Foot and Langley, *MI9: Escape and Evasion 1939–1945*, 135.

Chapter 10

1   Dear, *Escape and Evasion*, 93

2 Frank, *Tower of Skulls*, 342.
3 Four excellent sources are: Frank Owen, *The Fall of Singapore* (New York, NY: Penguin Books, 1960); Peter Elphick, *Singapore: The Pregnable Fortress: A Study in Deception, Discord and Desertion* (Edinburgh: Coronet Press, 1995); Alan Warren, *Singapore 1942: Britain's Greatest Defeat* (Singapore: Talisman, 2002); and Frank, *Tower of Skulls*.
4 Frank, *Tower of Skulls*, 340.
5 Geoffrey Brooke, *Singapore's Dunkirk: The Aftermath of the Fall* (Barnsley: Pen & Sword Books Ltd., 2003), 246.
6 The Japanese 25th Army had approximately 30,000 troops. Malaya Command had 85,000 although many of them were not front-line troops.
7 Frank, *Tower of Skulls*, 345.
8 Dear, *Escape and Evasion*, 80.
9 I feel compelled to venture a word or two on the difficulty of establishing place names in this narrative. Depending on the source, spellings differ widely. Riau is in some cases spelled Rhio; Sambu is rendered as Sabu, Priggi Raja appears as Prigi Rajah, etc. I decided to use the modern spelling to aid any readers with tracing the routes mentioned in this chapter.
10 Major H. A. "Jock" Campbell of the Kings Own Scottish Borderers later rose to the rank of lieutenant colonel and received an OBE, among other decorations. See: Charles Cruickshank, *SOE in the Far East* (Oxford and New York, NY: Oxford University Press, 1986), 66–7.
11 Captain Ivan Lyon of the Gordon Highlanders led two canoe raids on Singapore Harbor in 1943 and 1944 respectively. The first raid was a spectacular success that sank 39,000 tons of shipping, the second a gallant failure. None of those who took part in the second raid were ever heard from again. By the end of his life, Lyon was promoted to lieutenant colonel and received a DSO and an MBE. See: Geoffrey Brooke, *Alarm Starboard! A Remarkable True Story of the War at Sea* (Barnsley: Pen & Sword Books Ltd., 2009), 386–7.
12 Cruickshank, *SOE in the Far East*, 66.
13 Priggi Raja become Sungai Bela after Indonesian independence.
14 The Ayer Molek Rubber Company is still in business as of 2021.
15 Brooke, *Singapore's Dunkirk*, 65.
16 Ibid., 21.
17 For a brief biography of Admiral Ozawa see: Military Wikia, "Jizaburo Ozawa," https://military.wikia.org/wiki/Jisabur%C5%8D_Ozawa.
18 Brooke, *Alarm Starboard!*, 197.
19 Nearly 800 out of 1,300 officers and men were rescued. For a detailed account of the sinking of HMS *Prince of Wales* and HMS *Repulse*. See: Owen, *The Fall of Singapore*, 55–65.
20 Brooke, *Singapore's Dunkirk*, 216–7.
21 Brooke, *Alarm Starboard!*, 260–1.

22 Brooke, *Singapore's Dunkirk*, 82.

23 Ibid., 80–1.

24 For a short history of Admiral Nagumo see: Military Wikia, "Chuchi Nagumo," https://military.wikia.org/wiki/Ch%C5%ABichi_Nagumo.

25 For a detailed discussion of the attacks see: Military Wikia, "Indian Ocean Raid," https://military.wikia.org/wiki/Indian_Ocean_raid.

26 Liddell Hart, *History of the Second World War*, 237.

27 Present-day Mumbai.

Chapter 11

1   WO 343/1/213/2/BAAG, 14.

2   For an excellent example of the Chinese ability to deny the Japanese control of the country beyond the range of their own guns see: Frank, *Tower of Skulls*, 110–2.

3   Kweilin is the Romanized version of Guilin. See: Wikipedia, "Guilin," https://en.wikipedia.org/wiki/Guilin.

4   From the transcript of a speech given by Sir Lindsey Ride at a reunion of BAAG personnel in Hong Kong, in the Great Hall of Hong Kong University on July 25, 1952. See: WO 343/1/213/1/BAAG, 13.

5   Waichow is now officially known as Huizhou. See: Wikipedia, "Huizhou," https://en.wikipedia.org/wiki/Huizhou.

6   WO 343/1/213/1/BAAG, 53.

7   Dear, *Escape and Evasion*, 105.

8   Ibid., 107.

9   Ibid., 107. See also Foot and Langley, *MI9: Escape and Evasion 1939–1945*, 268.

10 Dear, *Escape and Evasion*, 110.

11 Major General Sir Walter Cawthorn, Director of Military Intelligence at Headquarters India during 1944, sent a letter to be read at the 10th BAAG Reunion. He lamented their lack of public recognition but heaped praise on their achievement. See: WO 343/1/213/1, 21. For a biography of MG Cawthorn, see: Australian Dictionary of Biography, "Sir Walter Joseph Cawthorn," https://adb.anu.edu.au/biography/cawthorn-sir-walter-joseph-9715.

12 Foot and Langley, *MI9: Escape and Evasion 1939–1945*, 265.

13 Many escape organizations incidentally collected intelligence not related to establishing or maintaining escape routes. However, it was not a primary mission.

14 Cruickshank, *SOE in the Far East*, 158.

15 Foot and Langley, *MI9: Escape and Evasion 1939–1945*, 265, 268.

16 Ibid., 265.

17 WO 343/1/213/1/BAAG, 14.

18 WO 343/1/213/2/BAAG, 1.

19 WO 343/1/213/1/BAAG, 7, 9.

20 Dear, *Escape and Evasion*, 111.

21 From the transcript of a speech given by Sir Lindsey Ride at a reunion of BAAG personnel in Hong Kong, in the Great Hall of Hong Kong University on July 25, 1952. See: WO 343/1/213/1/BAAG, 15–6.
22 WO 343/1/213/1/BAAG, 16.
23 The Kempetai (sometimes spelled Kenpetai) combined the role of military police and counterintelligence corps. Their brutality was a byword throughout occupied Asia and the Pacific Islands.
24 Foot and Langley, *MI9: Escape and Evasion 1939–1945*, 267.
25 Ibid., 268.
26 WO 343/1/213/1, 16.
27 His full name was Alfonso Rudolph Wichtrich, the son of a German father and a Mexican mother. See: Archives.gov, "JFK Releases," https://www.archives.gov/files/research/jfk/releases/2018/180-10144-10019.pdf.
28 A. R. Wichtrich, *MIS-X Top Secret* (Raleigh, NC: Pentland Press, Inc., 1997), 20.
29 Ibid.
30 Ibid, 22–30.
31 Yunnan Province forms part of the southeastern border of China. It touches on Vietnam, Laos, and Burma (Myanmar). At the time it was sparsely populated, mountainous, and covered in jungles.
32 OMF, "The Lisu of China" https://omf.org/us/resources/people-and-places/famous-missionaries/james-o-fraser/lisu-people/.
33 Wichtrich, *MIS-X Top Secret*, 39–40.
34 French Indochina comprised modern-day Vietnam, Laos, and Cambodia.
35 Shoemaker, *The Escape Factory*, 233.
36 Wichtrich, *MIS-X Top Secret*, 100–5.
37 Ibid, 114.

Chapter 12

1 In German, *Stalag* is a contraction of *Stammlager*, itself short for *Kriegsgefangenen-Mannschaftsstammlager*, a literal translation of which is "war-caught (i.e., POW) team main camp." It usually applied to camps for noncommissioned officers and privates.
2 Airey Neave, *They Have Their Exits* (Barnsley: Pen & Sword Books Ltd., 2003. Kindle), location 488.
3 Ibid., locations 786–92.
4 Gefreiter is equivalent to a private in the US Army.
5 Neave, *They Have Their Exits*, location 1147.
6 Ibid., location 1420.
7 Ibid., location 1509.
8 Ibid., location 1678.
9 Neave, *Saturday at MI9*, location 537.
10 Ibid., location 564.

11 Neave, *They Have Their Exits*, location 1732.
12 Ibid., location 1738.
13 Airey Neave, *The Escape Room* (New York, NY: Doubleday & Company, Inc., 1970), 24.
14 Ibid., location 1787.
15 Neave, *Saturday at MI9*, locations 702–801.
16 Neave, *The Escape Room*, 36.
17 Neave, *They Have Their Exits*, location 2045.
18 Ibid., location 2141.

Chapter 13

1 Pacific Wrecks, "Cabcaben Airfield," https://pacificwrecks.com/airfields/philippines/cabcaben/index.html.
2 Wikipedia, "2nd Infantry Division (Philippines)," https://en.wikipedia.org/wiki/2nd_Infantry_Division_(Philippines).
3 Edgar D. Whitcomb, *Escape from Corregidor* (Washington, D.C.: Henry Regnery Company, 2017. Kindle), 57.
4 Ibid., 107.
5 Don Sixto Lopez had the distinction of having fought for Filipino independence against the Spanish, Americans, and Japanese.
6 Whitcomb, *Escape from Corregidor*, 140.
7 Ibid., 146.
8 Ibid., 152.
9 Ibid., 159.
10 Ibid., 169.
11 Ibid., 185.
12 Ibid., 190.

Chapter 14

1 The Vickers Vildebeest was a biplane able to conduct daylight bombing and torpedo operations. It had a crew of two. See: BAE Systems, "Vickers Vildebeest," https://www.baesystems.com/en/heritage/vickers-vildebeest.
2 205 Squadron was formed in Singapore in February 1928. It began active patrolling with the outbreak of war in Europe, flying Wildebeest aircraft. By the time war broke out with Japan, the squadron had been equipped with PBY Catalinas. The squadron suffered heavy losses and was disbanded in March 1942 in Australia. See: Rafweb.com, "No 201 – 205 Squadron Histories," https://www.rafweb.org/Squadrons/Sqn201-205.htm.
3 Singapore Evacuation, "Civilian Evacuation Lists," https://singaporeevacuation1942.blogspot.com/2007/03/hin-leong-1942.html.

4 Dictionary of American Naval Fighting Ships, "Wakefield," https://www.history.navy.mil/research/histories/ship-histories/danfs/w/wakefield.html.

5 Charles McCormac, *You'll Die in Singapore* (Singapore: Monsoon Books, 2015. Kindle), 27.

6 Ibid., 28.

7 Ibid., 49.

8 McCormac, *You'll Die in Singapore*, 56. Refers to Collier's Quay. The actual name is Collyer's Quay. See: Wikipedia, "Collyer Quay," https://en.wikipedia.org/wiki/Collyer_Quay.

9 John A. English, *A Perspective on Infantry* (New York: Praeger Publishers, 1981), 204–5.

10 *Kampong* means "village" in Indonesian.

11 McCormac, *You'll Die in Singapore*, 110.

12 Oosthaven was renamed Bandar Lampung after Indonesian independence in 1949.

13 Paul Brickhill, *Escape or Die* (London and Sydney: Pan Books, 1977), 43. *Tuan* is the Indonesian equivalent of "Sir."

14 Ibid., 44.

15 Ibid., 45.

16 The Distinguished Service Medal (DSM) was an enlisted award. After 1993, it was abolished and all ranks received the Distinguished Service Order (DSO). See: "JSP 761 Honours and Awards in the Armed Forces," https://ndm-pr.webs.com/jsp761%5B1%5D.pdf.

17 An RAF squadron leader is the equivalent of a major in the USAF. See: Wikipedia, "Comparison of United Kingdom and United States military ranks," https://en.wikipedia.org/wiki/Comparison_of_United_Kingdom_and_United_States_military_ranks#:~:text=US%20%22Enlisted%22%20and%20UK%20%22Other%20ranks%E2%80%9D%20compared%20,%20Sergeant%20aircrew%20%2010%20more%20rows%20.

18 McCormac, *You'll Die in Singapore*, 220–1.

Chapter 15

1 Dictionary of American Naval Fighting Ships, "Quail," https://www.history.navy.mil/research/histories/ship-histories/danfs/q/quail-i.html.

2 Depending on the source, the facilities at Cavite are referred to as the Naval Base or the Naval Yard. This work will use the term Naval Base.

3 Edwin P. Hoyt, *The Lonely Ships: The Life and Death of the U.S. Asiatic Fleet* (New York, NY: David McKay Company, Inc., 1976), 153.

4 The Hall of Valor Project, "John Henry Morrill," https://valor.militarytimes.com/hero/21408.

5 The Department of Military Art and Engineering, United States Military Academy, *The West Point Atlas of War, World War II: The Pacific* (New York, NY: Tess Press, 1959), Map 121.

6   Hoyt, *The Lonely Ships*, 298.
7   J. F. Meeker earned the affectionate title "Chief Cook and Bottle Washer" from Morrill. See: John Morrill and Pete Martin, *South from Corregidor* (New York, NY: Simon and Schuster, 2018. Kindle), 172.
8   Ibid., 54.
9   Ibid., 47.
10   Buda manufactured diesel and gasoline engines for farm and marine use from 1881 to 1953, when they were bought out by Allis Chalmers. Tractor Fandom, "Buda Engine Company," https://tractors.fandom.com/wiki/Buda_Engine_Co.#Applications.
11   Morrill and Martin, *South from Corregidor*, 58.
12   Military Wikia, "Lewis Machine Gun," https://military.wikia.org/wiki/Lewis_Machine_Gun.
13   Morrill and Martin, *South from Corregidor*, 73.
14   The taffrail is normally found at the stern of a boat.
15   Hoyt, *The Lonely Ships*, 298.
16   Morrill refers to it as Malikaban. See: Morrill and Martin, *South from Corregidor*, 76.
17   US Department of Commerce, "Coast and Geodetic Survey 1930," 120.
18   Hoyt, *The Lonely Ships*, 299.
19   Morrill and Martin, *South from Corregidor*, 84.
20   Ibid., 86.
21   Ibid., 86.
22   Ibid., 88.
23   Morrill refers to it as Tobangas Bay. See: Morrill and Martin, *South from Corregidor*, 92.
24   Hoyt, *The Lonely Ships*, 299.
25   Morrill and Martin, *South from Corregidor*, 94.
26   Hoyt, *The Lonely Ships*, 300.
27   Morrill and Martin, *South from Corregidor*, 108.
28   Ibid., 134.
29   Hoyt, *The Lonely Ships*, 300.
30   Morrill and Martin, *South from Corregidor*, 151.
31   Ibid.,157.
32   Ibid., 163.
33   Ibid., 164.
34   Ibid., 167.
35   Ibid., 173.

Chapter 16

1   Eggers, *Colditz*, 216.
2   Chancellor, *Colditz*, 372–3.
3   Eggers, *Colditz*, 215.

4   Chancellor misidentifies the 273rd Infantry Regiment as belonging to the 60th Division. They were a subordinate unit of the 69th Division. See: Chancellor, *Colditz*, 373–8.

5   Eggers, *Colditz*, 216–7.

6   Chancellor, *Colditz*, 386–7.

7   Moosburg Online, "POW camp Stalag VIIA," https://www.moosburg.org/info/stalag/indeng.html.

8   Jim Lankford, "Stalag VII A: The Liberation," Moosburg Online, https://www.moosburg.org/info/stalag/14theng.html.

9   Durand, *Stalag Luft III*, 354.

10 Ibid., 355.

11 Breuer, *The Great Raid On Cabanatuan*, 160–1.

12 Hampton Sides, *Ghost Soldiers: The forgotten epic story of World War II's most dramatic mission* (New York, NY: Anchor Books, 2002. Kindle), 165.

13 Breuer, *The Great Raid On Cabanatuan*, 174–5.

14 Sides, *Ghost Soldiers*, 294–8.

15 Ibid., 319–21.

16 Ibid., 322–4.

17 Breuer, *The Great Raid On Cabanatuan*, 177–8.

18 Ibid., 193.

19 Sides, *Ghost Soldiers*, 390–6.

20 Ibid., 397–8.

21 D. M. Giangreco, *Hell to Pay: Operation Downfall and the Invasion of Japan, 1945–1947* (Annapolis, MD: Naval Institute Press, 2009. Kindle), 554.

22 Wade, *Prisoner of the Japanese*, locations 3605–14.

23 Hornfischer, *Ship of Ghosts*, location 6534.

24 Wade, *Prisoner of the Japanese*, location 3614.

25 Parkinson and Benson, *Soldier Slaves*, 182.

26 Wade, *Prisoner of the Japanese*, location 3624.

27 Daws, *Prisoners of the Japanese*, 373–8.

28 Ibid., 340.

29 Parkinson and Benson, *Soldier Slaves*, 183.

30 Daws, *Prisoners of the Japanese*, 342–3.

31 Hornfischer, *Ship of Ghosts*, locations 6653–62.

32 Wade, *Prisoner of the Japanese*, location 3678.

Chapter 17

1   Richard B. Frank, *Downfall: The End of the Imperial Japanese Empire* (New York, NY: Penguin Books, 2001), 321. By the time of the September 1945 formal surrender ceremony on the deck of USS *Missouri*, most of Japan was reconciled to their fate.

2 Daws, *Prisoners of the Japanese*, 375.
3 The author knows this from personal experience. In 2004, while in Okinawa on business at the Marine Base, I saw a group of Japanese high school students from Tokyo touring the museum dedicated to the battle of Okinawa. The curator, a retired Marine sergeant major who spoke fluent Japanese, gave a short lecture to the students. They were absolutely spellbound. Some of them wept openly. All the while, their teachers were downstairs. At the end of the presentation, I spoke to one of the teachers. He told me that for them to teach about the war was *kinjiru*—forbidden. So, they would bring the students here on their senior field trip to learn the truth. Later, the sergeant major confirmed that he would normally have between six and ten groups of students per day during the school year. He also showed me a standard history text. The entirety of World War II was covered in about six pages. See also: Daws, *Prisoners of the Japanese*, 24–5.
4 George Macdonald Fraser, *Quartered Safe Out Here: A Recollection of the War in Burma* (Pleasantville, NY: Akadine Press, Inc., 2001), xix–xx.
5 For an excellent first-hand account of the daring rescues effected by the Coastwatchers see: Eric Feldt, *The Coast Watchers* (Cascadia, WA: The Normandy Press, 2019. Kindle).
6 According to the National Archives and Records Administration (NARA), 92,423 POWs returned alive from the European Theater and 19,202 POWs returned alive from the Pacific Theater. See NARA Accession Number 389-57-384. https://catalog.archives.gov/id/583428.
7 Whitlock, *Given Up For Dead*, 199.
8 Daws, *Prisoners of the Japanese*, 344.
9 Whitlock, *Given Up For Dead*, 202.
10 Iowa State University, "Robley Winfrey Papers," http://findingaids.lib.iastate.edu/spcl/arch/rgrp/11-2-51.html.
11 Wade, *Prisoner of the Japanese*, location 3893.
12 His obituary reads: "Lt. Henling Thomas (Tom) Wade died peacefully on 5th March 2015, age 94. Born in Shanghai, China, Tom attended Bedford School in England and became a journalist with the Shanghai Times. In 1940, he volunteered for the British Army and served as an intelligence officer (2nd Lieutenant I.T.A., 2nd Battalion, Loyal Regiment) in Malaya. Wounded in action, he was taken prisoner with the fall of Singapore in 1942. Tom's account of his brutal POW experience was published in his book, 'Prisoner of the Japanese: From Changi to Tokyo'. The much loved husband of Audré and father of Mark, Simon and Cathy, he will be greatly missed." See: Telegraph.co.uk, "Telegraph Announcements, Wade – Henling Thomas Arthur," http://announcements.telegraph.co.uk/deaths/189681/wade.-henling-thomas-arthur.
13 Felton, *Operation Swallow*, 257.
14 Hillenbrand, *Unbroken*, 365.
15 McCormac, *You'll Die in Singapore*, 233.

16 David Sears, "Escape From Corregidor: The Story of Edgar Whitcomb," Historynet. com, 2021, https://www.historynet.com/escape-from-corregidor-the-story-of-edgar-whitcomb.htm.

17 Perry County News, "Edgar Whitcomb," https://www.legacy.com/us/obituaries/perrycountynews/name/edgar-whitcomb-obituary?id=18037883.

18 Wikipedia, "Reinhold Eggers," https://en.wikipedia.org/wiki/Reinhold_Eggers.

19 Whitlock, *Given Up For Dead*, 168.

20 Moore, *As Good As Dead*, 275.

21 Daws, *Prisoners of the Japanese*, 153–4.

Selected Bibliography

BAE Systems. "Vickers Vildebeest." Accessed November 14, 2020. https://www. baesystems.com/en/heritage/vickers-vildebeest.

Barnett, Glen. "Sailing Into the Unknown." Accessed January 18, 2021. https://www. historynet.com/sailing-into-the-unknown.htm.

Behr, Edward. *Hirohito: Behind the Myth*. New York, NY: Villard Books, 1989.

Breuer, William B. *The Great Raid On Cabanatuan: Rescuing the Doomed Ghosts of Bataan and Corregidor*. New York, NY: John Wiley & Sons, Inc., 1994. Kindle.

Brickhill, Paul. *Escape or Die*. London and Sydney: Pan Books, 1977.

——*The Great Escape*. New York, NY: W. W. Norton & Co., 1950.

Brooke, Geoffrey. *Alarm Starboard! A Remarkable True Story of the War at Sea*. Barnsley: Pen & Sword Books Ltd., 2009.

——*Singapore's Dunkirk: The Aftermath of the Fall*. Barnsley: Pen & Sword Books Ltd., 2003.

Brune, Peter. *Descent Into Hell: The Fall of Singapore—Pudu and Changi—the Thai–Burma Railway*. Sydney, Melbourne, Auckland, London: Allen & Unwin, 2014. Kindle.

Bryan, Carol A. "Lieutenant-Colonel Sam Derry, Newark-On-Trent most decorated war hero, holder of the Military Cross and Distinguished Service Order." Accessed March 9, 2020. https://newarkcemeteryuk.wordpress.com/2012/05/22/lieutenant-colonel-sam-derry-of-newark-on-trent/.

Chancellor, Henry. *Colditz: The Untold Story of World War II's Greatest Escapes*. New York, NY: HarperCollins Publishers, Inc., 2001.

Charles, H. Robert. *Last Man Out: Surviving the Burma-Thailand Death Railway: A Memoir*. St. Paul, MN: Zenith Press, 2006. Kindle.

Churchill, Winston S. *Their Finest Hour*. London: Rosetta Books, LLC, 2013. Kindle.

Coggins, Jack. *The Fighting Man: An Illustrated History of the World's Greatest Fighting Forces*. Garden City, NY: Doubleday & Company, Inc., 1966.

Counts, Major Laura C. "Were They Prepared? Escape and Evasion in Western Europe 1942–1944". Thesis, Air Command and Staff College, 1986. Kindle.

Cruickshank, Charles. *SOE in the Far East*. Oxford and New York, NY: Oxford University Press, 1986.

Daws, Gavan. *Prisoners of the Japanese: POWs of World War II in the Pacific*. New York, NY: William Morrow and Company, Inc., 1994.

Dear, Ian. *Escape and Evasion: POW breakouts in World War II.* London: Rigel Publications, 2004.

Derry, Sam L. *The Rome Escape Line.* New York, NY: W. W. Norton & Company, Inc., 1960.

Dumais, Lucien. *The Man Who Went Back.* London: Futura Publications, 1975.

Durand, Arthur A. *Stalag Luft III: The Secret Story.* Baton Rouge, LA: Louisiana State University Press, 1988.

Eggers, Reinhold. *Colditz: The German Viewpoint.* London: New English Library, 1973.

Eisner, Peter. *The Freedom Line: The Brave Men and Women Who Rescued Allied Airmen from the Nazis During World War II.* New York, NY: HarperCollins Publishers, Inc., 2004.

Elphick, Peter. *Singapore: The Pregnable Fortress: A Study in Deception, Discord and Desertion.* Edinburgh: Coronet Press, 1995.

English, John A. *A Perspective on Infantry.* New York, NY: Praeger Publishers, 1981.

Evans, A. J. *The Escaping Club.* London: John Lane, 1934.

Feldt, Eric A. *The Coast Watchers.* Cascadia, WA: The Normandy Press, 2019. Kindle.

Felton, Mark. *Operation Swallow: American Soldiers' Remarkable Escape from Berga Concentration Camp.* New York, NY: Center Street, The Hachette Book Group, 2019. Kindle.

Flanagan Jr., Edward M., Lt. Gen USA (Ret). *Angels at Dawn.* New York, NY: Berkley Books, 1986.

Foot, M. R. D. and J. M. Langley. *MI9: Escape and Evasion 1939–1945.* Boston, MA: Little, Brown and Company, 1980.

Frank, Richard B. *Downfall: The End of the Imperial Japanese Empire.* New York, NY: Penguin Books, 2001.

——*Tower of Skulls: A History of the Asia-Pacific War: July 1937–May 1942.* New York, NY: W. W. Norton and Company, 2020.

Fraser, George MacDonald. *Quartered Safe Out Here: A Recollection of the War in Burma.* Pleasantville, NY: Akadine Press, Inc., 2001.

Froom, Phil. *Evasion and Escape Devices: Produced by MI9, MIS-X, and SOE in World War II.* Atglen, PA: Schiffer Publishing, Ltd., 2015.

Giangreco, D. M. *Hell to Pay: Operation Downfall and the Invasion of Japan, 1945–1947.* Annapolis, MD: Naval Institute Press, 2009.

Gold, Hal. *Japan's Infamous Unit 731: Firsthand Accounts of Japan's Wartime Human Experimentation Program.* North Clarendon, VT: Tuttle Publishing, 2019. Kindle.

Grossman, Dave, LTC. *On Killing: The Psychological Cost of Learning to Kill in War and Society.* Revised Edition. New York, NY: E-Reads, Ltd. Publisher, 2009. Kindle.

Handy, Ned and Dr. Bill Grey. *Grey Ghost: The Story of a Professional Soldier's Epic 3,000 Mile Journey of Escape and Evasion in World War II Occupied Europe.* Indianapolis, IN: Dog Ear Publishing, 2018. Kindle.

Hanson, Victor Davis. *The Second World Wars: How the First Global Conflict Was Fought and Won*. New York, NY: Basic Books, 2017.

Harries, Meirion and Susie Harries. *Soldiers of the Sun: The Rise and Fall of the Imperial Japanese Army*. New York, NY: Random House, 1991.

Heaps, Leo. *The Evaders: The Story of the Most Amazing Mass Escape of World War II*. New York, NY: William Morrow and Company, Inc., 1976.

Hillenbrand, Laura. *Unbroken: A World War II Story of Survival, Resilience, and Redemption*. New York, NY: Random House, 2010.

Hitler, Adolf. *Mein Kampf*. Stone Mountain, GA: White Wolf, 2014. Kindle.

Hornfischer, James D. *Ship of Ghosts: The Story of the USS* Houston*, FDR's Legendary Lost Cruiser, and the Epic Saga of Her Survivors*. Annapolis, MD: US Naval Institute, 2006. Kindle.

Hoyt, Edwin P. *The Lonely Ships: The Life and Death of the U.S. Asiatic Fleet*. New York, NY: David McKay Company, Inc., 1976.

Hunt, Ray C. and Bernard Norling. *Behind Japanese Lines: An American Guerilla in the Philippines*. Lexington, KY: The University Press of Kentucky, 1986.

Hutton, Clayton. *Official Secret*. New York, NY: Crown Publishers, 1961.

Hymoff, Edward. *The OSS in World War II: The Complete Story of America's First Wartime Espionage Service, The Forerunner of the CIA*. New York, NY: Ballentine Books, 1972.

International Committee of the Red Cross. "Convention relative to the Treatment of Prisoners of War. Geneva 27 July 1929." Accessed September 7, 2019. https://ihl-databases.icrc.org/applic/ihl/ihl.nsf/Treaty.xsp?action=openDocument&documentId=0BDEDDD046FDEBA9C12563CD002D69B1.

International Committee of the Red Cross. "Convention (IV) respecting the Laws and Customs of War on Land and its annex: Regulations concerning the Laws and Customs of War on Land. The Hague, 18 October 1907." Accessed September 7, 2019. https://ihl-databases.icrc.org/applic/ihl/ihl.nsf/Treaty.xsp?documentId=4D-47F92DF3966A7EC12563CD002D6788&action=openDocument.

Jackson, Charles R., Sergeant Major USMC (Ret.). *I Am Alive! A United States Marine's Story of Survival in a World War II Japanese POW Camp*. New York, NY: Random House, 2003.

Kaminski, Theresa. *Angels of the Underground: The American Women Who Resisted the Japanese in the Philippines in World War II*. New York, NY: Oxford University Press, 2016.

Konstam, Angus. *British Motor Gun Boat 1939–45*. Oxford and Long Island City, NY: Osprey Publishing Ltd., 2010. Kindle.

Liddell Hart, B. H. *History of the Second World War*. New York, NY: G. P. Putnam & Sons, 1970.

McCormac, Charles. *You'll Die in Singapore*. Singapore: Monsoon Books, 2015. Kindle.

Middlebrook, Martin. *Arnhem 1944: The Airborne Battle*. Boulder, CO: Westview Press, 1994.

Miller, Col. E. B. *Bataan Uncensored*. Grand Rapids, MI: The Hart Publications, 2018. Kindle.

Moore, Stephen L. *As Good As Dead: The Daring Escape of American POWs From a Japanese Death Camp*. New York, NY: Caliber, 2016.

Morrill, John, Lieutenant Commander, USN, and Pete Martin. *South from Corregidor*. New York, NY: Simon and Schuster, 2018. Kindle.

Murray, Williamson and Allan R. Millett. *A War To Be Won: Fighting the Second World War*. Cambridge, MA: The Belknap Press of Harvard University Press, 2001.

National World War II Museum. "Guests of the Third Reich—Global Conflict." Accessed September 2019. https://guestsofthethirdreich.org/global-conflict/.

Naval History and Heritage Command. "Dictionary of American Naval Fighting Ships—USS *Quail*." Accessed December 30, 2020. https://www.history.navy.mil/research/histories/ship-histories/danfs/q/quail-i.html.

Naval History and Heritage Command. "Dictionary of American Naval Fighting Ships—*Wakefield*." Accessed November 14, 2020. https://www.history.navy.mil/research/histories/ship-histories/danfs/w/wakefield.html.

Neave, Airey. *The Escape Room*. London: Biteback Publishing Ltd., 2013. Kindle.

—— *They Have Their Exits*. Barnsley: Pen & Sword Books Ltd., 2003. Kindle.

—— *Saturday at MI9*. Barnsley: Pen & Sword Books Ltd., 2010. Kindle.

——*Little Cyclone*. London: Biteback Publishing Ltd., 2013. Kindle.

Owen, Frank. *The Fall of Singapore*. New York, NY: Penguin Books, 1960.

Pacific Wrecks, Inc. "Cabcaben Airfield". Accessed July 18, 2020. https://pacificwrecks.com/airfields/philippines/cabcaben/index.html.

Parkinson, James W. and Lee Benson. *Soldier Slaves: Abandoned by the White House, Courts, and Congress*. Annapolis, MD: Naval Institute Press, 2006.

Pether, Michael. *Singapore 1942*. Accessed November 14, 2020. https://singaporeevacuation1942.blogspot.com/2007/03/hin-leong-1942.html.

Potts, J. R. "USS Lapwing (AM-1)". Military Factory.com. Accessed January 18, 2021. https://www.militaryfactory.com/ships/detail.asp?ship_id=USS-Lapwing-AM1.

RAF Web. "Air of Authority – A History of RAF Organisation." Accessed November 14, 2020. https://www.rafweb.org/Squadrons/Sqn201-205.htm.

Reynolds, Bob. *Of Rice and Men: From Bataan to V-J Day, a Survivor's Story*. Davo City: Mindianao Publishing, 2019. Kindle.

Russell, Baron Edward Frededrick Langley. *The Knights of Bushido: A history of Japanese war crimes during World War II*. New York, NY: Skyhorse Publishing, 2008. Kindle.

Sadler, A. L. *The Code of the Samurai: A Translation of Daidoji Yuzan's Budo Shoshinshu*. Rutland, VT: Charles E. Tuttle Company, 1996.

Sage, Jerry. *Sage: The Man the Nazis Couldn't Hold*. Wayne, PA: Miles Standish Press, 1986.

Samenow, Stanton E., Ph.D. *Inside the Criminal Mind*. New York, NY: Broadway Books, 2014.

Shigesuke, Taira. *Code of the Samurai: A Modern Translation of the Bushido Shoshinshu*. Translated by Thomas Cleary. Rutland, VT: Tuttle Publishing, 1999.

Shoemaker, Lloyd R. *The Escape Factory: The Story of MIS-X, the Super-Secret U.S. Agency Behind World War II's Greatest Escapes*. New York, NY: St. Martin's Press, 1990.

Sides, Hampton. *Ghost Soldiers: The forgotten epic story of World War II's most dramatic mission*. New York, NY: Anchor Books, 2002. Kindle.

Simmons, Kenneth W. *Kriege: Prisoner of War*. New York, NY: Nelson, 2019. Kindle.

Slim, Field Marshal Viscount William. *Defeat Into Victory*. London: PAPERMAC, 1986.

Stewart, Sidney. *Give Us This Day*. New York, NY: W. W. Norton & Company, 1999.

The Department of Military Art and Engineering, United States Military Academy. *The West Point Atlas of War, World War II: The Pacific*. New York, NY: Tess Press, 1959.

Tiger, Lionel. *Men in Groups*. New Brunswick: Transaction Publishers, 2009.

Tiger, Lionel and Robin Fox. *The Imperial Animal*. New York, NY: Dell Publishing Co, Inc., 1971.

Toliver, Raymond F. *The Interrogator: The Story of Hans Joachim Scharff, Master Interrogator of the Luftwaffe*. Atglen, PA: Schiffer Publishing Ltd., 1997.

Tsunetomo, Yamamoto. *Hagakure: The Book of the Samurai*. Translated by William Scott Wilson. New York, NY: Kodansha America, Inc., 1983.

Tuohy, William. *The Bravest Man: Richard O'Kane and the Amazing Submarine Adventures of the USS* Tang. New York, NY: Ballentine Books, 2006.

US Department of Commerce, Coast and Geodetic Survey. *United States Coast Pilot, Philippine Islands Part II: Palawan, Mindinao, and Sulu Achipelago, Second Edition*. Washington, D.C.: US Government Printing Office, 1930.

Vinen, Richard. *The Unfree French: Life under the Occupation*. London: Allen Lane, 2006.

Wade, Tom Henling. *Prisoner of the Japanese: From Changi to Tokyo*. Nashville, TN: Kangaroo Press, 2011. Kindle.

Warren, Alan. *Singapore 1942: Britain's Greatest Defeat*. Singapore: Talisman, 2002.

Whitcomb, Edgar D. *Escape From Corregidor*. Washington, D.C.: Henry Regnery Company, 2017. Kindle.

Whitlock, Flint. *Given Up For Dead: American GI's in the Nazi Concentration Camp at Berga*. New York, NY: Basic Books, A Member of the Perseus Books Group, 2005. Kindle.

Wichtrich, Lt. Colonel A. R. *MIS-X Top Secret*. Raleigh, NC: Pentland Press, Inc., 1997.

Williams, Eric. *The Wooden Horse*. New York, NY: Harper & Brothers Publishers, 1949.

Witbanks, Bob. *Last Man Out: Glenn McDole, USMC, Survivor of the Palawan Massacre in World War II*. Jefferson, NC: McFarland & Company, Inc., Publishers, 2004.

Index

References to tables are in *italics*.